Mary T. Browne

∴

Fireside

PUBLISHED BY SIMON & SCHUSTER INC.
New York London Toronto Sydney
Tokyo Singapore

∴ *LOVE* ∴

in Action

A SPIRITUAL APPROACH
TO FREEDOM AND
HAPPINESS

FOREWORD

If you're like me, you get a lot of information about the ways of the world by reading books, talking to friends, reading magazines, watching T.V. Maybe you read Shakespeare, or books by John Irving. Or talk to your lawyer, investment banker, or trusted business associate. Maybe your family or your significant other will provide that pearl, some wit of insight or knowledge.

Mary Browne's information base is not from the same perspective as the "traditional" paths, and a lot of us are very uncomfortable with advice that comes from a tacitly spiritual base. But, I've known Mary, both as a friend and a professional. Her advice has always been helpful, straight, and in one way or another, very practical and often profound. I think that Mary is a very smart lady and her book deals with just about everything that's important in a helpful, straightforward, and provocative way. . . . So read this book—it's as unique as the woman.

One more thing about Mary. It takes courage to write a book like this; it takes confidence. For good old-fashioned reasons, the easiest thing to do when someone says that they have psychic gifts is to say that they are quacks, that they are crazy, because their ideas don't quite fit into the neat, rational world we think we inhabit.

You may not buy everything that Mary says, but don't dismiss this.

It will make a difference.

Owen Lipstein

INTRODUCTION

I was born with a psychic gift. Some people are born to be great singers, doctors, or scientists and some are born to serve with a gift such as mine. People with a gift to see the future have existed since the beginning of mankind.

Working as a professional psychic for the past eight years, I have seen hundreds of private clients, most of whom have come to me in great distress, having already talked with therapists or with their friends. Often they have sought help from various sources before making an appointment to see me. My work seldom attracts those who are seeking sheer phenomena. Most people come to me in the hope that my special ability will shed some light on their problems. Skeptics deny the existence of psychic gifts, but my clients have experienced firsthand the proof that such gifts do indeed exist. It is their personal testimony that I present as my credentials.

The first truly psychic experience I remember occurred when I was seven years old. My great-aunt owned the town's funeral parlor. One day she asked me to come over to answer the phone for her. She had to be away from her office and didn't want to leave it unattended in case an emergency arose. I went there with her promise of fifty cents as my payment. After telling me exactly what to do in case a call came in, she left. I sat in her office and stared at the phone, taking my job quite seriously. Not much time passed before I became restless and fidgety, so I decided to take a look around the funeral parlor.

I walked into the main hallway that had doorways on either side leading to individual funeral chapels. I was drawn to one of the rooms on the left where a wake was scheduled later in the day. It was still early, so no member of the deceased person's family had yet arrived. Still feeling a bit too timid to enter, I stood outside the room in which the casket lay, perceiving a silence that had the quality of quiet one feels upon entering a church. Flowers and the smell of incense filled the room. Suddenly I saw an arrangement of flowers appear to float in the air. For a moment the flowers seemed suspended in space, and then, ever so gently, they began to move through the room. I closed my eyes, then opened them again, expecting the apparition—which must surely have been a figment of my imagination—to have disappeared. Not so. The flowers were still floating in air. I then saw the ever-so-faint shadow of a woman holding the bouquet. I had not seen her at first, or maybe she had not appeared until this moment. I am certain that I saw her and that the scent of lilacs had not been present until she appeared. She smiled radiantly and waved with one hand, then replaced the flowers in their original spot next to the coffin and disappeared. At that point I walked into the room, only to discover that the woman holding the flowers was the same person lying in the coffin.

I didn't feel fearful; instead, I felt great excitement flowing through me. At that moment, I was filled with certainty that there was no death. I had seen a woman who was supposed to be dead looking quite alive and happy. When I told my grandmother what had happened, she merely nodded as if she understood. She told me not to mention it to anyone because most people would not believe me. "You have a gift. Be grateful for it," she said. I told no one else about it, not even my great-aunt who owned the funeral home.

The backyard of my grandmother's house was where I first became aware of the beings that believers call elementals and nature spirits, or "the little people," fairies, and elves. I was seven years old and thrilled to know that fairies and elves really existed. These tiny "folk" stood about three inches high and played among the tomato plants and rows of corn. These darling little ones seemed to be very happy and oblivious of my presence as I spent hours at a time watching them.

Grandma would ask me what I was doing. "Watching the fairies and the elves dig in your garden," I would reply. I wonder now what she must have thought about a child who talked about spirits and elves and fairies as if they were the most normal things in the world. A few times I tried to get a friend to see the fairies, but invariably the friend would laugh at me, so I finally learned to keep it to myself. I was quite content to watch my little friends and felt no need to convince anyone else of their existence. I knew what I saw and was happy to be among them.

One dear childhood friend of mine has reminded me that my ability to locate missing objects with great accuracy began when we were children. Someone would say, "I can't find my keys." I would answer, "They're behind the third book on the shelf in your bedroom." Off the person would go to see if the lost keys were there. Inevitably the person would return holding the keys and say, "How did you know?" My reply would be, "I just knew." I could not explain how I knew since usually I had been nowhere near the person's house. This happened so often that those who were close to me became used to it and took my ability for granted.

Upon finding a journal I wrote when I was twelve, I was surprised to read: "I know that I have lived before and that I will live again." It seems that I believed in reincarnation before I had even heard the word.

I was indeed a strange child but very creative. I sang at a very early age and was always interested in drama. I put on plays in my grandmother's basement and dreamed of leaving Iowa and going to New York to be in the theater. I read everything I could find about the theater and dreamed I was Sarah Bernhardt or Gertrude Lawrence. (Was this the memory of a past life? I doubt it, but it is food for thought.) After graduation from high school I went to the University of Iowa to study music and drama. At the university I had a part-time job working in a bookstore, and it was there I was first exposed to books on metaphysical subjects, especially works concerning reincarnation and life after death. The interest remained with me after I left Iowa and moved to New York.

My first years in New York were divided between pursuing the theater and studying metaphysics. I was always doing both. My psychic abilities were becoming sharper, and I developed an overwhelming desire to help people. Sitting through auditions, I could always tell who would get a part just by looking at the actors waiting for their turns to read. Often we had to wait a few hours to be seen by the director, and I spent that time giving psychic readings to people I met there. It would just happen: I would start talking to someone, and psychic information would come through. Others in the room would hear what I was doing, and before long a crowd gathered around me. Actors are known to be very open-minded so they were quite accepting of my gift and grateful for the readings.

There is an old saying that when the student is ready, the teacher appears. At this point in my life I desperately wanted some guidance but did not know where to find it. I did not need anyone to teach me to be psychic, I was born with that gift, but I did need help in learning how to handle my abilities and how to use them in the best way possible. Knowing that the proper teacher was not to be found in the Yellow Pages, I waited and studied on my own. I became very interested in the teachings of Manly P. Hall and, later, Helen Petrova Blavatsky. Through their great work I found the truth I had been looking for: a synthesis of science, philosophy, and religion.

Again I had reached a point where I felt I must channel my energies into helping people, and by word of mouth my clients came to me. I have never advertised my services or allowed anyone to interview me about my abilities. But from the moment I decided to become a professional psychic, I had more clients than I could handle. I then closed the door on my theatrical pursuits and devoted all my time to the work about which I have written here.

I worked with clients for one year before I found the teacher I was seeking. I will call him Lawrence, but this is not his real name. I alter certain facts about him in order to honor his right to privacy and anonymity, but I have altered nothing about his teachings and philosophies.

How have I come upon the information contained in this book? Most of it has been drawn from the troubles of humanity, as reflected in the needs of my clients; the majority of them have come to me seeking a point of view that gives them insight into the problems of their daily lives. By giving them information about what I see in their future and what may be affecting them from their past, I am able to discuss with them the things I feel would be helpful to them in handling whatever day-to-day crises may arise.

Learning to Be Free

Many people desire freedom; they desperately seek it but without success. If you are depressed or fearful, or addicted to something, your freedom is stolen from you. But by learning selflessness and the importance of service, your freedom can and will be restored. I have never met an unhappy person who was living a life of service. Freedom comes through selfless living. By the same token, I have yet to meet a happy, fulfilled person who is self-consumed.

This is not a book to be read only by those who believe in the gifts of psychics. This book is for anyone seeking a point of view to support him or her through the trials and experiences of daily living. Again and again in these pages, I will stress the need for action, and love in action *is* the act of serving.

Man learns by example. A child learns to walk and talk through imitation. Throughout this book my teachers Lawrence and Sir William serve as great examples of people who through many incarnations have worked out the issues of their lives and found their freedom. They are now totally selfless men whose only motivation is to serve humanity. The doctrines of reincarnation and karma that will be explained subsequently are the metaphysical teachings which form the basis of their philosophy and mine.

The concept of reincarnation embraces the notion that man lives not just one but many lives. He returns to the Earth repeatedly until he reaches perfection. An acceptance of the law of karma means believing that we are governed by the laws of cause and effect. It means that each person lives the life he or she has earned. If you accept this teaching, then it follows you believe there is no such thing as a victim. We attract only situations that we have created ourselves.

Psychic phenomena is a tool to help and serve others. For many people the word psychic carries weird and negative connotations: images of gypsy fortune-tellers looking into crystal balls, and so forth. One of my goals is to dispel such misconceptions. A great deal of time and energy is wasted in trying to prove that psychics are frauds when they could be spent benefiting from the teachings and wisdom.

Since I am a psychic counselor and not a psychotherapist, this book is concerned mainly with metaphysics. Yet it is a self-help tool for working through psychological as well as spiritual issues. It is also a book of common sense, containing illustrative case histories of many of the people who have come to me for counseling. People come to me for various reasons. A few have come merely out of curiosity. Some have specific questions, such as, "When will I meet the man or woman I will marry?" and "Which job offer should I accept?" One client told me, "I came to see you today because I am trying to find God."

Shortly after that client's visit I decided to write this book. I feel that all of us, whether we are aware of it or not, are trying in our own ways to find God. I believe that God is within each and every one of us and that the God within us shines most brightly when we are involved in a life of service.

This is not a book you should read once and then put on the shelf; it should be used for reference. The twelve chapters cover many aspects of our lives; for example, if you are having a problem with a personal relationship, it may help you to look at the chapter on relationships to get some perspective on your particular problem or concern.

Many books have been published recently on spiritual development. Many of them focus on how to fulfill your desires for money, ambition, or sex. This book does not focus on showing the reader how to get what he or she desires. It is my hope the reader will learn through this book that the goal is to desire nothing and that a life of service is the greatest tonic for all of one's problems.

This book will show how it is possible to be selfless without being a martyr or a "doormat." Through examples of real people and their struggles, I hope to take the mystery out of metaphysics while leaving the sacredness intact. I have been asked by hundreds of clients to guide them toward books that will help them to understand the purpose of life. They constantly tell me they do not understand many of the books written about metaphysics. They become frustrated by their inability to understand, and then it seems impossible. I feel that this book will help to clarify many metaphysical subjects for the neophyte.

The point of life is growth. The Earth is a great schoolroom for the individual soul's development if you let it be so. Everything is all right in the long run. Life may appear very difficult or even totally overwhelming, but with understanding there can be great peace. If we learn to understand that this one life is but a drop of water in the great sea of time, we will become calm. If we can know in our hearts that everything is a test for the development of the individual, then we will have no reason to be upset all the time. We have eternity before us. There is plenty of time to learn to grow and find happiness. We are not running a race to become the most spiritually developed person. We can only hope to do the best we can with whatever situation is presented to us.

During an age such as the one we are living in, the opportunity for spiritual growth is enormous even as we face difficult times and will probably face more difficulties on the road ahead. We must reach toward our higher selves in order to cope with the problems of the age.

There are many ways to perceive any given situation. It does not matter what happens but only how we react to what happens. The choice lies in our own hands. I place emphasis on the idea of free choice throughout this book. The idea I am offering the reader is that you can and will have a happy life if you live a life of service and learn to be selfless. This concept has been a tremendous help to the hundreds of clients who have come to me over the last ten years.

This book is my gift to all those who are trying to be free.

∴ I ∴

The Maya of
Depression

I have found depression the most common problem of the people I meet and counsel. There have been hundreds of books written about it, and there seem to be just as many theories about what causes it. It seems to me that most people succumb to depression when they are thinking about themselves and don't have something they want or can't have their own way about something. The basic root of depression lies in selfishness.

Let's say you wake up with the blues. You try to get out of bed but find it very difficult. You lie there consumed with thoughts about what isn't going right for you, and you don't feel motivated to do anything. The phone rings. It is a close friend, and she tells you she has just fallen in her apartment and thinks she may have broken her leg. She needs your help to get to the hospital. Do you say, "I can't help you, I am too depressed"? Or do you say, "I'll be right there"? You probably jump out of bed, get dressed, and rush over to help your friend get to the hospital. You become busy with her needs for the next few hours, and during that time you forget about your own depression. Why? You have replaced the depression with the needs of another person. You've been so busy helping a person in need that you've had no time to think about yourself.

The I-I-I Syndrome

The I-I-I Syndrome is the term I've adopted for what I feel is the basis for most causes of depression. "I am lonely," "I do not have enough money," "I want people to love me more," "I feel helpless"—these are just a few examples of the I-I-I Syndrome. There can be no peace for you when you are consumed with thoughts of yourself and of your personal desires. If you take time to think about this, you will see the truth of it. How can you be depressed when you are thinking about the needs of another person? Your mind will not be able to hold on to the depression when it is focused on something other than its own desires. This is not to say we should live our lives as one grand avoidance of issues that make us feel bad. Yes, disturbing things will crop up. How can we live on a planet that is full of misery and not be affected by it? But you don't have to become depressed in order to share the pain of suffering humanity. I'm certain many of you have heard that it is good to keep yourself occupied if you're going through a difficult time. This is great advice. You must not allow yourself to fall into depression. There is too much to be done to waste your sacred energy this way.

Do a little experiment with me. Observe just how many times each day you use the word *I* and listen to the conversations of others. How often do you hear those around you using the word

I? Try to retrain yourself not to think the word *I* first. Replace *I* with *you.* Look at everyone you meet and be interested in what they are feeling and thinking. Don't allow yourself to stay consumed with thoughts of yourself.

I have a client who has been battling cancer for the last five years. The cancer metastasized to her brain. This lovely woman has two small children and a husband she loves very much. She faces the day-to-day uncertainty of not knowing if she will see her family and friends again. Yet she is always concerned about the feelings of others. The first words out of her mouth are always "How are you today?"

I remember visiting her at the hospital after surgery. She was asleep when I arrived so I sat quietly next to her bed and waited. When she woke up, the first thing she said was, "Mary, you look tired. Thank you so much for being here." Then she asked if I had eaten.

Her foremost concern is always with what effect her illness is having on her friends and family. In fact, many of our discussions center on the best way to handle the sadness and depression of the friends and family who visit her. She laughs and says that she has no fear of death. She sees her illness as a learning experience for her soul's development. Yes, she loves life and is doing everything in her power to become well, but depression has no place in it. Her concern for others carries her through even her most terrifying moments.

Those who are suffering often become stronger through serving others. We can learn by their example. I don't think it is necessary to put one's hand in the fire to prove that fire does burn, and we don't have to become seriously ill in order to learn selflessness. We can be fortified by the courage of those around us. We can look at the troubles of others and be grateful for what has been given to us. If we are truly grateful, it is not possible to be depressed. Don't look at the suffering of others and say, "How terrible!" and then run off and complain about the things you don't have. The gratitude you feel for all that has been given to you will lift you above depression.

The Fantasy of Depression

It is with the help of my friend and teacher Lawrence that I first came to an understanding of the true nature of depression.

I first met him on a glorious spring day while I was sitting on a bench in the park. I love the outdoors, but sitting in the park was unusual for me because I seldom have time to enjoy it. On that morning I felt compelled to go there. It was as though nothing could keep me away. I took a book with me, but I really did not feel like reading. All I could do was sit and take in the sunshine. I could have been preoccupied with a number of stressful situations, but on this day all seemed calm and peaceful. Feeling a cool breeze, I looked up. A man was standing next to me. I experienced a strange sensation of recognition; I was certain I knew this man but could not remember where I had seen him before. He looked at me and smiled. The urge to speak came over me, but it did not seem appropriate. A moment passed, then he sat down next to me.

He sat quietly for a few minutes soaking in the sunshine, then he took my hand in a gesture of friendship. As he held my hand I felt no fear. A sentence flowed through my mind: "When the student is ready, the teacher appears." The man spoke to me: "My child, do not be afraid. You are deeply concerned about a friend who is very ill with cancer. You must not allow yourself to become overwhelmed because you are doing everything possible to help her. Your friend is learning much through her illness, and she is helping others. Do not doubt yourself, for you are on the right path. You suffer at times because you allow yourself to become enveloped in the maya of the physical world." He spoke in a deep, comforting voice.

Tears came to my eyes. I was filled with awe and gratitude. This man had just answered the questions that had been plaguing me. He had perceived my thoughts without conversation. A second of confusion passed over me as I thought of the word *maya*. "Maya means misconception or illusion," he said. There is an ancient story of a man who is walking down the street and jumps in fear as he sees a snake. He moves closer and sees that it is not a snake but a piece of rope. He laughs at himself when he realizes that he reacted to something that did not really exist.

"He was reacting to the maya. The reality was that he did not see what he thought he saw. People often become depressed over the possible outcome of a certain situation. If people reacted to what is and not to what they desire, they would not become depressed. Disappointment causes depression. If man learned to desire nothing, he would then be free of depression. Life on the Earth plane is full of illusion. It is like looking at a painting. What do you really see? It may appear to be a portrait of, say, a woman or a sailor, but what is it really? Is it not paint on canvas that produces the illusion of a woman or a sailor? Is paint not made of chemicals that are in turn composed of molecules which can be further broken down to atoms and then to subatomic particles and finally to pure force?

"Life, as we perceive it, is maya. Physical life does not last. The physical plane is a schoolroom for the soul's development. Everything that happens to us, every situation we attract to ourselves, is an opportunity for spiritual growth. The spirit of man is eternal. Physical life comes and goes. Realize that everything is an experience and that all is well, and you will not fall into depression.

"If you are thinking of others and of how you may best serve, there will be no place for depression. Think of what you have been given rather than of what you do not have, and you will not fall into the maya of depression. Your mind cannot hold two thoughts at the same time. If the mind is concentrating on service, it cannot be depressed. Do not leave yourself open to depression. Accept what is and do not despair because things are not the way you think they should be. You limit yourself by expecting. You may miss a side road that is much more beautiful. Nothing is perfect, for we are always striving to become better souls. In physical life we are asked to deal with problems every moment. So be it!

"Action is the greatest tonic for depression. Do something for another, and the depression will dissolve before your eyes. There are hundreds of ways to help and to serve. If you are presented with a problem that seems too difficult to handle on your own, seek proper help. Allow someone the privilege of helping you. This in itself is an action, the action of accepting help that is available. If psychological help is needed, seek a therapist. If it is a medical problem, seek a physician. Do not feed the depression by going over and over the things in life that are not perfect. Get busy serving and live for the now.

"Since the beginning, mankind has believed things that were not true. At one time people thought the world was flat. We now know that is not true, but at one time we believed it. As we grow and learn, our perception of the true, 'the real,' changes.

"The true spiritual man, the God in embryo, is never depressed. The true man is aware of the continuation of life and the need to learn through various experiences. The real man does not feel victimized but is aware that he is fulfilling his destiny and that he has attracted all things to himself in order to learn. To act as a victim is to allow yourself to slip into the illusion, 'the maya,' that life is being unfair to you.

"For instance, say you are driving down the road and you think you see a turnoff. As you approach you see it is actually a circular drive that will put you back on the original path. When you drove toward it, you expected to be able to turn off one road and onto another. Will you become angry and overwhelmed because you did not see what was really there, or will you drive on until you reach a real exit? Think about this and your drive will proceed smoothly.

"For another example, let us say that one day you come home and find your husband is not there. You wait but hear no word from him. You start imagining all sorts of tragedies: He has left you for good and will never come back. He has been in a terrible accident. He has run off with another woman. He does not care for you any longer. You'd say to yourself that if he did, how could he make you suffer so? You start to cry and become hysterical. The time goes slowly. You feel on the edge of despair. This is very unlike your husband, you say; he has never gone out before without leaving a message for you. Your imagination takes off and you pace the floor. You think of all kinds of things you will say to him if and when he returns home. You are triggered into reliving past experiences that make you feel that way.

"There was the time your father did not return when he said he would. You have had lovers in the past who disappointed you by their insensitivity. The thoughts go on and on and you become frantic. You start thinking about how you will go on now that your husband has gone. Then, finally, the door opens and he is home. He apologizes for not being there sooner and not calling to tell you where he was. He says that he has been trapped in a stalled subway train for three hours. You start to laugh at yourself because you allowed yourself to create such a fantasy. You operated under the illusion that there had been a tragedy when it was merely an uncomfortable situation. You just went through three hours of maya. If you had only waited, you would have been fine.

"Suppose you wake up one morning with a headache. Instead of going back to bed, accepting the discomfort, knowing that it will pass, you start thinking that it must be something deadly. You remember a magazine article you read about brain tumors and you are sure this is an early symptom. Getting yourself into a terrible state, you start to allow cold fear to take over. You become so consumed with your fantasy that you don't even notice your headache has passed. You have just spent the last few minutes in a state of maya, operating under the illusion that there was something terribly wrong.

"You must get a grip on yourself when these feelings start to take over and not allow yourself to take off emotionally into an unreal state. This unnecessary stress will take years off your life. Wait to see the results before you decide that there is a tragic ending! Maybe things will turn out in a positive way. If you start fantasizing, use a sense of humor to lighten your load.

"Some people think depression is suppressed anger. You would not be angry if you did not allow yourself to live in a state of constant expectation. Disappointment usually causes anger and the resulting depression. Keep yourself open and do not allow yourself to decide the outcome of any situation in advance. There will always be times of sadness and times of great joy. There will be days that seem more fruitful than other days, but all days bear fruit when one is involved in the learning process. Each day we are given the opportunity to learn and to serve, and that is wonderful."

Lawrence stopped talking and sat watching some children at play. He smiled as he watched them. The children were involved in a game of tag, and their squeals of delight were a joy to hear. The sun was bright, and I felt as if I were sitting in a church, not in the park. Looking at Lawrence, I felt reverence. What a remarkable man! Somehow I had attracted the interest of this soul. How fortunate! I had known that teachers like Lawrence existed, and my own inquiries into metaphysics had helped to prepare me to meet this great man. But nevertheless, I was astonished by his advanced level of spiritual development, far beyond that of any person I had ever encountered. His calm dignity was unearthly. I could not tell his age, for he seemed vibrant and youthful but also wise, as if he had experienced a great many things. He was very handsome, but it was more than that: He radiated warmth and peacefulness, and energy seemed to flow forth from his very being. Feeling totally happy, I relaxed and waited, not wanting to break the spell by speaking!

A Frisbee flew by and landed near Lawrence's feet. He leaned over, picked it up, and laughed as he sailed it back to the child who had thrown it. "There is so much to learn from observing children at play," he said. "Didn't a very wise man once say that we must become like little children in order to grow?" He looked closely at me, smiled, and said, "What are you thinking, my child?"

After a moment I replied, "When I was younger, I used to have a difficult fight with my own feelings of depression. Walking down the street one day I looked up into a very blue sky. At that moment I realized I was allowing myself to be depressed and I could choose not to be. I was aware it was I who was choosing to be depressed and that everything was really all right. I was fighting with myself, and I did not want to do that any longer. Maybe this sounds a little strange, but it was then I stopped being depressed. Yes, there are sad times and times filled with worry, but these never depress me anymore. It is really a question of one's point of view."

He nodded. "Indeed it is, my child. If you hold on to the point of view that to live is to serve and if you do so lovingly, you will never become depressed. You will be much too busy to have time for depression. You, my child, are busy serving and growing. That will leave you no time to become depressed."

"Yes," I said. "I understand what you mean about depression being a fantasy, but depression is real to the people who are experiencing these feelings. How can I explain to them that their feelings are not real? How can I help those people who think that the physical is the only reality?"

"You must remind people that the physical does not last," Lawrence said. "Any situation that you attract is an opportunity to grow. It is a challenge for the individual to work through any test that life presents. Physical life comes and goes. The body ages and eventually passes over from physical life to spirit life. That is why the physical life is not real. What is real endures. The physical life is a temporary state of consciousness. One who understands this will not allow life's tests to cause depression.

"Repetition is a great teacher. Remember, we are merely offering a point of view. It is up to the individual whether or not to accept this viewpoint. We are not here to convince anyone. We are here to serve and to help through showing others a different perspective. All people are free to act or react in any manner they feel is right for them. Doesn't common sense as well as metaphysics teach one that selfless thinking is very freeing? Isn't it helpful to show people a road that has fewer pitfalls? They then may choose the road most suited to their individual development. Not everyone will agree, and that is fine. Do not worry about how people react, for that is their choice. You and I are here to offer this point of view. No single point of view suits everyone. This makes life interesting. Some people prefer vanilla ice cream and some prefer chocolate. It is good that both flavors are available for the individual to taste, but how does one find the best flavor without tasting them all? Yes, many people will say, 'I have tried vanilla and it is fine, so why bother to try chocolate?' Chocolate lovers will say, 'Look at what they are missing.' I say it is best to taste each one and then decide. Why limit yourself before you have had a chance to experience something new?

"Quiet thoughtfulness is not depression. Concern is not depression. It is similar to the contrast between assertiveness and aggressiveness. If one asserts oneself, it is positive. If one acts aggressively, others perceive this behavior as harsh and desperate. Sadness is not depression unless it becomes selfish and self-indulgent. There are many things in life that cause one to feel sad or even frustrated, but you do not have to allow yourself to succumb to the illusion of depression. This serves no purpose other than to make one feel hopeless. There is always hope, no matter what the situation, for each situation presents the individual with the opportunity to learn."

Lawrence stopped speaking, and a serene silence surrounded us. It had begun to get dark. Totally engrossed in the conversation as I had been, time seemed to me to have stood still. Lawrence took my hand and said that it was time for him to leave. He informed me that we would meet again in the very near future. "I will be in touch with you," he said as we walked out of the park. Lawrence hailed a taxi and opened the door for me. He bowed and said, "Until later." I got in the taxi and watched Lawrence stroll away. It had been an amazing day.

A woman named Elsie came to see me the next afternoon in a highly anxious state. She said she had sunk into a severe depression and could neither eat nor sleep. She had just lost her job of eleven years. There had been no warning signs, she said, and she felt that she had been treated shabbily and wanted to get revenge. "Revenge?" I said. "How can you think that way? I know you are upset, but don't you realize that vengeful feelings will just turn on you? You have good reasons to be upset, anyone would be, but let's examine what has really happened here."

Elsie started pacing the floor, talking about how unfairly she had been treated. She said she had given her life to the job, and no one had ever said "thank you" or appreciated her in any way. She said she felt as if she could not go on. She was in a panic about finances and had come to me to see if I felt that she would be all right. When I asked her if she had sought professional counseling, she became outraged. "I am not crazy!" she exclaimed. "I'm just overwrought."

"Elsie," I said, "nobody is saying you are crazy. Do you think a person must be crazy in order to seek help? You tell me you're depressed and can neither eat nor sleep. You're very worried about money, and you're holding on to thoughts of revenge. It just seems to be common sense that you need someone to talk to, to help you sort all this out. I can help you, but I'm not a therapist.

"First of all, Elsie," I went on, "can you truthfully say that you had no warning of any kind that there were problems at work?"

She became very quiet and tears welled in her eyes. "My boss hated me because I was a woman. I would yell at him because he was so stupid."

"You were yelling at your boss, Elsie, and you didn't realize that there were problems?"

"Well," she said, "he was always angry because I was late. I couldn't help it. I have a hard time waking up in the morning, and the trains are always so slow. I was only ten minutes late, or maybe twenty, but why was it a big deal? I still say it was because I was a woman."

"Did your boss also get angry at the men who were late?" I asked.

Elsie became quiet for a moment, then said, "Yes, I guess he did. But I still want to get him! How dare he fire me after all I did for him and his company!" She started to cry.

"Elsie, did you really like the job?"

"Like it? I hated it! I never wanted to work in an office. I just was too upset to leave and I wasn't certain what else I wanted to do."

"Whom did your boss remind you of, Elsie?" I asked. "I think he reminded you of someone else you wanted to please but were never able to."

"My ex-husband," she answered quickly. "He acted just like my ex-husband."

"Were you depressed throughout most of your marriage?"

"Yes, I was always depressed."

"Elsie," I said, "you are healthy, isn't that true?"

"Yes, of course. I've always been healthy."

"You have friends, don't you?" I asked.

"I have great friends."

"You have a place to live?"

"Of course I have a place to live," she exclaimed.

"Then, Elsie, I think you have no problems that can't be handled," I said. "You must work on changing your point of view so that you will be able to attract a happy work situation. Your attitude seems to be your worst enemy. You must stop looking at this firing as a tragedy and see it as an opportunity to get on with your life, to get a new job that is more suited to you. It will serve no purpose to be depressed since nothing can be gained by allowing yourself to be this way. If your anger causes you to act, then it is good. If your anger is turned on yourself or on your boss, it will only keep you depressed and ultimately make you sick. It is all experience, and it is all right. Let it go and get on to the next job. You will have no trouble attracting a new job if you let yourself be positive and get out there and look for one. You were miserable at the last job, so it was time to leave. If we aren't strong enough to make a decision, sometimes the decision gets made for us. In the long run you will see that this is all positive. You are now free to go on, and you are also being allowed to learn some valuable lessons." I took a deep breath.

"You're telling me to look at this as a positive situation?" Elsie asked. "You're saying that I have no right to hate my boss? You're saying I shouldn't try to get him into trouble? I am supposed to look at this and learn? I don't know how to do that." She sighed.

"Start to take responsibility for your actions, and you won't be depressed," I told her. "You will see that it was time to leave the job, and that's fine. Your boss will attract his own set of circumstances to deal with. You don't have to waste your precious energy wishing evil to befall him. In fact, you must stop that. It isn't wise and will merely cause you to feel worse in the long run. Your depression is a type of temper tantrum, Elsie. You don't like the way things have turned out so you're throwing a fit. Stop it, it is ridiculous. You're too big to be throwing tantrums, aren't you? Get on with your life, and you'll see that things will work out just fine! Consider the time you're wasting, thinking about how you've been wronged. I say you attracted this situation because you were being negative, and now you must go and attract a new, positive situation to yourself. It's all in your hands. You have free choice to decide how you will go on from this moment forward. Learn from all this, and it will serve you well. I still say you have no problems that can't be handled if you look at them from the proper viewpoint. You don't have time for depression; you must go out and get another job."

Elsie seemed to calm down and think about all this. We went on to discuss other job possibilities for her. She laughed a bit as she told me stories of the old job and also of her life with her ex-husband. She said she would try to think about things in a different light. She was not certain she would be able to, but she would try.

"That's all any of us can do, Elsie," I said, and I repeated that she needed to talk to a counselor to help her deal with her inner rage and feelings of uselessness. She left the session a bit lighter.

You Can Choose Your Own Mood

Many people demand their right to be depressed and unhappy, saying they're not in control of their moods. This is not true. You can look at any situation that arises and decide how you will handle it. Depression causes one to feel alone and hopeless. It is the height of self-indulgence when one allows the fantasy of depression to take control. Rarely are we really out of control. Your mood doesn't have to control you. In Elsie's case she had to feel angry, but she did not have to allow the anger to turn into thoughts of revenge. That was pointless and would do nothing but bring her pain. She may have a moment of euphoria while she plots her revenge, but this ultimately will not make her feel anything but miserable. How can we find happiness through inflicting pain on another? Jesus very wisely said that we must turn the other cheek. If you can realize the connectedness of all things, you will understand that what you do to another, you also do to yourself. An act or thought of revenge is an act or thought of violence turned on oneself!

I have a client named Sharon who, no matter what happens in her life, always conducts herself with the utmost dignity. Her life has been anything but easy, but you would never know that she has experienced great tragedy. Her unfailing concern for the comfort of those around her is reflected in her impeccable manners. Too many people have forgotten what good manners are. I don't mean the intricacies of etiquette; there are books that will tell you how to hold a teacup. To have truly good manners means to treat others with sensitivity and consideration. It isn't good manners, for example, to go to a dinner party in a blue funk and make the host and other guests uncomfortable. Use common sense; if you are in a bad state, then go to the party and act with consideration for others or excuse yourself and leave, or don't go. As difficult as you might imagine this would be to do, in the long run it's best for you and others! Rise to the occasion. Observe the dispositions of those whom you respect, and learn from their behavior. There is nothing phony or pretentious about good manners.

There are times in our lives when we are bombarded by troubles that seem intolerable. The loss of a loved one, financial ruin, great illness, the loss of a pet; these are just a few examples of difficulties we are asked to deal with. We all have a psychological history. There will always be incidents from our past that return to haunt us. Many people have had childhoods that were devastating; I have heard numerous stories of brutality, sexual abuse, neglect, and psychological torture. Some people deal with these horrors by becoming altruistic, transforming their painful feelings into a passionate desire to alleviate the suffering of others. This is excellent and helps one to transmute the pain into service. Other people are left unable to function in the world. If this happens to you, then of course you must seek the proper method to help you get through. There are times when antidepressant medication seems to be the only answer. This is the choice of the individual and should be undertaken only with proper professional medical care. Antidepressant drug therapy should not be used to avoid real issues. While it may be necessary to help get you through a very serious temporary situation, it will not solve the underlying problem. But medication is available to help us; there's no reason to endure pain unnecessarily. If you have an infection, take the necessary medication now before it turns into something more serious, then examine how you may have attracted the infection to you so that you can avoid illness in the future.

You must work on your character in order to live a productive life. You may not be able to integrate positive thinking and selflessness into your consciousness overnight. It may even take more than one lifetime to work out the traumas of an incarnation, so don't feel guilty for your lack of ability to deal with issues. Like depression, selfishness serves no purpose. Deal with your problems as you must, but aspire, even through your tragedies, to become selfless and of service to mankind. Each of us controls his or her own destiny. You may be confronted with problems that seem beyond your control, but it is within your power to deal with any situation that has been presented to you.

Don't Be Depressed, Do Something!

If you feel depressed, try to perform an action to help you get through this period. If you are busy, you will not have time to think about yourself. I have a friend who, when he is going through a difficult time in his life, will paint his apartment. When I call him and he is in the middle of redoing his living room, I always know that he must be going through a rough time. This is his way of using energy to do something. He has a great-looking apartment! He has found that the physical energy he expends in painting helps him mentally. What can I say? If it works, that's great. He will start out in a bad mood, but by the end of his painting he is usually feeling much better.

Some people exercise or go to a movie to take their minds off themselves. This is common sense. If you are feeling gloom and doom, then go out and do something. You will find that there are ways to help you get through. Don't just sit around feeling sorry for yourself. If you think about it, there are many things you have put off doing that would help you feel better if you did them. Clean the closet or clear out those drawers that you have neglected. Go out and volunteer to help at a hospital or at a soup kitchen, any place where your energy is needed. It will give you a sense of well-being and will help others at the same time. I repeat: If you have a bad day, do something. Do not allow yourself to wallow in your own negativity. The time will pass, and before you know it, you will be feeling much better. The best cure for depression is doing, doing, doing!

There is so much to be done on this planet to help others that it is overwhelming. There is no time to submerge into thoughts of yourself. Each of us is needed. Every one of us can do something to make this a better world. A client of mine who had been very depressed about the homeless people in the streets decided that each month she would donate twenty dollars to a soup kitchen. She does not make a lot of money, and twenty dollars was the most she felt she could give. I thought about this and realized that if every working person gave twenty dollars each month, there would be no hunger! This would be easy for most people and would serve the planet in a major way!

Don't become angry and overwhelmed about the plight of homeless people. Do what my client did and find a place to give a little money. If possible, also give a bit of your time. It is so easy to help, whereas it's difficult to sit around and be negative. Again, do something. No act of kindness is too small.

Where there is life there is hope. There is always a reason to go on. There is always help to be given. There is always something to learn. Life is sacred and wonderful. Your attitude will serve you well if it is an attitude of serving and of aspiring to become selfless. There's no time to be depressed. If something in your life is not working for you, so be it. There's something else waiting in the wings to help you in your quest for freedom. Get out of yourself and you will soar. Stay locked in the cell of your desires, and you will waste time that could be used to help others. Think of the Earth as a large schoolroom, and you will not easily fall into despair. Once you have learned one lesson, another lesson is given to you. Great!

I help a number of Native American families on a reservation in the Dakotas. At least three times a week, I receive a collect call from one of them. The situation on the reservation is appalling. The illness and hopelessness are beyond belief.

Recently, one of these people, a diabetic, had his second leg amputated. Diabetes is a very serious problem on the reservation because of a poor diet that is heavy in refined sugar. The man who had his legs amputated was only forty years old. He wasn't aware that he had this illness until he had a cut on his foot that wouldn't heal. Eventually he was told by doctors that he would die if the leg wasn't amputated. He had just begun to adapt to the loss of the first leg when the other one became gangrenous and also had to be cut off. When I phoned him in the hospital, he told me that for a while he had considered suicide. There had seemed to be no point in going on. His main concern was that he would be a burden to his wife and family. His wife had also been sick, with both cancer and diabetes; she had lost sixty pounds and had no strength. He talked on for a while and then said that at least he still had his mind and that he might be able to counsel others who had the same problems.

All the people on the reservation seem to have a capacity for laughter in the face of great adversity. They have nothing but are deeply grateful for any help that is offered.

Their economic situation is, of course, heartbreaking; this area of the country is going through a serious recession, and there has been a terrible drought as well. The Indians are always trying to find work, but there are no jobs. They are not lazy; one of the women goes from door to door offering to clean houses or do any odd jobs that are available. When people ask me why the Indians don't move to a place where they can more easily find work, I try to explain how economic and educational deficiencies are built into the reservation system. This, combined with the Indian's strong spiritual connection to the land, makes it difficult if not impossible for most of them to leave. Many who have tried find that they simply don't adjust to living away from the reservation.

These people have done me a great honor by adopting me into their tribe; I truly feel as if they are my family. Many of my clients have helped them, too, with contributions of various kinds. My friend Kathy, who has been very ill herself, is always helping my "family," sending frequent donations of clothing and money. The Indians constantly ask me about Kathy and send their love and prayers.

These sacred people have nothing but trouble. They are desperately in need of help of every kind, yet they are always interested in others. Though they aren't lacking for reasons to be depressed, it is amazing how they go on and try to make the best of things. Their great dignity, faith, and perseverance can serve as a shining example.

∴ I I ∴
Fear and Worry

"Hello, this is Laura. I was given your phone number by our mutual friend Lawrence. I was hoping I could make an appointment to see you in the near future."

Looking over my book, I told Laura that, yes, I could work her in at six o'clock that evening because I had a cancellation. After giving her directions, I told her I was looking forward to meeting with her.

Happy in the thought that I could do something for a friend of Lawrence's, I sat down to write. The work flowed. In fact, ever since I'd met Lawrence the writing became easier. He inspired me as I sat at the typewriter; I initially always wrote about our meetings as soon as I returned home.

I had discussed with Lawrence the fact that many of my clients seemed plagued with feelings of fear and felt hopeless when their fear buttons were pushed. I asked Lawrence how he thought people could best handle fear when it took over.

"Fear is worry about the outcome of situations. We must learn to accept what life presents us as a test of our spiritual development. If we can do this, we will be too busy with action to be submerged in thoughts of fear," he said. "There is a choice involved in all aspects of living. Each of us has moments of fear. Let yourself feel the fear, then go forward. It does not matter that you are afraid. What matters is that you feel fear and go forward anyway.

"The basic reason for existence is growth. Fear presents us with great opportunities for growth. Overcoming fear brings great spiritual freedom. Understand that everything is experience and that all of our experiences present us with opportunities to grow. A pure motivation to serve others will direct us on a straight path. If our motivation is the wise action, then fear will not sway us.

"Selfishness causes great confusion. Selflessness brings peace. Get yourself out of the way. 'What will happen to me?' is the wrong way to think. 'What may I do to serve?' is the question that expresses proper motivation."

The buzzer rang, shaking me loose from my writing, at exactly six o'clock. Laura was on time and dressed in pale green, which brought out the deep green of her eyes. As I looked at her, I felt a flash of pain, a feeling of deep sadness. Her eyes seemed dull and lifeless, despite their striking color, and her very being seemed suffused with pain.

Taking my hand, she thanked me for seeing her so quickly. "Lawrence has spoken very highly of you," she said in a soft voice. I asked her if she would like some coffee, and she declined. I showed her to a chair, sat across from her in my blue chair, and we began our session.

She looked lovely and fragile at the same time. I asked her if she had ever spoken to a psychic before. She said that she had spoken only to Lawrence at great length. She was a pianist and had first met Lawrence a few years before when he appeared backstage after a concert she had played. She had immediately felt comfortable with him. I told her I had felt the same way during my first encounter with him.

"I haven't come to see you because I expect you to produce psychic phenomena," she said. "I came because I felt you might help me so that I can go on with my music. I've been totally blocked, unable to write, for over a year. I've been very ill. I suppose you could say I had a nervous breakdown." Her already soft voice became quieter as she recalled this painful episode of her life.

"Laura," I said, "it isn't really unusual for one as sensitive as you to have the feeling that your nerves are disintegrating. You aren't alone. Many people suffer this type of nervous collapse. The nervous system is sensitive and can take only so much stress before it rebels. I've had times in my life when I had the feeling my nerves would snap, but I got through them. Maybe I had a walking nervous breakdown; I'm not certain what you would call it. People used to be embarrassed about this type of thing, considering it a sign of weakness; unfortunately, many people still are. They and their families try to keep it quiet. I believe that such a breakdown does not signify weakness but is merely the nervous system telling us 'Enough.' As a great musician you are more sensitive than most of us. The gift of music flows through you; a great deal of energy is channeled through you. You have to realize that many great artists suffer enormously. It is sad, but anguish seems to be part of the price an artist must pay for such a great gift. Life always produces balance at some point, and we are tested in proportion to our gifts. If we are given much, we will be greatly tested. This is the law.

"I feel that there is a serious problem in your relationship with your father. I sense an unresolved situation, and I think we should discuss it."

She put her face in her hands and began to cry. I paused before saying to her, "Laura, let it out. It's all right—tears can be very cleansing. Don't try to hold your feelings in. You must bring them forward in order to release the pain so that true healing can begin. I think there is something you haven't forgiven yourself for, something you shouldn't feel responsible for. We often neglect forgiveness when we are dealing with ourselves. It's often easier to forgive others than to forgive ourselves."

Laura looked up at me through her tears and smiled. When she spoke again, her voice was deeper, calmer, and steadier.

"My father was my music teacher as well as my manager. He had wanted to be a composer and a performer himself, but he was never successful at it. I think he saw the possibility of his dreams being fulfilled through me, but he was a tyrant, forcing me to practice until I thought my hands would break. I was never good enough for him. He always wanted it better. 'More feeling, Laura,' he would repeat over and over. When I made the slightest mistake, he became angry and refused to speak to me until I could play the music flawlessly.

"I can still see him standing over me, saying, 'No, no, not that way, you little fool.' He was relentless. I know he felt this was the way to teach. After brutalizing me, he would then turn around and buy me a lovely gift of some kind. I remember that he gave me a scarf once. All I wanted to do was tear it into little pieces and throw them at him, feeling that this might show him how he was always tearing at me. I was afraid of him and was always plotting ways to get away from him. From time to time my mother tried to get him to ease up on me, but she was afraid, too. She knew he would turn his anger on her, and she wanted to avoid that at all costs. My mother occasionally slipped into my room at night and told me to try to understand that my father just wanted what was best for me. She hugged me and told me that she loved me. I so much wanted to say to her, 'If you love me so much, do something. Don't allow this to go on any longer.' "

Laura paused, and I went to get her a glass of water. She took a few sips of water and continued: "In the long run, I don't really blame my mother. She wasn't able to stand up to my father.

"I started composing at the age of nine. My first piece was performed when I was thirteen. My father was so thrilled, you'd think he would have let up a little, but he didn't. I used to wish I had a life like other teenagers. You know what I mean: go to parties and have my friends over. But I wasn't able to establish friendships. My father insisted that I spend all my time practicing the piano.

"I was so shy that I think the other kids thought I was some sort of snob. I didn't know how to make friends, having spent all my time with my music. I was fifteen when I first met Brian. I was walking home from my school, the High School for Performing Arts. Brian came up next to me and started a conversation. I didn't know what to say to him, but he made things easy for me. He seemed to understand my discomfort, and he just chatted on, even though I didn't say much. Brian told me he had noticed me for the first time a few months before, had wanted to talk to me, but had been afraid that I wouldn't be interested in him. He said he had seen me play and that he was very impressed. He played the drums and was part of a band that played on the weekends. He asked if I would like to come and hear him one Saturday night.

"I started to feel more comfortable!" Laura said. "He was confident and calm, and I admired that. I told him that my father didn't like me to go out. He felt I'd be too tired to practice. Brian said, 'Don't you take time to relax and have fun?' 'Not really,' I answered. He wanted to know if I had any friends, and I told him I did have one friend, a girl named Martha. My father liked her because she came from a very good family. She lived in Connecticut, and once in a while my father allowed me to visit her on a weekend.

"When we reached my apartment, Brian shook my hand and said that he would see me at school the next day. It was one of the first times I can remember feeling really happy! I couldn't wait until the next day, but I knew I must not let my father know that I had been talking to Brian.

"Time passed, and I got to know Brian better. He was always warm to me and still seemed interested. He talked about music and told me about his goals. He said that he was really proud of me and kept asking me to come and hear his band. I searched my mind to come up with a way to hear him. I finally talked to Martha about it. She was delighted! She said she was always worried about the fact that I never seemed to be interested in boys. She worked out a plan to convince my father that I would be staying with her family for the weekend. Her parents were going to be out of town, but we didn't let my father know. Martha and I arranged to go to the club in New York where Brian's band was playing. I was terribly excited. We got there, and Brian was beaming as I sat listening to them. I had never been to a rock and roll club before, and I had a ball. We all stayed out until after four, and then a friend of Brian's who had a car drove us to Martha's house in Connecticut. I sat in the back with Brian, feeling that I was really in love.

"We arrived at Martha's house to find my father there. I was shocked, but I should have known he would call to check on me. He was in a rage and grabbed me. Brian tried to explain, but my father wouldn't listen. He ordered me into his car and we drove off. I will never forget the look on Brian's face. My father didn't speak right away but waited silently for half an hour. He then ordered me never to see 'that boy' again. I tried to explain that it had been a harmless evening with friends, but my father wouldn't listen. I should have stood up for myself and Brian more than I did. I should have told my father that I was going to start living my own life! In retrospect I can see so many things I could and should have done, but I wasn't able to do any of them at the time. I gave in, or I should say I gave up. I felt as if I could never stand up to my father. I just thought, What is the use? I was too afraid.

"My father told me that if I ever saw Brian again, he would send me to another school. So I started acting very cold and distant. When Brian saw me at school and tried to make conversation, I was horrible. Finally he stopped. Who wouldn't have? I continued with my music, pleasing my father but feeling miserable. Time passed and I had a string of successes, but nothing seemed to matter. I felt dead inside. I was never able to forget Brian.

"A little over a year ago I was in London giving a concert. Martha visited me backstage before the performance. She had married an older man with a lot of money, and they had been traveling in Europe where she had read that I was giving a concert. Surprisingly so, her behavior seemed a bit superficial and silly when she stopped in my dressing room. Then she said in a hushed tone, 'You must have been terribly upset when you heard about Brian. Isn't it positively dreadful?'

"I looked at her, totally confused. She sensed that I didn't know what she was talking about. She put her hand to her mouth and said, 'Oh, dear, you haven't heard. How awful of me.'

"I said, 'Martha, what are you talking about?'

"She told me that Brian had been killed in a car accident about four weeks earlier. It had been all over the New York papers. I just looked at her.

"The stage manager came and said, 'Five minutes, please.' I could hear the orchestra warming up. The room became blurred, and I felt as if I might faint.

"My father walked in at that moment and sensed that there was something wrong. 'Laura,' he said, 'what is it?' I could not speak. 'Get out,' he told Martha. He poured a glass of water and gave it to me, saying, 'Pull yourself together, Laura. The critics are all here tonight. This is a very important evening.'

"The stage manager came to the door and said, 'One minute.' I went to the door in a complete daze, unable to feel anything. Dizzy and disoriented, I looked at the orchestra and then heard the applause starting. My name had been announced and I had not heard it.

" 'Go on, Laura,' my father said. He almost pushed me onto the stage. I walked onstage, and all I can remember is the heat and glare of the lights beating down on me. I sat at the piano, and then the orchestra started. My hands wouldn't move. It was as if I was paralyzed. I couldn't hear anything.

"The next thing I knew I was lying in my dressing room with a doctor standing over me. My father looked stricken, almost in shock, but all he could say was, 'Oh dear, what will the critics say?'

"That was the last time I was able to go near a piano. No matter how hard my father tried, I would not go near it. I just looked at him and walked away. He took me to a psychiatrist and I would not talk. Finally, I was removed from my father. The doctor said that was my only hope for recovery. My mother cried about it a lot, but she finally took matters into her own hands and moved me in with a friend of hers. She told my father to leave me alone—he had done enough damage.

"In time I began talking a little, but I never really trusted the doctor. On a trip home from the doctor about a month ago, I met Lawrence. He was so kind and helpful and spoke to me at length."

Upon hearing Laura's story, I immediately felt there was a strong karmic relationship between Laura and her father. In fact, they seemed to have been married in a past incarnation. And, yes, there were lots of psychological implications. Theirs, in this incarnation, was an old, old story: the father trying to make up for his own failed goals and dreams through the success of his child. Although Laura had not seen Brian in years, she was still in love with him—loyalty being a fundamental part of her nature. But the loyalty also helped to perpetuate her destructive link with her father.

I explained to Laura what I meant by referring to it as a karmic relationship. I told her there is much about the way life is that most of us cannot see but must learn to appreciate. Relationships have their roots in karma, in reopening what is sown. But at the same time it is important that we not use karma as an excuse for our failure or a reason for our success. It is easy to shrug one's shoulders and blame karma rather than accept the challenge of increasing our own understanding of ourselves.

The worst was over, I said to her. Brian was not in any way dead. He had simply fulfilled this part of his karmic destiny, and it was time for him to "pass over."

"Laura, you will see him again," I assured her. "You must realize this. We all leave this planet at one time or another. It is in the hands of a force higher than ourselves. We miss each other and grieve for our loss, and that is natural. But you go on with your life and release your grief and your anger toward your father so that you can feel free. Brian was always very supportive of your work. He would be sad to know that you are so tormented by his passing that you stopped working. Yours is a gift that must be used to help humanity, and in time you will be able to go back to your music. I know it seems overwhelming now, but it won't always seem so. Great tragedies often produce great art. We sometimes produce our best work as a result of our greatest heartbreak. You must begin to think of the bigger picture. Your life is one of service, and it is through serving that you will be happy in the long run."

I went on to tell her she should not feel pressured by what I said. "If you need more time in order to truly heal, then you must take that time. You will be surprised, though, to see how much better you will feel when you are back at work. Try to work for just thirty minutes a day for the time being. I know you've been trained to work long hours to keep your gift polished, but that would produce too much pressure at this time. Start out slowly. Try to work for thirty minutes. Don't worry about whether you produce anything or not, just see what happens. You must understand that the gift comes through you. If you don't want to deal with your father at this time, that's fine. Separation is often a sign of growth. You still need to be away from him because seeing him is too painful for you."

I asked her if she was still seeing a therapist. She said that she had stopped for the time being because she didn't feel like going over her feelings again and again. I asked her if there was a music teacher in town whom she respected and I felt it might be good for her to study with a woman, given the painful nature of her relationship with her father. It might be easier for her to deal with psychologically.

I also told her that she had to start watching her diet. "You're much too thin, and this could be part of your problem," I said. "If you have a lot of trouble eating, then you must get a blender and start drinking protein drinks. This will help you regain your strength, which will help you feel more prepared to work again. It takes an enormous amount of energy to create. You must work to regain your physical strength, and you should consult a medical doctor about vitamin therapy to help you regain the strength of your nervous system. Your nerves have been pushed to their limit."

I also suggested a woman therapist I had known for the last eight years for whom I have a great deal of respect. I suggested that Laura see her because she still needed to talk about things. Laura seemed very eager to do what was necessary to get on with her life. She talked for a few minutes more about her fears, and then she laughed. It was the first time since she'd arrived that she was able to relax enough to laugh.

I went on to say that I saw her producing a new work within the next eighteen months. "Has music been going through your head when you wake up in the morning?" I asked.

She blinked in surprise and said, "Yes. For the last few weeks I've had a melody running through my mind. I awaken with it, and as soon as I'm totally conscious it seems to go away and I forget about it until the next morning."

"See," I said, "you're beginning to open up again." I suggested a book for her to read, *Theosophy Simplified* by Irving S. Cooper (Wheaton, Illinois: The Theosophical Press). I felt that she needed something tangible to take with her. I told her she could call me at any time, even in the middle of the night. Then I looked at the clock and realized that two hours had passed and that she had had enough for the time being. We knew we would see each other soon.

Laura stood up slowly and said that she felt much better. She told me she would call the therapist right away and would try to work on her music for thirty minutes each day. She said that seemed easy compared to her long-held belief that she had to work hours or not at all. I walked her to the door where we hugged each other. Her eyes brimmed with tears, but they were not the same as the tears of sadness, grief, and desperation she shed at the beginning of our session. These were tears of relief.

Pointing the Way

I thought about Laura for a long time after she left. It is very important in my work to be aware of how much a person can take at one time because everyone has a different capacity. Certain people who are very ill want to know every detail of the seriousness of their situation, while others do not want to hear everything at one time. I treat each client who walks through my door as an individual. There is no set formula in receiving and imparting psychic information. The responsibility of the psychic is to tune in to the person and speak to him or her in a way that is comfortable and productive. I have heard horror stories of psychic readers frightening clients so much that they left the reading in a state of panic. This is not helpful and can be very destructive. Firmness and honesty must be tempered with kindness and empathy when trying to help others.

Where there is life there is hope. Rarely is any situation hopeless. Every person is free, of course, to choose his or her own path. The psychic's gift is the ability to discern the direction that a person's life is taking. With this information the psychic can point out an alternate path that may make travel much smoother. For example, a man named Joe came to see me. I saw that he was heading for a possible heart attack if he did not change his life-style. I suggested that he have a medical checkup immediately and we discussed ways in which he could eliminate stress. He harbored negative feelings toward his son who had dropped out of school and kept asking Joe for money, and he needed to deal with that anger. Within one week after our session Joe consulted a doctor who found that his blood pressure was very high. With the doctor's help he started a diet and exercise program, and found a therapist to help with his family problems. Joe is fine today—two years after our reading.

Many people are frightened when they come to see me; they

think that a psychic is inevitably the bearer of bad tidings. They walk in thinking, Oh, God, Mary is going to tell me that something terrible is going to happen.

Common sense tells us that if we can see something bad on the horizon, we can take the necessary steps to avoid it. That is the benefit of having psychic information. Let's say you have a reading in which you are told that your brakes are in disrepair and could endanger you. You check the brakes, find out that indeed there is a problem, have them fixed, and thereby avoid an accident.

I relay psychic information in order to give my clients trust in my ability to help, then I try to guide them on a path to a better life. If a client has a psychological problem, I suggest that he or she seek psychological counseling. If I see that a client needs medical attention, I suggest a medical doctor. I do not allow people to become overly dependent on me but instead guide them to make their own choices. Many people who have never seen a psychic criticize psychics, calling us controllers. I never try to control or manipulate; I only suggest what I feel is most helpful. The individual chooses how he or she will proceed after receiving the information.

Let's say, for instance, that I see a woman in an unhappy marriage. She's depressed and feels that she can't go on in her situation if things don't change. I psychically see that she will soon divorce. Rather than say, "I see a divorce, and you might as well go ahead and file the papers," I say, "Unless you and your husband go for professional help and deal with your problems, I don't think your marriage will hold together under the strain. Try everything humanly possible to work this out. Give it some more time. Once you've done everything in your power to try to stay together, then you can choose to stay or get out."

The way the message is delivered is most important. If a medical doctor tells a patient that there is no hope for him, the patient will give up. If the doctor says, "The situation is very serious, but we will do everything possible to help you," he leaves the patient with hope. The patient then has a chance to put his life in order.

There are times when it is necessary for me to be very direct; in other cases I withhold information until the client is ready to hear it. Different people require different approaches.

Learning to Be Free

Many cannot believe it's possible to be fearless, nor can they conceive of a life of peace and tranquility. It is important for a person to learn that fear is natural but it does not have to terrify or paralyze.

"Just get through it." Those words were spoken to me by my grandmother. She would say, "No matter what situation comes up, you must just get through it." She said this again and again, and in time I saw the value of her advice. If you are afraid, you must persevere, and in time the fear will diminish. If we could learn not to worry about the outcome of a situation, we would not live in fear. How can we do this? Learn that all you can do is your best. In cases where you can't control the outcome of a situation, why try? It will create inner turmoil and wear you out.

Concern is positive; worry is useless. Worry dissipates your energy and leaves you exhausted. You must not allow yourself to worry. If it does overcome you, get busy with an action. Use your willpower to stop this bad habit; you can replace a bad habit with a new good habit. If you are busy doing something for someone else, you will not have time to worry about yourself.

"What if people laugh at me?" a client asked.

"So what if they do?" I replied. "You mustn't allow yourself to pay any attention to these types of people. If you are conducting yourself with spiritual development and character—acting selflessly—you won't be concerned with what other people think about you or your actions. We waste precious time thinking about our effect on others. If we achieve freedom from thoughts of ourselves, petty gossip won't disrupt us: Our point of view should be one of selflessness!"

I thought again of my friend Kathy and how she doesn't spend her days worrying about dying. She lives each moment as if it were the only moment. She is always cheerful and selfless, a person free from fear and worry.

Speaking Up

My thoughts were disrupted by the sound of the telephone. I had been sitting for an hour deep in thought after Laura's visit. I picked up the phone and a voice said, "My child, I would like you to meet me for a light supper if that is possible."

"Lawrence?" I replied, surprised to hear his voice.

"Yes," he said. "I was thinking about you and felt that we should meet."

Lawrence told me where he would be, so I hung up the receiver and left. Upon arriving at the cafe, I saw Lawrence sitting at a corner table. He rose and held out a chair for me. I was comfortable in Lawrence's presence. I was in awe of him but felt no fear.

His first question was, "How is your friend Kathy?" I reported on her progress and remarked that her fearlessness was inspiring.

"Yes," he said, "your friend is a remarkable woman. Many people are being served by her great example."

I told Lawrence that during our most recent phone call, Kathy had said, "I am not afraid anymore." She had struggled through a tunnel of fear. In the beginning there had been shock and terror, and she had been paralyzed with fear about having cancer. Through talking and learning about life after death, she had been able to release the fear.

"Please tell your clients that I was very afraid and that it has not been easy for me," she said. "I want to help them understand that through knowledge you can learn to be fearless." I told her that I would pass her message on.

. . .

"Thank you for seeing Laura so quickly," Lawrence said. "She is a remarkable woman, very talented. She will serve the planet well through her music. I felt that you could be a great support and comfort to her. In time she will heal and her fear will dissolve. Then the music will flow from her."

The waiter came to take our order. After he'd left I said, "Lawrence, many of my clients are afraid to speak up when they feel they're being treated unfairly. They are insecure in the workplace about mentioning such treatment to their superiors. They're afraid they'll lose their jobs if they speak up. How can they best handle this?"

"If your motivation is to make the situation better, then you shouldn't be afraid to speak up. There is a time and a place and a way in which to speak up. Speak with courtesy, love, and understanding, and you will not offend your employer. Don't wait until you're upset and out of control before you speak up. This will only cause misunderstanding and bad feelings. Do not fear speaking up if you are doing so as a service—in this case, to make the job situation more pleasant and productive.

"Employers, for their part, should try to be aware of the feelings of their employees. This takes little time and makes people feel that they are valued. Good bosses are aware of their workers' feelings and should give the workers an opportunity to voice their views in a constructive manner. Open communication helps to make a work environment a happy one. Employers are responsible to their workers, and they have the privilege of making their workers' lives more pleasant by providing a positive work environment. Good employers know that speaking up will help keep workers' dignity intact.

"This applies to a person's personal life as well. You must not, for example, waste your time being afraid that your loved one will leave you if you tell him or her that you are not happy about the way you are being treated. The relationship is not worth preserving if you are being treated shabbily. Respect yourself. People often don't become aware of their behavior until it is pointed out to them.

"You stand to lose if you suppress your anger. The body reacts to the buildup of rage by succumbing to illness and breaks down if anger is not released in a positive and productive manner. Think before you speak, but by all means speak up.

"Do not fear the outcome if your only desire is to help. There are times when speaking firmly is the most productive way, but this does not give you license to be cruel. It is possible to be firm without being unkind."

We chatted for a few more minutes, and Lawrence asked for the check. The evening was clear and cool as we left the cafe and strolled for a few blocks sharing the silence.

I awoke the next morning to the sound of the phone ringing. "Mary, this is Leo," said the male voice on the line. "I met with you two weeks ago, and I was wondering if I could talk to you for a minute."

"Yes, Leo, go ahead."

"I'm having a terrible anxiety attack, and I don't know what's the matter with me. I feel frightened, as if something terrible were going to happen to me. It doesn't make any sense, but I've been feeling like this for the last few hours."

"Leo, you need to do something. Take a walk or call a friend to meet you for breakfast. Don't just sit there and allow the anxiety to take over."

I felt it would help him if he became active. It wouldn't solve the problem, but it would change the focus from anxiety to action.

"My wife is away on business," he continued. "I feel lonely when she's away."

"Leo, you're feeling a sense of abandonment, as if your wife has deserted you, but don't you realize that this isn't true? She hasn't left you; she'll be back soon."

As we talked further, Leo told me his mother had died when he was ten years old, and after that his greatest fear had always been abandonment. When he connected his wife's business trip with this childhood fear, he began to feel calmer and realized that although this knowledge wouldn't make the anxiety go away, he could keep it from immobilizing him.

I smiled in amazement as I hung up the phone, realizing that once again I had been able to immediately use the information Lawrence had just given me.

There are times when we are hit with feelings of fear for which we can't find a logical reason. If you wake up in a panic, talk to someone. After you have talked the situation over, do something—anything to take your mind off the problem.

Replace the anxiety with action, and it will go away. Do something for someone else, and the fear will begin to dissolve. This advice may seem simple, but it is very useful. You cannot think of yourself and help someone else at the same time. The helping will replace the wrong thinking. "What may I do for you?" is the question to ask yourself if you want to live fearlessly.

Fears from Past Lives

One client told me she had a terrible time keeping her appointment with me; she actually felt unable to leave the house. Days would go by during which she simply could not go out the door. Sometimes she got dressed and reached for the door, but fear would take over and she would not be able to open it. Having been in therapy for seven years, she felt she had made some progress: "I must be doing better, or I would not have been able to come to see you today." I said it was certainly a positive sign that she had come to see me even though she felt fear.

"You must have faith in your ability to overcome this problem," I told her. "You are making progress. In time you will find that you're no longer afraid at all."

Unlike Leo's case, there was no apparent reason for this woman's fear. She could remember nothing from her childhood that might have caused her to feel this way. Even her therapist was perplexed because he could find no psychological basis for her problem.

"Did you ever think that your problem could stem from a past life experience?" I asked. "The possibility has occurred to me," she replied. "I'm certain that I can't find a rational, logical reason for my terror."

I don't feel that we should use past lives as an excuse for all of our problems. Rarely do I suggest to a client that I see a past life experience, but sometimes this information is given to me. In this woman's case I saw a very clear picture of a past life experience, so I gave her the information.

"I see a prison that you escaped. The building looks very old, possibly sixteenth century. I feel that you were involved with a group of resistance fighters. Even though you escaped, you were in constant terror of being found and returned to this prison. Does this make any sense to you?"

She looked very surprised, then she said quietly, "I have had dreams ever since I was a child that I was in hiding. Waking up in terror, I thought that at any moment I might be taken away and put in a cell with no light. It's possible that these could be a memory of a time past. Why don't I remember this more clearly?"

"The mind is not capable of remembering that far back," I said, going on to explain my statement.

"I see your point," she said. "If I can't remember all of this life, then it makes sense I can't remember past lives."

"That's right," I said. "Some people remember past lives, but this is not common. We must not use past life readings to excuse us from dealing with the issues presented to us in this life. I gave you this information because I felt it would help you release the fear of being put in prison, and this has already happened. It won't happen again. If this reading is accurate, you will be able to integrate the information immediately."

She left feeling much better. We had uncovered some very valuable information that would help her. Her fear was brought over from a past life, but most of our fears have their roots in things that have happened to us in this life. If the past life reading is accurate, the subconscious will react by releasing the fear.

My friend Kathy phoned to tell me that she had her own psychic experience. "It was wonderful," she said. "I dreamed that my mother was standing next to my bed. She was smiling and reaching her hand toward me. She told me not to be afraid, that she was waiting for me. You know my mother passed over five years ago. I always knew I would see her again." Kathy sounded happy and calm as she told me of her experience.

"Your mother wanted to help you so that you wouldn't have any fear of passing over. A person who truly understands that there is no death but only a change of form will have no fear of death."

I received a message to meet Lawrence at a restaurant. He was waiting for me at a table when I arrived.

"It's wonderful to see you again so soon," I said, taking his hand. We ordered some tea and talked of the events of the last few days.

"I spoke to Laura, and she seems much happier already," Lawrence told me. "She has been working on her music for a half hour each day. I'm delighted that she is hopeful about her future once again. Thank you for helping her."

"I'm very happy that I was able to and that I could do something for you."

"Just keep helping others in any way you can. That will stand as a statement of your gratitude."

I nodded in agreement, then asked him, "Lawrence, are you ever afraid?"

"No," he said, smiling. "I am too busy dealing with the immediate situation to allow myself to feel fear. There is no time for fear because there is too much to be done.

"I met a famous actress who was so afraid every time she performed that she would vomit before the curtain went up. I asked her what she usually thought about before the performance, and she told me her thoughts were that people would say she had no talent and had a lot of nerve getting up to perform. I told her that she should think about the privilege she had been given to perform. After our chat she never again became ill before a show.

"If we work on developing a selfless point of view, fear will diminish and, in time, disappear. This cannot always be achieved in one lifetime. The true test of good character is to proceed with the wise action, fear or no fear.

"Surrender to your higher self. This part of man lives with no desire other than a passion to serve. This passion is a light that radiates from within the soul. There is no fear if this light is glowing.

"Mother Earth is crying for balance. She is no longer able to handle the flow of negativity being directed toward her. Through our greed and selfishness, we are destroying her ability to sustain and nourish us, or even, perhaps, to support life at all.

"Each person must become more aware that we are all connected to the whole, and that we are all responsible for everything," he said.

As I walked home, Lawrence's words were whirling through my head. It is possible to have a more harmonious planet. It is possible to think positively. Selflessness and service are the only answers.

I passed by homeless people who were living in the street. I gave two of them a dollar. This would buy them a cup of coffee and an hour of warmth as they sat in a coffee shop. It is an indictment of our society that there are people living in the streets. We must not be afraid to help them or fear that we will be taken advantage of. We should not fear that people will expect too much help nor be afraid to look at the suffering of others. We cannot pretend the suffering does not exist. We must stop thinking about our fears and do the very best we can to alleviate the suffering of others.

Let us live as examples for others. Let us think of nothing but service, and our fears will dissolve. Let us go forward and allow harmony to reign!

∴ III ∴
Money

We are living in a world that is consumed with the issue of money. Wars are fought, people are destroyed, and people commit suicide because of it. How many horror stories do we hear about people not being able to go on because they have experienced financial ruin? One of the greatest tests of our personal development is how well we handle money.

We are conditioned by social attitudes to judge people according to how much money they have—it has become the measure of success or failure. I have listened to panic in the voices of people terrified of being poor. I've talked to people who run out and buy very expensive things because they fear that if they do not purchase them now, they will not be able to afford them later. There are people who look down on others who don't care so much about money. They see these free spirits as lazy and nonassertive.

People also hold on to money too tightly: "My father scared me as a child by telling me that we were poor. I never knew if we had money because my mother said that if I didn't eat my dinner there would be no money for snacks." I have heard my clients say, "What will happen to me when I am old if I am without money?" These statements express great fear of the consequences of having no money.

People also feel a lot of guilt because of money, especially if it has been given to them. But if you have been given money, it is because you have earned the right to have it, either in this life or in a prior one. It is that simple. The law of karma says, "You get what you earn." The spiritually minded person will accept wealth with gratitude and use it to live comfortably and to help others.

Theodore has a huge trust fund left to him by his grandfather, and he has spent twenty years in therapy trying to learn to deal with it. Relentlessly guilty, feeling that he did nothing to earn it, he spends a great deal of time and energy trying to act as if he were poor. He is afraid that people won't like him if they know how much money he has.

I explained the law of karma to him. Then I went on to discuss with him the ways in which he could use his money to help others. As we talked I realized that he had an interest in the environment, and as the discussion continued, he decided that he could help in his concerns about the environment by starting a newsletter. He is now happily publishing his monthly newsletter on environmental issues and, involved in service, he no longer feels the need for therapy.

Money and Karma

The doctrine of reincarnation teaches us that we do not live one life but many. This philosophy, which is also the basis of my teaching, tells us that man returns to the Earth plane or the physical world until he has perfected himself. Man is, in essence, a composite of all his lives but must learn to focus on how best to live the present life.

I am often asked, "How can I understand this life if I don't remember my prior lives?" You can learn the most about your past lives from observing your present life.

Some people who visit me tell me of their grand past lives. They often seem to think they were somebody famous. Cleopatra is a favorite, as are Charles Dickens and the Brontë sisters. When I asked how they came upon this information, they told me they had had a past life regression, a process in which a metaphysician gives a reading that tells about past lives. I stress that anyone can tell you anything and claim that it is a past life reading, but be careful whom you consult. Only a few gifted people are capable of giving this type of information.

Examine why you want to have a past life regression. How can it serve to make you a better person? What can you learn from this knowledge? All you need for your personal development is right in front of you, in the here and now. You are living the life you have earned. You have earned the good, and you have earned the unpleasant. You will earn your happiness by living well now.

It takes many lives to work through our selfishness, but we have eternity in front of us, so be patient. It is a sacred process, and we have as much time as we need.

The law of karma teaches us that whatever happens to us, for good or ill, is just. We attract only what we have earned through our personal choices in this life and all of our past lives. Since it has taken us many lifetimes to accumulate the karma whose effects we experience in this present life, it should be obvious that in this one life there is simply not enough time to work through all of that karma. We can only hope to do our best with whatever circumstances are presented to us now. The individual chooses the pace at which he or she develops. This is not a race; there is no competition. If you try to push yourself to develop faster than you are ready for, you will only create inner havoc and will feel unbalanced. You should be neither lazy about your development nor obsessed with becoming more "spiritual."

Face your physical circumstances and learn from them. The

past has happened; you cannot change that. You can change your attitude and behavior today and in the future.

Giving Freely

If you have been incarnated with money, be grateful and humble. The test of your development is how you handle what you have been given. It is much easier to be wealthy than to possess wisdom. Most people can have money if they are willing to sacrifice enough in order to attain it.

Giving away your money so that you can have a plaque on a wall with your name on it, for example, is not really giving with the proper motivation. It is giving in order to gratify your ego. It is a selfish act.

Morton, a very rich client of mine, donated money to have a wing built on a hospital because he wanted the wing named after him. "They will remember me when I am gone," he told me proudly.

"What difference does that make?" I asked. "When you pass over to the other side, you will not be patted on the back by the Almighty because you have a hospital wing named after you. You will be judged by the motivation behind your acts of so-called generosity."

"Well," he said finally, "I am not going to give my hard-earned money away without people knowing about it."

The proper spiritual motivation for giving is to help others who are less fortunate, but Morton could not let go of his desire for recognition.

How many people will give money freely if they receive no tax benefit or if they are not applauded for their generosity? Merely having wealth is not a sign of spiritual development.

Some ways of giving are more helpful than others. It is more helpful, for example, to give people the tools to raise their own food than to give them the food itself—and to educate is an excellent way to give.

Find a charity you can believe in. It is your choice—there are thousands of ways to help through the giving of your finances. A great many people have told me wistfully, "I wish I could help people." Just help them, I say, in whatever way you can. No help is too small. You don't have to give up everything and live an ascetic life in order to help mankind. You can help in any way that is presented to you. If each working person gave ten dollars a week, the world would be freed from a tremendous amount of suffering. It doesn't have to be a grand gesture in order to be a worthwhile one—you can help in little ways. Rather than cry when you read the list of the neediest cases at Christmas time, get out your checkbook and give whatever you can afford. Just help in some way!

Handling Your Finances

There are three great tests in the physical world: good looks, good health, and money. These must never be taken for granted.

Don't look at the suffering planet and become so overwhelmed that you do nothing. Don't ever feel that your contribution does not matter. It matters to your development and to the people you are helping.

What is worse than a miserly person who is always trying to get something for free? What is worse than going to dinner with a friend who finds it almost impossible to pay a check? What is worse than people who accept a service and then procrastinate about paying for it? Which of us has not performed a service and then had to wait and wait, until we were in the embarrassing position of having to ask for payment? Do not place another person in the position where he must beg for payment. This is outrageous. If you accept a service, then you accept the responsibility of paying for it. If there are circumstances that make payment difficult or impossible, explain the problem to your creditor and devise a plan for eventual payment.

Lighten Your Load

I cannot stress enough how much it would help you spiritually to try to lighten your load of physical and financial responsibilities. Humanity becomes stressed by the pressure of financial slavery. Too many times we become involved in the "more, more, more" syndrome. We have to work harder to make more money so that we can possess more things. We have to find ways to invest our money so that we can reduce our tax payments. All of this produces a state of intense anxiety. Think before you buy! Weigh the pros and cons of your purchase. What is the use of spending your whole life worrying about money? This saps your precious energy and creates turmoil in your life. Yes, it is nice to be comfortable, but at what price? What can possibly be the price of your freedom? If you are always worried about the physical, you are never free. Yes, life is to be enjoyed, but why work until you drop just to have more possessions? Simplify your life! Ask yourself if you have enough time to enjoy things or if you are always on a merry-go-round. When you get one financial problem cleared up, do you have ten more to deal with? Live within your means. Too few people do this. Learn to say no to yourself and to others if some prospective purchase will put you in financial stress. Debt and possessions take away your freedom.

Sometimes the urge to spend develops into a compulsive pattern and a problem that requires therapy. Therapy and counseling groups have been started to help people deal with compulsive spending. Shopping can be an addiction much like alcoholism, and both have similarly destructive potential. If you must spend money, spend it on the needs of others. Give money for groceries so that a soup kitchen can continue to feed the hungry. Get involved in volunteer work. This way you will not have the time to run around shopping for things that you don't need.

Every action you perform is important. If you mishandle

money in this life, you will be severely tested in the next. You are responsible for your life.

If you owe money, repay it! If circumstances make this impossible, deal with the issue truthfully and do the best you can. If you must get a second job in order to pay your debts, do so. It is better to pay five dollars a week on a debt than to say, "Five dollars won't help. I'll wait until I can pay a larger sum." Five dollars will help! It will show that you are responsible and serious about paying what you owe.

Bankruptcy

Bankruptcy can be a difficult spiritual decision, bearing karmic implications. If you have done everything humanly possible to avoid it, only then should you consider bankruptcy. What do I mean by everything? Have you taken a second or third job in order to pay off these debts? Have you spent one dollar unnecessarily instead of paying a bill that was lying on your desk? Have you contacted all those to whom you owe money and tried to work out a schedule of payment? Have you changed your life-style to reduce your monthly outlay of money?

I have seen many people who have done all these things and still are not able to keep up their payments to debtors. In these cases, bankruptcy is an acceptable spiritual decision.

The circumstances that cause personal financial devastation may be out of our control.

The national economy can even change, and cities that are booming can suddenly become frighteningly quiet and financially moribund. In many cases, the problems we attract do not result from gross overspending but from external circumstances. Sometimes a person takes a responsible risk on a completely legitimate business deal, and then it does not work out positively. My client Jim found himself in this situation.

Jim was in a very depressed state when he came to see me.

He had used all his savings and had taken a second mortgage on his home in order to start his own business. Jim lives in a state whose economy has suffered greatly in recent years, but he had researched the deal for many months and the prospects for success looked excellent. Working eighteen hours a day trying to keep the new business going, he was losing weight and was anxious all the time. He took his children out of private school, sold his expensive car, and put his house up for sale (but was unable to sell it due to a depressed real estate market). The bills kept piling up, and there was no business coming in. He was very worried about what people would say if he declared bankruptcy, and he lay awake at night trying to solve his problems.

Jim had tried everything possible before finally deciding to declare bankruptcy, and through this crisis he learned some valuable lessons. First, he was able to free himself from the worry of what people would say about him. Second, he learned what was important in his life: peace of mind.

Jim did not make his decision lightly, and today he is doing fine. He was finally able to sell his house, which reduced his debt to the bank, and found work with a friend. He now lives without undue pressure.

Bankruptcy should not be used as an easy way out. There are few things more outrageous than a person who runs up debts and says, "Oh, well, I can't pay these bills, so I'll declare bankruptcy," then continues to go to expensive restaurants and buys whatever he wants with no remorse. This is a form of stealing, and the karmic price attached to it is severe.

I have a client who has had cancer for the last five years. When she was first diagnosed, she had no health insurance. She had come to this country from England shortly before she became ill and wasn't able to afford insurance. The bills were staggering, as medical bills tend to be, and because of her illness she has not been able to work except for short periods. She has a wonderful husband who is working as hard as he possibly can, and each month they pay as much as they can toward the balance of these bills.

These people do not spend one unnecessary dollar, and I have never heard her complain during all this trouble. I also have never heard this couple discuss the issue of bankruptcy. Whenever she is well enough, this dear person is working. Nothing is too menial for her if she has the strength.

I flew out to see her after she had a recurrence of the cancer, finding her in a very weakened state. She was lying in a hospital bed looking very frail, but her eyes lit up when she saw me. She clasped my hand tightly and said, "Mary, I'm so happy to see you. When you called to say you were coming, I was thrilled, but I'm worried about the cost. We don't have the money to pay you back for your expenses, but as soon as we do . . ."

"Please don't concern yourself with that," I said. "I'm very happy to be here and to help you in any way possible."

She asked me to open a drawer in her bed table. On opening it I saw a package wrapped in red paper. She told me to open the package, and inside was a beautiful sterling necklace. I looked at her in surprise, and she said, "The necklace belonged to my mother. It is the only piece of jewelry I have that is of value, and I would like you to accept it. There's no way I could ever repay you for the help you've given me, but in this small way I can show you my gratitude."

My first impulse was to decline the gift. Her mother was no longer living, so I knew the necklace had great sentimental value for her. But then I realized it was very important to her that I accept the gift because it was her way of compensating me for my service to her. The necklace means more to me than any other gift I have ever received.

This is a very good example of a person who is spiritually developed in her handling of money. She does her best at all times in handling her debts, and it is not within her nature to declare bankruptcy, even though in her case it would be completely acceptable. She is generous, and no matter how little the amount seems, she pays some money to everyone she owes. Her dream is to be debt free.

Be sure you have done everything humanly possible to pay your debts before you consider bankruptcy. If you owe money, you are responsible for your debts. You are living on money that is not yours, and possibly causing others great discomfort when you don't pay your debts. If you have a deep psychological problem with spending, seek help. Don't continue living on the edge, for that will only cause you great heartache. You can't remain a child forever. Children don't have to worry about money, but you have to accept financial responsibility as a sign of adulthood. In other words, grow up! Think before you spend money on a luxury item. Can you afford this or will it put you under undue pressure? You don't have to live your life in a pressure cooker because of your desire to buy things. Lighten your load. Don't complain about money all the time. Don't be consumed with the issue of money.

Many people have dropped dead because of their desire to obtain ever more material wealth. Heart attacks are frequently the result of this desire. I see many clients, especially from the financial world, who are crazed because of their desire to acquire more and more money. They have no time for their families and are quite miserable.

Often these poor souls drink too much in an effort to find release from the pressure. But they also feel a real high from wheeling and dealing. Their whole destiny is defined by the almighty dollar. They die prematurely because they have never taken the time to rest or eat properly. They pass over from the physical world to the spirit world, never having had the opportunity to spend their money or to know their children. This is tragic and unnecessary.

You don't have to live like this. If you do, you are living a life that is totally consumed with the physical, and the physical world is a fantasy that doesn't last.

I visited a client in the hospital after he had a heart attack. Terribly weak, he was connected by tubes and wires to all sorts of life support equipment. When I arrived he was upset. He wanted me to find a phone and call his office to see what was going on there. The doctors had deliberately not put a phone in his room, knowing that complete rest was the only hope for this man. I told him that his office could handle things, so I refused at first. He became so upset, though, that I became afraid and finally did as he asked. When I returned and told him that things were going smoothly in his absence, he calmed down. For the next twenty minutes I tried to help him see the folly of his way of thinking. It did little good.

My friend Lawrence would say, "We have eternity in front of us, so perhaps in his next life this poor man will see that there is indeed a better way to live."

My client was released from the hospital with a warning that he must change his life-style drastically. He didn't listen but returned to work with the same intensity as before, and suffered a second, more serious heart attack. It is now impossible for him to walk even one block. He didn't have to attract this situation. He had plenty of warning, and one would think the fear of almost passing over would have awakened him to see what was really important. But we must not stand in judgment of the way people handle their finances because this is a big test for all of us.

I asked Lawrence how one retains a spiritual viewpoint while living on this material plane. He replied, "How many hours a day do you spend thinking about the physical, and how many do you spend thinking about your spiritual development? Of course, we must take care of our physical needs. We must pay bills, prepare food, and do all the necessary things to sustain life and to be as comfortable as possible. But if physical needs dominate your thinking, they will consume your time and energy and leave you exhausted. Focus on your spiritual development and balance will reign."

Prosperity Consciousness

"You too can have a Mercedes" is the claim of many metaphysical groups that profess to be spiritual. Their method is sometimes called "prosperity consciousness" and is concerned with finding ways to attract money into one's life. Meditation practices and visualization are often used in such groups to focus on a desired amount of money.

Visualization is a method of creating a picture in the mind's eye and concentrating on that picture until one is able to produce the desired object. Meditation is a means of clearing the mind of all thoughts in order to focus on a single point or object. A spiritually developed person does not visualize or meditate. in order to attract material things or to escape the troubles of life! Whether or not they are aware of it, people who use these techniques are practicing a form of sorcery. Sorcery or "black magic" is used by one who attempts to use the forces of nature for his own personal gain.

People who practice "holding the thought" to attract some type of prosperity, as I described it above, are courting disaster. If you attract wealth to yourself by this method, you are stealing from the universe. The universal law of karma teaches that you get only what you earn. All that is yours will come to you; you don't have to manipulate to get what is yours. Any use of metaphysics for self-service is black magic, and the only difference between black magic and white magic has to do with one's motivation. White magic involves doing for the good of humanity.

Clearly there is a difference between "holding the thought" and thinking positively. If you are thinking positively, your thoughts are productive and kind. You are not thinking about getting; you are thinking about serving. A positive person is concerned with the well-being of everyone, not just with his or her own desires. Your thoughts create your whole life. If you desire something continuously, you may very well attract what you desire, but you are also taking on negative karma.

If you work hard and keep yourself focused, you can earn a great deal of money. Mankind has become lazy, desiring to get, get, get, in the easiest possible way. A person will pay hundreds of dollars to attend a New Age workshop that teaches how to get the most for the least amount of effort. But workshops have nothing to do with spiritual development and character. You risk your sanity by taking courses to open up your psychic centers in order to win wealth and success.

There are certain so-called spiritual teachers who advocate meditating on your chakras, the seven energy centers that, according to Hindu belief, run vertically along your spine and correspond to the seven successive centers of being, as well as emotions, colors, sound vibrations, and physical organs. The idea is that in doing this you will free blockages in the chakras. This will relieve you of stress and help solve problems that relate to these centers. For instance, if you have a sexual problem with your spouse or lover, you can solve the problem by meditating on your sexual chakra, seeking harmony in your sex life. You risk becoming unbalanced by practicing this type of meditation. It isn't wise to allow yourself to be induced into a trance state—a sleeplike, hypnotic condition—and have your psychic centers opened up by someone without proper training or without the proper motivation.

You are not protected by your ignorance of the laws. Just because you are not aware of something does not mean you are not affected by it. Let's say you're a member of an isolated tribe that has just arrived in New York. One of the laws of your tribe states that if someone insults you, it is your duty and your right to kill the person. If someone insults you while you're in New York and you kill him, the police will come and take you to jail. You may not know that you did something wrong, yet all your protestations of innocence won't keep you from being tried for murder.

Manipulating Reality

Jenny is twenty-seven years old and attractive. When she first came to see me two years ago, she was nervous and talked non-stop. She kept repeating, "I just don't understand why my life isn't working out the way I want it to. I'm doing everything possible to get what I want and what I feel I deserve. I meditate for two hours every day and read my tarot cards every night." There are seventy-eight cards in the tarot deck that are used for fortune-telling.

"Jenny," I said, "I am perplexed. Where did you get the idea that you should try to manipulate things to get them the way you want them?"

"Workshops I've attended teach you that if you dwell on an image intensely, you can get the thing you picture. I've also stopped eating meat and all animal products in order to keep myself lighter and more able to attract what I want."

"What do you want, Jenny?" I asked.

She shrugged. "Not to have to work. And I want Kevin to love me."

Kevin had repeatedly said to her that he had no interest in pursuing a relationship with her.

"Jenny," I said, "I really don't think that Kevin wants to be involved with you."

"I don't care," she snapped. "I want him, and I know that if I concentrate long and hard enough, I can make him change his mind."

I shifted to her other desire. "Why do you think you shouldn't have to work?"

"I was taught that the universe would provide for me. Working would interfere with my meditation, yoga, and visualization practices." She was pacing back and forth as she spoke.

I asked her what kind of work she normally did, and she told me that she was trained to be a nurse but was living on a small trust fund. She was worried because the fund was running out, and unless her meditation began to achieve the desired effect soon, she would have to find a job.

"How did you become involved in these workshops?" I asked.

"I read an article in a magazine that told me I could have anything I desired as long as I totally believed that I deserved it. I was unhappy at my job and didn't want to work any longer. I was desperate because Kevin wouldn't pay any attention to me. So I went to the first workshop, and a second and a third."

Several times I tried to tell Jenny what she was doing was dangerous and completely selfish, but she would always reply adamantly, "I don't care what you say. I know I can get what I want."

I suggested that she stop all meditation, start to eat meat, and see a therapist to help her deal with her obsessive nature. "Jenny," I told her, "you are trying to escape the responsibilities of life. The law of karma is that you get what you earn. If you have earned something, it will be yours. It would help you to go back to nursing; it is a service profession, and helping people will take your focus off yourself and your desires. If you begin to eat meat, you will feel less 'spacey' and more grounded."

Jenny wanted to hear that she could get Kevin and that she wouldn't have to work for a living. She left the session angry.

I heard from her six months later. She had had a nervous breakdown and was now recovering. She saw three other psychics after our session, hoping to hear something different. Kevin had told her strongly that she needed help, and he changed to an unlisted phone number. She said that she had begun seeing things: "I was seeing flashing lights and faces staring at me from the mirror. I was also hearing voices that told me it was all right if I wanted to kill myself."

She called her mother, who put her under the care of a psychotherapist. Now she was working part-time and putting the pieces of her life back together. She no longer did meditation and visualization exercises, and she was eating a healthy, balanced diet. She thanked me for the advice I had given her. She now saw the foolishness and danger in her past actions.

Money, like all aspects of our lives, is a test. Just because you have had trouble earning a living does not mean that karmically you must have trouble earning money throughout your entire current incarnation.

If you conduct yourself in a manner that reflects spiritual development and character, you won't be obsessed with the issue of money. Realize that money can be a serious trap. You can become so involved with the making of it or the desire for it that you fail to perceive things that are most important to your development. You must not think that you can get what you want by manipulating natural forces. Work and enjoy what you do. Love work, for that is your service. If you find that you can't make a living doing a certain job, find another. Gladly do whatever is necessary! This will surround you with a very positive vibration. You will not be negative and frustrated if you live with this point of view. Be grateful if you do well financially and can help others through your good fortune. If you have problems with money, face these problems.

Don't wallow in self-pity. Don't judge your life against someone else. Just because someone else is more successful financially, this doesn't mean you're doing something wrong. People become angry, resentful, and bitter because they think others have more than they do. Your life is your life. Your karma is your karma. Resentment will cause you nothing but trouble and illness if you allow yourself to hold on to it.

Why are some people born rich while others are born poor? Why do some people have to struggle while others seem to do things effortlessly? Each one of us is incarnated with tests that are necessary to our soul's development. Accept this and learn from your personal circumstances. Stop dwelling on what you don't have or on what someone else has. These circumstances have nothing to do with you. Don't allow yourself to worry about what people will think of you if you don't have a lot of money. It doesn't matter what people think. What matters is how you are living your life. If you have acquired wealth through good fortune or hard work and if you can help others through your wealth, how can you be miserable?

Many of us have known people who have committed suicide when their physical circumstances seemed perfect. This demonstrates that no perfection is possible when one thinks purely in terms of the physical and the material. You can't buy inner tranquility. Possessions take away from your freedom. Balance your physical life by not making it a life-and-death struggle to acquire things. There is never enough for a greedy individual. It is an endless cycle that leads to nothingness.

James is a very wealthy man who started a computer software company twenty years ago. He has vast real estate investments and is the chief stockholder in a very solid bank. He is always doing something to help people, but he is very quiet about it. He doesn't make grand gestures so that people will know how generous he is. If James hears about someone in need, he simply does something about it.

I told James about a couple who were having a difficult time paying for their son's college education, and James arranged to pay the boy's tuition. Not only that, he refused to tell the family what he had done. He asked me to act as a go-between but made me promise not to give the family his name. The family was overwhelmed by this gesture. They wanted to thank him personally but accepted his desire to keep his identity unknown.

The son graduated from college, and as soon as he was working he arranged to help a student who could not pay his expenses. James was very happy when he heard about this.

There are many people who could do the same thing James did and never feel any financial pressure. What a privilege to be able to help someone complete his or her education!

Think about the times in your life when someone helped you.

Wasn't it wonderful? Wouldn't it be great to do this for someone else? Most of us have gone through good times and bad times. Let's remember this and help whenever we can.

Learn to Be Generous

Only through helping others can we be truly free. Helping financially is one way to be a freer person.

If you don't know how to handle money, you must learn if you wish to become a truly loving person. If you were incarnated into a family that didn't teach you as a child to be balanced with money, then learn now. Learn through observation. If you are not a generous person now, that doesn't mean you can't become one. Try not to live in boxes; this means you think things must be a certain way—the way you learned they should be. If you have learned that money is essential to your happiness, unlearn it. If you have learned that you should keep all your money to yourself, unlearn it—the sooner the better. If you have learned to judge people according to the money and possessions they have, unlearn that right now.

That you have lived in a certain way for a number of years does not mean you must continue to live in that way. A good life is constructed by breaking entrenched habits. If you have bad money habits, break them. The getting of money is, for some people, a "real high." This is pathetic. See money for what it really is: a way to help others and yourself. This is part of learning to be selfless. Through helping you will learn to be of service.

Start in some small way. If you can give ten dollars a week, that will get you started on the road toward being a generous person. Do not give because you think it will come back to you if you do. This motivation is not a spiritual one. Tithing—pledging a fixed portion of one's income to a worthy cause—is a good way to show gratitude for one's good fortune, but it is dangerous to do it believing it will return to you tenfold. It doesn't represent a spiritual insurance policy but is a selfish way of looking at generosity.

If you believe in the worth of a particular organization, then by all means give to it. All charitable organizations need funds to survive and to help people. Numerous churches and groups help many through your donations. Give to a group you believe in.

Psychotherapy

The Earth plane is the stage for the emotions. Our spirits become incarnated on the Earth in order to work out our emotional natures. The great masters Jesus, Buddha, and Zoroaster had reached a point of personal development where they were totally conscious of all motivation and free of any unresolved subconscious problems. This is why they are called masters. This process of working through our emotional natures takes many lives. It is a sacred learning process, and it is a difficult one because it is painful. Most people will go to any lengths to avoid pain.

Psychotherapy can be a very positive method of working through emotional problems. It is often impossible to handle a situation until one brings the problem from the unconscious to the conscious level. Once a problem is brought to consciousness, one can work on either dissolving it or balancing it.

Say, for instance, that you cannot control your spending; you have tried and tried, yet you are compelled to spend money you don't have. You can't find a conscious reason for doing this. Rationally you know it is wrong and you should stop. Logic is not helping you. You finally go to a therapist and in the therapy process you talk about whatever you feel you need to discuss. (A good therapist will guide you to examine the issues that are difficult for you to confront. He or she will listen and help you to free yourself of your accustomed patterns of dealing with or evading problems.) Through your discussions with the therapist, you realize that your spending disorder stems from feeling you were neglected as a child. You felt that your father showed love by buying you something. Now when you are feeling lonely or unloved, you buy yourself something. Realizing this will help you to recognize the problem and thus be better equipped to conquer it.

A synthesis of psychology and metaphysics is the most effective method of helping people deal with the problems of living. Once you realize the psychological basis for the problem, you can accept it and use service and selflessness to help you get through it.

Money can bring us a measure of freedom if used properly. Otherwise it creates bondage! If you have money and give of it freely, you will feel a sense of well-being. Every one of us will pass over from the Earth plane to the plane of the spirit. Once you are in the world of the spirit, no one will be interested in how well you did financially; only your character and spiritual development will count.

Be Grateful for Prosperity

When you pass over, you will see every moment of your incarnation pass before you. Yes, every moment. You will have to look at your life, and face the way you lived it. Is this a frightening thought to you? If it is, then start today to change your point of view to one of selflessness. Perform acts that make you proud of yourself. Think before you act. Think about the way you have behaved, and improve yourself. Stop thinking of this one life as being all there is. It is only a short trip for each one of us. We all have the opportunity to grow and to help. It's really wonderful! It doesn't matter to the Almighty (or whatever we call the God force within us) whether you were the president of a large corporation or an unskilled laborer—you will be judged by your actions, not by your station in life.

When we see our lives from a purely material viewpoint, it makes little sense. There seems to be great unfairness in how wealth and resources are divided among us. Some people are born with nothing, some with everything. In each incarnation we have a different physical body, a different name, different social circumstances, perhaps a different sex. We have earned whatever has been given to us. Nothing is unfair in a perfectly organized universe ruled by universal law. Stop thinking that life has been unfair to you. You have attracted particular difficulties so that you can gain knowledge and understanding. The purpose of life is growth.

∴ IV ∴
Sex

Sex between two people who love each other is the merging of souls, but otherwise sex can be a trap. We've all heard countless stories of people who were devastated by sexual relationships, and frequently these are people who have mistaken their sexual attraction to someone for love. They go to bed with a person they don't know very well, make assumptions about their feelings, and then don't understand why they never hear from the person again. "How could he do that to me? What does he think I am?" they ask, wanting to feel that they've been involved in a tragic love affair when what they have really encountered are the results of their own dishonesty.

It is difficult for us to admit that we enter into relationships because of physical attraction alone. But if we think about it, doesn't it stand to reason that it takes time to love another person? Sexual attraction is powerful, but love takes time because it involves learning.

Many people, through the sexual act, try to renew their connection with the God force within them. Life has become so overly consumed with the physical that we have forgotten the spiritual. We feel lost, empty, and lonely. Through that powerful and immediate feeling of total union with another person, we can feel a sort of connectedness that approximates our forgotten sense of unity with the God force.

If we turn our gaze on what is within each of us, we won't look to sex to give us a sense of completeness. Sex as a release from one's feelings of separation can be dangerous as well as unsatisfying, especially now when sex can put you in potentially life-threatening states of disease. What does this tell us? To think before we act! You need food and water to live, but you can live without sex. It may be uncomfortable, but until you meet a person with whom you feel you can develop a true relationship, you should not become sexually involved. This is common sense and must be taken seriously. If we are careful about sexual involvement, we won't have to live in fear.

Sex can be a teacher as well as a destroyer, and much can be learned through intimacy especially: our strengths and our weaknesses, caring and consideration, how to feel deeply.

If sex were not interesting, who would bother with it? But it should not be overly discussed because this reduces it to a totally physical act. It should be an act of feeling, a spiritual act. There is nothing quite as beautiful as sex that is the outcome of true loving feelings. Sex as an act of love is love in action because it is an act of giving, not only of one's body but of one's spirit. If you think about the needs of your partner, you will not be burdened with worries that your sexual relationship is not good enough. You will not be consumed with thoughts of your personal desires. You will be happy being next to the person you love.

It is time to return to the idea of courting. There was a time when hopping into bed with someone was not acceptable behavior. Before the so-called sexual revolution, sex was delayed until the two people felt certain they wanted to be in a committed relationship. The Victorian era has passed as all ages pass, but have we gone too far in the other direction? If you are busy using your energy to serve and to create, you won't be overwhelmed with the desire for sex. It will be a part of life rather than life itself.

Romance is thrilling. There is nothing like it. We feel wonderful when we are in love. If the attraction passes, we think we are "out of love." We must try to use the term *in love* less often. If we don't, we are likely to confuse love and sex, which are not the same thing.

You can have a very romantic evening without ending up in the bedroom. "What am I supposed to do? My boyfriend will leave me if I don't go to bed with him," a client told me.

"Let him leave if that is the way he feels," I replied. "Under no circumstances should you ever feel forced to go to bed with anyone."

If you are dating someone who is pressuring you to have sex but you do not feel it is right, end the relationship. It is not a good relationship if the other person isn't willing to take the time to get to know you. If two people have a good relationship, they will have mutual respect for each other and there will be no feelings of pressure. You must not worry about what someone will think of you. You must be true to yourself. Adult behavior is responsible behavior, especially in regard to sex in the age of AIDS. It is unfortunate that we must live in mortal fear of an act that is a natural part of being human.

Rhonda came to see me because she said that she loved her husband of ten years, but she was no longer "in love" with him. "I just don't feel interested in him sexually. It's not exciting anymore. My husband is a terrific person, and he takes good care of me and our son. We have a lot in common and are best friends, but he lacks sex appeal." She went on to say more about how wonderful her husband was and how great their marriage was, except that it lacked sexual excitement.

"What about your husband? Is he interested in a sexual relationship?" I asked.

"Oh, he's still very interested. I try not to hurt his feelings. I tell him I'm tired, and he never pressures me. He's always totally understanding."

"Rhonda," I said, "it sounds to me as though you're married to a wonderful guy. Is it possible you're thinking too much about yourself and that you would be happier if you thought about your husband's feelings and needs? Maybe you should plan a trip together. Romance has to be kept alive; it will burn out if it is left unattended. If you love this man as a friend, and it seems that you do, then you must think of his needs and not dwell on your own personal discomfort. How do you think your lack of physical attention affects him? He's acting as if he is all right, but he must feel sad and rejected. It sounds as though he is aware of your feelings and your comfort. It isn't important that sex be totally exciting to you. It *is* important that you become aware of your partner's needs."

Rhonda thought for a moment, then said, "Oh dear, I never thought about it that way. My husband must feel terrible. He's always so very patient with me, and I took this for granted. Do you think it's possible to put romance back into the marriage? I thought that if sex had become uninteresting, there was little you could do about the situation."

"Rhonda, do you want to leave your husband?" I asked.

"Of course not!" she exclaimed.

"Then you must think about his needs and be affectionate toward him. It is selfish of you to be unresponsive. It's not easy to be passionate if you don't feel that way, but it will test your development to be loving to him."

Rhonda got up and started pacing the room. Then she stopped, smiled, and said, "There's a wonderful little town in Vermont where my husband and I used to go when we were first married. I'll make plans for the two of us to go there for a long weekend. My husband mentions this town every so often, and I've just ignored him. I think it would make him happy."

When Rhonda left, she was clearly energized. She had never taken the time to think that maybe she needed to put some life back into her marriage. Many people I've spoken to over the years have had the same problem. They wanted romance and excitement but didn't take the time to make plans that would help this process along. Everyday living takes so much of our attention that we often don't think things through. If you really love your partner, you will take the time to consider his or her happiness.

Lou was a man who had suppressed his feelings for many years. He was born into a family that didn't communicate with one another. They never discussed their feelings, thus Lou did not know how to express his. Lou was a chef at a fine restaurant and had channeled all his energies into his work. Feeling desperately alone, he came to see me, hoping I could shed some light on his future. He was well respected and worked sixteen hours a day. That is, until he met a woman he wanted to date. Wringing his hands, he said, "I've never felt this way before, and I don't know how to handle my feelings. I'm so attracted to her that I clam up every time she comes near me. I'm a bit short with her, and I think I have hurt her feelings. I try to be nice, but somehow everything comes out of my mouth with an edge to it."

I smiled. "Sounds to me as if there is a great deal of physical attraction. Does that frighten you, Lou?"

"I just don't know how to handle myself and my feelings," he said. "I feel clumsy and inept with women."

I nodded, then said, "I think you had a sexual experience with someone who was very critical of you, Lou. That experience made you feel inferior." I paused, then asked, "Why don't you tell me about the girl you fell in love with when you were sixteen? I think she was blond, five foot three, and had a dimple in her left cheek."

Lou started to laugh. "I forgot that I was talking to a psychic. You're right. When I was sixteen, I fell in love with a girl named Gwen. She was lovely. I'd had a crush on her for months before I had the courage to speak to her. One day at a school function I found myself sitting next to her in the bleachers. It took me twenty minutes to say a word to her. She seemed totally self-assured, and I couldn't imagine her wanting to talk to me. Before I knew what had happened, she agreed to go with me after the function to get something to eat. I couldn't believe I was really sitting in a restaurant with Gwen. It seemed unreal. As I walked her home, she held my arm. We reached her door, and I kissed her. She pulled away quickly and said, 'Ick! You smell like onions.' I was so embarrassed that I ran away as quickly as I could. The next day at school I saw her talking to a group of friends. They started giggling when they saw me. I was never able to talk to Gwen again."

"Lou," I said, "that was a terrible experience, especially for one as sensitive as you. Not all women are like Gwen. You were both children, and I'm sure that contributed to her insensitivity. I'm certain she had no idea how she hurt you. Take your time getting to know this woman you've met. You could ask her to lunch or to a movie, but you mustn't feel personally rejected if she turns you down. How can she reject you if she doesn't even know you? There are always risks involved when we try to get to know a new person. Don't think about yourself and your fear. Ask her to do something the same way you would ask a person to whom you weren't physically attracted. It's amazing how afraid we become when we feel attracted to someone. I think this woman will be delighted to go out with you. Don't rush yourself—there's plenty of time to get to know her."

I told Lou I thought it would be wise for him to talk to a good therapist. I suggested my friend Alice who, besides being an excellent therapist, is also a young and attractive woman; I thought a therapeutic relationship with someone like her might help him to work through his fear of rejection.

After he left, with Alice's phone number in his address book, I reflected that he would be fine, but it saddened me to see him in such great pain. Seemingly small incidents can leave people scarred. When you're young, you are often insecure about your attractiveness. How many people are afraid of touching someone because they have been hurt before?

The incident with Gwen became the vehicle to help Lou work

through his feelings of lack of self-worth in relation to the new woman. In time he would learn to communicate his feelings, both physically and emotionally. He would attract a person into his life who would help him; I was sure of that. We attract people to ourselves when there is something we need to learn. Lou had to learn that he was a valuable person worthy of being loved. His sexual feelings helped him become aware that he needed to work on himself. When he met someone for whom he felt desire, he began to look within himself. It was painful to him but important to his development.

Sex and Spirituality

I awoke the following morning with a strong feeling that I must see Lawrence to talk with him about the sexual issues my clients had been raising lately. I went to a coffee shop where we had met before. I felt certain he would be there and he was.

"You were picking up my thoughts," he said, smiling. "It's good that you are so receptive."

After finding a table in the corner, we ordered breakfast. The coffee shop was very busy, but I felt as if we were alone. I told Lawrence about the clients I had been seeing and that I was intrigued so many were coming to talk about their sex-related problems. I told him that at times I became overwhelmed. "I really need your help, Lawrence."

"It is my privilege to serve you. There is much to be learned by studying people's perceptions of sex." He sipped his coffee. "Misuse of the Kundalini force has caused mankind to become overly involved with sexual desire." Kundalini is the Sanskrit word for the Hindu concept of a serpentlike force that rests at the base of the spine. This force can be drawn up through the spine and channeled into creative energy. If properly channeled, it becomes creative, such as with music and poetry. If misused it can cause man to become unbalanced; an example of this would be a preoccupation with sexual desire and overemphasis on man's lower nature. Man is composed of a physical self and a spiritual self; this is one of the basic concepts underlying my teaching. The spiritual self is also known as man's higher body. The physical represents man's lower nature. It is very dangerous to do exercises, mainly breathing exercises, whose purpose is to guide the Kundalini force. You have a choice as to how you channel the energy that is within you. If you keep your mind focused on service and selflessness, you will not allow yourself to dwell on the lower nature, the animal part of yourself.

"When two spiritually minded souls fall in love," Lawrence continued, "there is a rich blending of soul and body. Sex as mere recreation must be stopped. We are being warned by the prevalence of sexual diseases on the planet that an imbalance has been created. Man is being asked to reevaluate his needs."

Lawrence and I discussed a few individual situations that I had found confusing. I told him I thought it was shocking that so many people were totally consumed with their desire for constant physical gratification. Lawrence nodded and then spoke.

"Sex can be beautiful when it is the expression of deep love. At this time on the planet there are many reincarnated souls from ancient Greece and Rome. A study of the history of that period reveals that there was an overemphasis on the physical. It's interesting that activities such as marathon running are as popular once again as they were in ancient Greece and Rome. Narcissism ruled at those times, as it similarly does now. Man aspired to possess the perfect physical vehicle. Once again we see that mankind is seeking confirmation through the physical at the expense of the spiritual. Sex has become a confirmation of self for us. We feel worthwhile only if we feel desired sexually. We must instead find our confirmation within our higher spiritual nature. If we work on serving and loving as well as on creating, the focus will shift away from our sexual nature. We will be too busy working on our character to be overly consumed with thoughts of sexual desire. Instant gratification is just that: a momentary thrill and it's over. Then what? We are left to look at ourselves." Lawrence stopped speaking as the waiter came to offer more coffee.

"Lawrence, what are your feelings about celibacy?"

"Celibacy is not a prerequisite to spiritual development. I once had a student who felt that he could not reach spiritual enlightenment if he engaged in sexual relations, even with his wife. He spent an enormous amount of time forcing himself to be celibate when he was not ready to live a sexless life. He did not take the feelings of his wife into consideration. She had not chosen to live a celibate life. If she had chosen that path, she would not have entered into marriage. If one has outgrown the desire for sex, then fine, but celibacy should never be forced. If you have truly outgrown the need for sex, you will not have to discipline yourself to control your sexual urges—they will not be there. Many great spiritual teachers have married and had families; that did not hinder their development. Great lessons can be learned through intimate relationships with souls whom we deeply love. Take time to attract relationships with people you can trust and with whom you can grow. Learn to take time with those you encounter in order to discover their true character."

The spell that Lawrence cast as he spoke was broken by the sound of rising voices coming from a table close by where a man and a woman had begun to argue. Lawrence studied the couple and then said, "Jealousy has no place in a truly loving relationship. Many people mistake jealousy for caring. How can we be jealous if we desire nothing but happiness for the one we love?"

The waiter walked by, and Lawrence asked for the check. We talked for a few more minutes. He assured me that we would see each other again in the near future. We left the coffee shop, and I watched as he walked briskly away.

Possessiveness

As I walked home I thought of all the people I had encountered who had been taken over by jealousy. They thought jealousy was a statement of true love and behaved viciously and vindictively over the ending of a personal relationship. It amazed me that these people had once felt they loved the person they were now trying to destroy.

Passion can be destructive or creative. Possessiveness is an outcome of jealousy. One becomes possessive of a person with whom one is having a physical relationship. This emotion has nothing to do with love, for one would never try to possess someone whom one loved selflessly. When you love a person truly, you want your loved one to feel happy and free.

A woman named Martha came to see me. She was being tortured by her ex-lover. She couldn't go anywhere without being followed by him. She was frightened of him and didn't know where to turn. Unable to tolerate his possessive behavior, she had ended the relationship. At first she thought it was nice and that he wanted to be with her all the time, but as time went on she found herself feeling like a prisoner. Having tried everything she could think of to solve the problem, she finally called it quits. Her lover refused to accept her decision and was harassing her. When she became frightened, she called the police. We discussed ways to deal with this situation. I told her she must be very firm with him and not allow herself to be immobilized or panicked by fear. Eventually her ex-lover stopped trailing her, but it was a terrible ordeal.

Possessiveness shows deep insecurity on the part of the one who is acting in this manner. You cannot possess another soul; it is sheer folly to try to do so. People need space, and this fact will be respected in a balanced, loving relationship. Many couples would stay together much longer if one party did not try to control the actions of the other. Discipline yourself to stop asking your partner about his or her every thought or movement. In other words, lighten up!

A client of mine used to call her husband seven or eight times a day. He could hardly get his work done because she was always interrupting him. He finally blew up and told her that if she didn't trust him, she should leave him. She stopped her possessive behavior, and they began to get along just fine.

Soul Mates

I arrived home to the sound of the phone ringing. The person on the line was one of my clients, a woman named Jo, who told me she had an important question to ask me: "What are your feelings about the concept of soul mates?" she sputtered.

"Why do you ask, Jo?"

"I met a new man, and I'm certain he's my soul mate. I saw him walk into the room, and it was instant recognition." She sighed.

"Sounds to me like a clear case of sexual attraction," I said.

"Couldn't he be my soul mate, Mary?" she asked.

I knew she wanted me to agree, but instead I said, "I don't believe in the concept of soul mates. A lot of people spend all their time looking for their true soul mates, thinking there is one person out there who is the other half of their soul. Since we are complete within ourselves, it doesn't follow that our other half is running around the universe waiting to be discovered by us. There are many people for us to love, not just one. Jo, I think you've let yourself fall into a romantic fantasy. Face the fact that you have a physical attraction to this man you met and don't try to make it metaphysical."

Jo started laughing and admitted the guy was pretty cute.

I added, "Since there are many people to love, we attract a certain person at a particular time because we have something to learn. You must learn to love with no conditions and no expectations. Let go of the idea of the soul mate and take time to get to know this fellow."

"But Mary," Jo interjected, "I just feel that this man is my one true love."

"Jo," I said, "save yourself a lot of heartache and try not to confuse physical attraction with love. Relationships that have their basis in physical attraction seldom last very long. Many marriages end once the initial attraction is over. People tend to abandon their partners much too easily. If you love another soul unconditionally, you will not expect anything in return. Remember, the God force within each of us loves unconditionally. We humans, though, seem to expect a return on giving and loving."

Jo finally agreed to take the time to get to know this new man. She said she was a bit disappointed that I did not think he was her soul mate, but she understood what I meant.

To love all people and all things is to be a free person. Never to expect but to learn to accept what is given to us is to love with our divine self. It takes many lives to learn this. We must aspire to greatness of the soul, and in doing so we will be given many jewels. We must love with acceptance, not criticism. It is easy for us to love those who seem lovable; there is no test involved in this kind of love. The test comes in loving those who are difficult to love.

I spent a few quiet moments in contemplation. Everyone should spend some time each day thinking loving thoughts. It should be a warm, pleasant experience. If we can spend a little while thinking of nothing but of feeling goodwill toward all, it will surround us with a loving vibration that will carry us smoothly through any difficulties that may arise. It is a person of good character who can turn the other cheek no matter what others do.

Incompatibility

Janet had been married for almost two years and was sure her husband was seeing another woman. She didn't need a psychic to tell her that this was the case. She had hired a detective to follow her husband, and he had given her the proof she felt she needed. Janet was quite depressed when she arrived. She didn't seem angry but deeply hurt. I offered her some tea and we began talking.

"We haven't been happy for a long time," Janet began. "I

tried to ignore it, but I can't do so any longer. I intend to see a divorce lawyer because I can't go on this way. It's too dangerous. I can't believe my husband would do this to me. If he had simply asked for a divorce, I would have given him one. He doesn't have to subject me to the possibility of contracting some social disease by his sleeping with another woman."

"Have you told him of your feelings?" I asked.

"Not yet," she replied. "I knew I had this appointment with you, so I thought I would wait until I'd seen you."

"I'm worried that you may act too hastily. You must stay calm," I said. "You're very calm right now, as if you were in a state of shock, but you will explode in anger when the shock wears off."

"I just wish he had been honest with me," Janet said quietly. "I would have listened. I've never tried to make him stay. Any time I tried to express my feelings about problems in our marriage, he became affectionate with me, as if that would solve everything. We've always been quite physically attracted to each other. Sex was not our problem; communication was. We never talked to each other much."

"Don't you think you should try to discuss this situation with your husband before you run out to file for divorce?" I asked. "Maybe a marriage counselor would help the two of you work out your communication problems. If you haven't worked on this issue, you haven't done everything in your power to see if this marriage can still work."

She sighed and shook her head. "It's no use," she said, and she became very quiet. I was not certain how to proceed. You cannot force someone to want to work out his or her problems, and Janet didn't seem open to trying therapy.

"You must have had things in common besides sex, or how could you have stayed in this marriage as long as you have?" I asked. "Do you love this man? If you do, I think you should go to him and try to talk this out."

She shrugged. "I'm not sure I even know what love is. I married him because I felt that I couldn't live without him. In retrospect I think the major interest was sexual. I should have waited to get to know him better, but I was overcome with passion, so I married him within four months of meeting him. He was always interested in sex. I was complimented. Silly, wasn't it?"

"I think you're being too hard on yourself, Janet. Silly isn't the right word. Maybe you were impulsive, but which one of us has not acted on impulse sometimes? But sexual attraction isn't enough to base a marriage on."

"How does the old song go?" she asked. "To-may-to, to-mah-to, po-tay-to, po-tah-to—that was us. I like the country, he likes the city. I like to stay at home, and he likes nightlife. The things we do not have in common could fill a book. I don't blame the other woman. My husband can be very attractive. He probably made her feel as if she were the only woman in the world for him. He did that to me, and I now see that I'm not the only woman. I know who she is—she works in my husband's office. I've met her socially at parties and liked her the few times we met."

Janet was vehement that she did not want to go on living with her husband. Nothing I said could convince her otherwise. It was her decision; I merely wanted her to look at the total picture. Janet was certain there was not enough to base a marriage on. She would find a lawyer and then she would tell her husband about her divorce plans. It was obvious that she had entered into a marriage with someone she did not know well enough. Sexual attraction had convinced her she was "in love." If she had only waited until she got to know this man better, she could have avoided this divorce. I felt that Janet would be fine. She had character and good insight. She left the session certain that she would leave her husband.

The next time I spoke to Janet was six months later. She was living alone and seemed glad to be on her own. Her husband made a fuss but had not contested the divorce. Janet went into therapy to help herself avoid making the same mistakes again. Feeling clear and strong, she was taking time to get to know new people but was in no rush to have a personal relationship. She had met three interesting men but had not gotten involved with anyone yet. Enjoying dating, she did not need to settle down with one person at this time in her life. She was spending weekends at her cousin's country home, and this was a delight to her. In the future she hoped to be living in the country full-time. For the time being she was taking life one day at a time.

There are many Janets in the world, people who become involved in a relationship or marriage before they have taken the time to get to know the other person well. Attraction blinds them to potential problems, and thus they are heartbroken or angry when the relationship turns out to be less than perfect. Sex, to many people, is confirmation. They feel confirmed that they are attractive or desired. We must learn that our confirmation must come from within, not from externals.

AIDS

Billy was twenty-six years old and had everything to live for. He was a beautiful blond and blue-eyed young man. I met Billy three years ago when he first arrived in New York from his native Georgia. For him it was a dream come true; he had wanted to live in New York since he was a teenager, and he had finally made it. Billy was quite a flirt. He flirted with everyone, men and women alike. His innocent beauty made it easy for him to fall into casual sexual relationships, and he pursued this life-style with enthusiasm. When I warned him not to take his relationships lightly, he would laugh and say, "You're only young once." When I stressed that promiscuity was unsafe, he didn't respond; I don't think he even heard me.

Billy's father had neglected him. Billy had tried everything to gain his father's attention and approval, but nothing had worked. His father seemed to care only for his older brother, a more "manly" type. Billy always got by because of his looks. People melted when they looked at him—everyone except his father. I think Billy spent his life trying to receive confirmation from father figures. Each time I met with him, he was involved with yet another older man. He desperately wanted some type of security and was unable to find it within himself.

Billy wanted to be an actor and had been fortunate enough to get work almost immediately upon his arrival in New York. He loved the theater and theater people.

The last time Billy came to see me, he looked thin and pale. I was worried about him. He seemed to be a bit vague, as if it was difficult for him to concentrate. We talked about his work and his relationships. I remember coming down hard on him about his affairs. I begged him to stop being promiscuous because it could not lead to any kind of happiness. He laughed and said, "I am being careful."

"Not careful enough," I emphasized. "You must work on your personal development and character, Billy."

"I'm trying," he said, and then he told me about all the self-help books he was reading.

"Books are great tools of support, Billy, but the important thing is how you use the knowledge in the books to live a fuller, more productive life!"

Billy thought about this and agreed. I must tell you that Billy was always trying to help people. He was especially interested in helping the elderly. He would go to various nursing homes in the city and entertain the patients. His greatest virtue was that he loved to make people happy.

But he was very insecure and felt that he was not worthy of being loved. Nothing anyone said to the contrary could reach him. He constantly needed confirmation that he was physically attractive. His looks were an obsession with him. He wanted everyone to love him, and he confused desire with love. When Billy left that day, I felt very sad for him. He was a terrific person but so unhappy. I was deeply concerned about his health and had told him during the session that I felt he should get a checkup and a series of blood tests. I didn't want to scare him, but I felt that he must do this to protect himself and those with whom he might become involved. He assured me that he was having "safe sex" and that there was nothing to worry about, but he promised to have a medical checkup.

Time passed, and there was no word from Billy. Then late one afternoon I received a phone call from a friend of his. Billy was in the hospital and was asking to see me. He had AIDS, and the doctors did not think he would live much longer. He had contracted pneumocystic pneumonia and was having difficulty breathing.

Saying that I would go immediately, I canceled my appointments and left for the hospital, feeling heartbroken. Billy was a wonderful person who had desperately sought love and approval. He had done a lot to help others but had never been able to see his own self-worth. His desperate pursuit of fulfillment and validation through others, a pursuit that led him into a preoccupation with the physical side of life, had caused this tragedy.

Walking into the hospital, I felt the urge to cry. I was directed to his ward, where the nurse asked me to put on a gown and a pair of gloves. I did so and entered. There was oxygen equipment by Billy's bed, and he was being fed intravenously because he could no longer eat on his own. This beautiful boy looked like an old man. He could not have weighed more than ninety pounds. I tried to smile as I reached out and took his frail hand.

"Thank you for coming," he whispered. "I've been waiting for you. I wanted to tell you that I appreciate all you tried to do to help me. When you first talked to me, I thought you were overreacting. I thought nothing bad could happen to me since I was young. I now know I'm going to die and that this could have been avoided if I had grown up and stabilized my personal life. Please tell your clients about me. Tell them this doesn't have to happen to them."

We both started to cry, and after a while he went on: "My family has been called. I know my father won't come. My mother will be very upset, and I wish she didn't have to go through this."

"Your mother loves you, Billy, and she will want to see you and be with you."

The room was full of flowers. I commented on this, and Billy smiled and exclaimed, "I have some great friends!" He then asked me to tell him about life after death. "Is it really true that I will see people I knew on Earth?" he asked.

"Yes, Billy, you will be met as soon as you pass over. I think your grandmother is waiting for you."

Billy seemed comforted by this. "I loved my mother's mother.

I never knew my dad's mother. Gram was always my best friend.
It will be wonderful to see her again!"
 We talked about this a bit longer. Billy seemed to be getting
tired so I asked if he would like me to leave. "Don't leave yet,"
he said. "Sit with me a while longer." I sat next to the bed,
holding his hand. He fell asleep, and I stayed with him as he
rested. Once he awoke and said, "I'm not afraid, Mary. Don't
worry about me." I left him when he was sleeping peacefully. This
was the last time I saw him. He passed over three days later. His
friend called to give me the news. Billy had died in his sleep. His
mother and father were at his bedside.

You can't live without food or water, but you can live without sex.
That statement kept repeating itself in my mind. Sex can be
beautiful, but we must keep the beauty alive by attracting only
relationships that are based on love. We can learn that the energy
used in sexual relationships can also be focused energy. If we are
busy serving and loving all whom we encounter in an uncondi-
tional way, we will not be preoccupied with thoughts of sex.
 Think before you act. If you are attracted to someone who
seems terrific, shouldn't you get to know that person before you
allow the relationship to become physical? Is sex so important that
you are willing to risk your life for it? Certainly we all need
affection, but affection can be given and received without having
a sexual encounter.
 If you are involved in a personal relationship, don't allow sex
to be a priority. It is *part* of loving, not love itself. If you think
about the needs of your loved one and that person is thinking
about your needs, balance will reign!
 The God force lives within each of us. We are never alone.
There are times when we feel that we are, but this is an illusion
born of our physical nature.
 Sex can teach us great lessons. I met a woman who was
terrified of sex. She was thirty years old and had never had a close
personal relationship with anyone. If someone touched her, she
panicked. This poor woman had never been held as a child. She

told how she would lie in her bed screaming, but no one came to her. I told her that she needed to talk to a good therapist, because the problem was deep-rooted. "You don't have to live your whole life with this fear," I told her. "It will take time, but you can overcome this terror. It will help if you think of others, and it would serve you well to spend time at a children's home. There you would experience holding a child who needs affection. If you were terrified of the water, I wouldn't suggest that someone throw you in so that you would swim or else drown—but in this case I think it would be best to put one finger in the water first. In time you will be able to place both hands in the water, and sooner or later, if you keep working on this problem, you will be able to put your whole body in the water."

Taking this advice, she volunteered at a children's hospital. It was very difficult at first, but in time she was able to give a great deal of affection to these children. She entered therapy and was able to accept affection from her therapist. She is slowly overcoming her fear. Now she can give me a hug when she sees me. She has had several dates and has been able to give her dates a good-night kiss. In time she will be free of her terror.

Sexual Abuse

I am shocked at the number of my clients who have been sexually abused. Most cases involve women who have been abused by their fathers, uncles, grandfathers, and brothers, as well as family "friends."

But it doesn't happen only to women. My client Mark was abused sexually by his older stepbrother from the age of five to eleven. The stepbrother told him that if he ever told his parents, he would kill him. My client was finally released from his terror when the stepbrother left home to go into the army. My client is still terrified of his stepbrother and does everything he can to avoid contact with him. He still has not had the courage to tell his parents about this. He has recurring nightmares in which he is running from his stepbrother, but he is never able to get away from him. I suggested that he go into therapy or join a group that helps people who have been abused.

Sexual abuse violates not only the body but the emotions and the spirit of the person who has suffered the torture. All the people I have met who have been abused live with terrible guilt. They suffer from great fear and feel a sense of worthlessness. They have come to believe that in some way they were responsible.

"I should have told my parents even though my brother threatened to kill me," Mark said. "I somehow feel that I allowed this and that I could have fought him. I allowed myself to be a victim."

"Mark," I said, "you must forgive yourself and realize that you were only a small child when this started. You were afraid, and you didn't know how to handle the situation. If we could live our lives over again, we would all do many things very differently. You must realize that this is over and that you don't have to live in fear any longer. You must seek proper psychological counseling to help you resolve your feelings to the best of your ability." I stopped speaking because Mark had begun to cry.

"Tears can be very cleansing," I told him. "Never be afraid to cry. This will help to release the pain. In time, healing will take place and you will live with greater freedom."

There is help available to those who have experienced the horror of sexual abuse. People are coming forward with their stories, and this is helping many others not to be afraid to speak of their personal trauma.

Ginny had been sexually abused by her father. She became a woman who measured her worth by how many men wanted to have a sexual relationship with her. She knew this was not right, but she couldn't stop herself. Having tried therapy and found that it did not help to break her obsession with sex, she felt hopeless. Unable to sustain a committed relationship with a man, she felt empty and lonely. As a young girl she had tried to confide in her mother, who refused to believe her and pretended that nothing was wrong. Ginny finally gave up trying to convince her mother.

After leaving home at the age of sixteen, she settled with her aunt in another state. "My mother was relieved to have me leave," Ginny said. "I was a reminder that she did not have a happy marriage with my father. My mother was a weak woman who felt that she was not able to make a living on her own."

Ginny was too humiliated to confide in her aunt. Ginny began to believe that sex was confirmation. She started to have casual sexual relationships with boys, and when her aunt caught her having sex, she threw Ginny out of the house. The aunt had no idea of the psychological basis for Ginny's behavior.

Devastated by her aunt's rejection, she decided that she would "make it" on her own. Having taken secretarial courses in high school, Ginny was able to find an office job. Working hard and with the help of a few high-powered men with whom she had affairs, Ginny eventually became an executive. It was at this point in her life that I met her. She had achieved a great deal of professional success but was tormented by her promiscuous behavior and her inability to stop.

I spoke with her and suggested a therapy group that helped with similar problems. Ginny is now very much involved with this group. Having been able to talk about the past to people who have gone through similar experiences, she is releasing the guilt and learning why she has behaved in a manner that has not made her happy. Several talks with her mother have also helped. She finally confided in her aunt who was very understanding. Ginny does not see her father and is at peace with that decision.

Sexual abuse has been brought out into the open, which is important because people need to understand that they are not alone and that there is help available. Many people try to deny the existence of this problem because it is too disturbing for them to face, but it is very real to the Ginnys of this world.

If a child tells you that he or she is being abused, do not turn your back. Find out what is going on, and never feel that you should not interfere. It is the responsibility of all of us to do whatever we can to stop this from happening. Take action if you hear about this situation. We must protect our children from this horror! We cannot turn our backs and pretend that these atrocities do not exist. If Ginny's mother had listened to her daughter, she could have prevented a great deal of suffering.

Obsession

Lizzie became obsessed with her desire to continue a relationship that her lover had told her was over. She refused to believe him and came to see me, expecting me to tell her that this relationship would continue. She didn't get what she was looking for.

"Lizzie, you're obsessed," I told her. "You're fixated on your desire to possess your boyfriend. This is not good for you. You could become unbalanced if you don't let these negative thoughts go. If you are fixated, you must force yourself not to dwell on this desire. Think of other things, such as all the things in your life that you have to be grateful for. This will help you to let go of the obsession and begin to think clearly."

Trying to be as kind as possible, I told her I did not see her getting back with her lover. "Why do you want to try to force him to see you?" I asked. "If the man is not interested, don't you think you should let him go and get on with your life? I realize this may not be easy, but you are causing yourself a great deal of unhappiness."

Lizzie refused to listen to me and demanded that I tell her the relationship would continue. "He told me he loved me," she yelled. "How could he have changed his mind?"

"People change, Lizzie. You must learn not only to listen to what people say but to observe what they do. Anyone can say anything. The true test of a person's character is in his actions. Are you angry at yourself, perhaps, for believing this man when he told you he loved you?"

Ignoring this question, she wanted to know if I thought her lover was seeing another woman.

"Lizzie, that isn't important," I said. "The important thing is that you come to terms with the end of the relationship and realize that there are many good things waiting for you. You'll make yourself ill if you continue in this manner."

"I was very attracted to him, and I know he was attracted to me," she said. "How could he change his mind? I will not allow him to change his mind! I'll see another psychic who will tell me I can have him back."

"By all means, Lizzie, go to someone else," I told her. "I hope you find what you are looking for, but I think you're looking in the wrong place. The answer lies within yourself. Don't expect to hear what you want to hear."

She left in a huff, and I never heard from her again. I hope she was able to work out her problems. She thought that she would be fine if she got her lover back. This was not true, of course, but our egos often get in the way of our ability to perceive reality. We feel that we have been wronged and will get what we think we deserve. This approach to life's setbacks will bring no happiness. Look within yourself for your strength.

Like all things, sex is part of creation. In the true spiritual sense, sex is a part of love in action, the expression of the love within us toward the love within another person. We cannot connect to our higher selves unless we learn to lose ourselves. We achieve true spiritual happiness by not thinking of ourselves. Physical pleasure is momentary. Spend time on what brings lasting happiness. Service frees us from the slavery of preoccupation with the physical. Yes, we are human. Yes, we have human needs. But let us not confuse our needs with desires. Let us make all actions that we perform selfless actions. Does this seem difficult? It is really much more difficult to stay trapped in a life that is not truthful. The purpose of life is growth, and the purpose of sex is to express love. Associate with people of character and you will not be constantly heartbroken. Think before you act. This takes a little time and will save you a great deal of suffering. Do not become one of the trapped, for you do not have to do so. Keep yourself free by loving in the true spiritual sense of the word. Love is the spiritual side of all of us.

∴ V ∴
Addictions

Webster's dictionary tells us that addiction is the act of devoting or surrendering oneself to something habit-forming. Just as the word surrender defines addiction, it also provides the key to overcoming an addiction: One must surrender to one's higher self. It is the lower nature, the physical person, that is addicted to the habit-forming substance or behavior. If one keeps one's thoughts on a higher level, it is much easier to overcome an addiction. To think on a higher level is to think of the spiritual aspect of oneself and of how one may best serve humanity. If your thoughts remain those of beauty and of service, your mind will not dwell on desire; thus it will be able to release the addiction and live a life of freedom.

Each person is incarnated onto the Earth plane with tendencies that must be overcome. One person may be able to take one drink and stop while another finds that he cannot stop after one drink. One person finds food an obsession while another has to remind himself to eat. Each person has to deal with individual problems and his or her individual karma.

If you are addicted to something, your freedom is stolen from you. Once you are able to control your need for the addictive substance or behavior, your freedom is regained. A life of service is the best tonic for an addiction.

Addiction results from the desire to fill an emptiness in ourselves; replace your desire for an addictive substance with your passion to serve, and you will not have a moment of emptiness. If you find yourself unable to control your desire for an addictive material, face this and surrender to the God force within.

You Are Not Alone

Know within your heart that you are not alone. Many people have had to acknowledge that they could not control their addictions. The physical world is full of temptations. These are the dragons within that must be slain, and you can slay them. Many of my clients over the years were able to earn their freedom from an addiction. In the beginning they felt it was hopeless, and they often tried and failed. What did they all have in common? They did not give up.

If you have tried to stop something twenty times and have been unable to do so, try for the twenty-first time. Patience, discipline, and prayer will serve you. Never lose your sense of humor, no matter how impossible things appear, for this will give you added strength.

Forgive yourself. People feel ashamed when they cannot control themselves. Sometimes we feel embarrassed to reach out for help because we feel that we should be able to deal with our problems ourselves; this will interfere with your ability to overcome your addiction. Facing the fact that you have a problem is the first step toward freedom.

I have been asked why it is that people who come to me with an addiction leave the session and find that they are able to muster the strength to overcome it. They want to know what I do that seems to work faster than therapy.

When I work with clients who have an addiction, I am very truthful. I tell them straight out that they are addicted, and then I say I know with certainty that they have the strength to face and overcome their addiction. No matter how many excuses they come up with to justify their need for an addictive substance or behavior, I remain firm in my resolution that they can learn to live without it.

A spiritual realization supersedes the psychological. I explain to the client that life is sacred and that the physical does not last. The spirit is eternal and must be treated with dignity and respect. The body is very important because it is the vehicle that carries the spirit. We must treat the body with reverence, and it is not reverent to put harmful substances into it.

I show the client a picture of his or her life as it would be if free from the addiction. Then I try to guide the client toward the proper support group. I have even picked up the phone during a session and called Alcoholics Anonymous to get a list of meetings that a client can attend. I have given a client the name of a good therapist and I have given clients a book to read, such as *Theosophy Simplified* by Irving S. Cooper (Wheaton, Illinois: The Theosophical Press) or *The Power of Positive Thinking* by Norman Vincent Peale (New York: Fawcett-Crest). I then tell the person to call me if necessary—support is essential. People need to know that they are not alone, that there are people standing by to help. I cannot do it for my clients—they must do the work for themselves—but I can teach, support, and help them to find the courage they will need.

One of my clients was finally able to free herself from her desire for cigarettes. The first three months were very hard. She called me twice a day to say, "I'm dying for a cigarette." Her desire to quit, however, was stronger than her desire to smoke, and she persevered. In time she was able to tell me, "I can't believe it, but even the thought of a cigarette makes me sick. I have no desire to smoke. I cannot even tolerate the smell of cigarettes. I didn't think this was possible, but I now see myself as a non-smoker."

She had integrated a positive change in her behavior and no longer struggled with her desire to smoke. Four years later she is still not smoking. In her case, integration replaced discipline. There was no force involved; she simply no longer wanted to smoke.

There are times when a person is ready to quit something and is able to carry out that decision immediately. This is when the spiritual self, the higher self, makes the decision and the physical self follows with little trouble. This is not always the case, but it does happen. The person says "Enough" and is able to give up an addiction with little effort. Each person earns freedom in his or her own way and time.

Remember, the point of life is spiritual education for the soul's development. We must be aware that we will be incarnated with the same problem over and over until we are able to free ourselves from it. This freedom must be earned on the Earth plane, the schoolroom for the soul's education.

Don't dwell on past failures but look toward future success. You can decide at any moment to take charge of your life. Nothing is impossible. Difficult, perhaps, but not impossible.

As you start on your path of freedom, keep yourself away from the addictive substance. It will not serve you in the beginning to put yourself in a bar if you are trying to stop drinking. In time, after you have the problem in control, you will be able to sit with someone who is having a drink and not be tempted to have one. At this time, you will find that integration has replaced discipline.

Integration

Self-discipline implies force. Let's say that you must lose weight. You desire to eat cake or ice cream, but you force yourself not to.

You walk by the bakery, telling yourself you will not go in and purchase the jelly doughnut that you see as you walk by. The desire for the doughnut is overpowering, and you finally break down and buy it. As you eat it, guilt sets in, causing you to feel angry and defeated. You were not able to force yourself to stay away from the doughnut. If you had fully integrated your decision to lose weight, you would not have had to fight your desire for the doughnut. The desire simply would not have been there.

In the beginning stages of overcoming your problem, you may well have to use discipline, but as you see the results of your dieting, you will feel so good that you won't want foods which make you feel heavy and unattractive. When this happens, you are free. You no longer need to force yourself to do something that is difficult.

Addiction to Alcohol

Kari had called earlier in the morning, sounding desperate. She walked through the door and began to sob, obviously in great pain. "I have tried, but I haven't been able to stop drinking. I don't know how I can go on. Last night was horrendous. This morning I thought I would die if I didn't get some help. I've had your phone number for six months, but I wasn't able to call until now." She stopped speaking and put her head in her hands.

As I observed her, I thought, But you have called now, at a point of total desperation, at a time when you are ready to stop.

"Kari," I told her, "you will find the strength. Coming to talk to me is the first step to overcoming this addiction. You must let go and ask your higher self for the help that lies within you."

Kari had started drinking in her teens. It had seemed harmless at first—weekend parties and social drinking with friends. Slowly she started drinking more and more until she found that she could not control the alcohol; the alcohol was controlling her. She had attended an AA meeting to try to get support but had found it uncomfortable. "I felt as if everyone were staring at me. I also felt that I was very different from the other people there," she commented.

Kari's parents had been drinkers. They had the usual five o'clock cocktail and then wine with dinner and liquor after. Trying to talk to her mother about her problem was useless because her mother refused to accept that her daughter had a drinking problem.

There had been times when Kari had not had a drink for a few weeks, but then she would visit her parents and end up drinking with them.

"Once I started drinking, I wasn't able to stop until I passed out. I wanted to be one of those people who could have a drink or two and then stop. I had a date last night with a very nice man, and I decided I was not going to drink. He ordered some wine, and I thought, One glass won't hurt. I proceeded to get very drunk and started kissing him in the restaurant. I don't remember what happened after that. I woke up lying on the floor of my apartment. I'm so embarrassed, I could die."

"Kari, you cannot overcome this problem alone," I said. "You need support and understanding. Many people have been in your situation, and they have learned to handle their addiction to alcohol. You want to stop or you wouldn't have come to see me today. I'm going to call AA and find out where the meetings are being held today. I know you have tried this before, but at that time you weren't ready."

I went to the phone and got a list of the meetings and their addresses. Watching Kari, I could see that she was beginning to calm down a little. I talked to her about loving herself and learning that she could be free. She had not been ready to stop before, so she had made up all kinds of excuses and was very judgmental of others. She had seen herself mirrored in the other people at the first AA meeting she attended and had not been ready for that.

"You must face the fact that you are an alcoholic. You cannot control your drinking, so you must stop right now. It is not easy to do this, but it is possible. If you reach toward your higher self, the part of you that is spirit, you will find great inner strength.

There will be a battle between your higher self and the physical part of yourself that is controlled by your desires. Realize that your higher self is going to win the battle. You will find great happiness through overcoming an addiction, and your freedom will be restored. Responsibility is a key word: You are responsible for your actions. No one can force anyone to take a drink."

Kari left that day and went to an AA meeting. Calling later to tell me how it had gone, she said that she had been given love and support. She had gone out with three people from the meeting, and they had stayed with her throughout her first day of sobriety.

Three years have passed since that first meeting with Kari. She has not touched a drink in that time and has helped others on their road to being free from alcohol addiction. Each time I see her, she seems happier. Her desire to drink is gone. The first weeks were very difficult and a lot of self-discipline was needed, but in time integration replaced discipline. This is the key to staying successful.

Kari is just one example of a person who has overcome an addiction. She had tried and failed many times before she realized success. The important thing was that she did not give up. If you do not succeed, you must try again. No matter how many failures you have had, keep trying and you will eventually make it. Sooner or later your attempts will bring positive results.

Overeating

When I met Marvin, he weighed three hundred pounds and seldom left his apartment. He had no self-esteem and was very depressed. At the time he came to see me, he had not seen a therapist for seven years. He felt that it did not help, so he gave up. Marvin was a talented painter who could not paint and felt lethargic and unmotivated. Each morning he would tell himself that he was going to stay on a diet; he did fine for three or four hours, and then ate everything in sight. After he consumed the food, he felt totally depressed and then ate more and more.

I told Marvin, "The body is a vehicle that carries the spirit. You must respect your body as the divine instrument it is. You must think about the needs of the body, as opposed to your desires. Ask yourself, 'What is the need? What does my body need in order to function at its best?'

"As long as you make dieting a huge issue, you will not be able to stay on your diet. Start each day with the question, 'How may I best serve my body?' This body has been given to you as a sacred trust. It should be treated as one. Your problem, Marvin, is not an easy one to overcome. Many people with a problem as great as yours have been able to conquer their addiction to food. Communicate with others who have felt the same way you do. This will give you great support, and you will not feel alone."

Marvin openly blamed his mother for his condition. "She was always telling me how fat I was and that she was embarrassed to be seen with me. Watching everything that I put into my mouth, she would yell if I ate something fattening. I had to sneak food and I became expert at it."

I realized that he was trying to get back at his mother by overeating, but he was harming only himself. No matter what his mother had done, he was responsible for his own behavior. He could overcome this problem if he sought proper support and learned that life is good for each of us if we do not consume ourselves with selfish thoughts. Marvin's overeating was selfish.

"It is easier to stop overeating than it is to keep living in your self-imposed prison, Marvin," I said. "Start in small ways. You cannot change your habits overnight, but you can begin by saying that you will try to attend one support meeting each week. You can also get more exercise. Start by walking. Don't try to run a marathon the first day out, just take a leisurely walk every day. Soon you will begin to enjoy this exercise, and it will be a pleasure, not a burden."

He thought this over, and I continued: "Marvin, I think you are a terrific person and a very talented artist. You have been given a gift and you have a lot to be grateful for. Think of the good things in your life. The situation seems bleak at the moment, but it can get better immediately if you start on your new program of health, which includes healthy thinking."

I waited for Marvin's reaction. I had not wanted to hurt him, but I felt strongly that he must do something about his weight because it could be dangerous to his health.

"I will try again," he said finally. "I'm not certain it will work, but I will try again. Do you really think I'm a talented artist?"

"I certainly do. And you could be an excellent artist if you would put more energy into it."

We talked more about his mother. "I really do love my mother, but I feel very angry with her," he told me.

"Your mother didn't know how to handle your problem," I said. "I'm not saying she did the right thing, but we must try to understand her point of view. She's no longer standing over you—you are now in control of what you put into your mouth. It will take great patience and commitment, as well as learning to love yourself, to take the weight off and keep it off. These virtues can be learned by taking things one moment at a time. Don't keep reliving past failures. Good, healthy nutrition and positive support are the keys to your success. Right thinking— the kind that is positive, productive, and kind—will help you stay on course."

A year after our meeting, Marvin called. He had lost sixty pounds and felt like a new person. He had joined Weight Watchers and a walking group. Having gone back into therapy, he understood much better why he had escaped through eating.

He was counseling teens who had weight problems and was enjoying helping others. At times he still slipped and ate too much, or ate for the wrong reasons. He accepted these little setbacks and was able to get back on the track swiftly.

"I have a painting that I would like to send you," he said. "My art has gotten better, and I am loving painting again."

After Marvin hung up, I thought, What a great example of how you can change your life by changing your point of view.

Now much more self-assured and much healthier, he was enjoying life and helping others to do the same.

Addiction to Sex

Nadia was addicted to Lionel; she was totally obsessed with this man. At the time of our first meeting, she was emaciated and had a skin rash. She had just broken up with him for the seventh time. She kept repeating, "I cannot live without him."

As I looked at her, I psychically saw that she had been physically abused many times. I asked her about this.

"The violence was only occasionally. I would not tolerate it if it happened all the time," she said.

"You shouldn't have tolerated it at all. Have you no self-respect?" I asked.

"I can't go on without him," she repeated, not seeming to have heard what I said. "The sex is so good. I've never been attracted to anyone the way I am to Lionel. When he was violent, he was very sorry afterward, and then became very loving."

"Why have you come here today, Nadia?" I asked. "What is it that you think I can help you with? You've stated that you can't live without Lionel. But this simply isn't true. You could live very well without him! Your life could be much better if you let this relationship go. You don't want to hear this, but I must say what I feel will help you. I must warn you that if you keep on with this relationship, you will end up being badly hurt, physically and mentally."

"I tried to live without him, but I wasn't able to. I miss him when he's not around. He is a wonderful lover."

"It sounds to me as if you are addicted to sex with Lionel," I said.

"What is wrong with enjoying sex?" she snapped.

"Nothing is wrong with it unless it is dangerous and emotionally unhealthy. Look at yourself, Nadia. You look terrible. Your body has broken out in a rash from nerves, and you look as if you are starving to death. I'm very worried about you."

"I came to see you today because you're a psychic, and I want you to tell me when you see us back together." She stared at me and waited for my answer.

Cases often come to me that are beyond my expertise. This woman needed a professional psychologist. I knew that all I could do was warn her about what I saw and try to help her see the dangers involved in staying in such an unhealthy relationship. She needed to be taught that she could let this relationship go and be a happier person.

She became reflective and then said, "There are times when I feel this is not good for me. I can't stop thinking about him, and it is interfering with the rest of my life. I don't like to be alone, and sex is very important to me. He always promises that he will never hit me again, and he can be very sweet at times."

"Nadia," I said, "just because you are not with Lionel does not mean you will be alone. There are many people for you to spend time with. Can't you let go of your desire for a moment and look around to see what you are missing?"

"Other people don't give me what Lionel gives me," she replied.

I told her of the possibilities I saw for her if she was able to overcome this addiction. I saw that she had always wanted to travel; if she applied, she would be able to get a job with the airlines. I also told her that she would feel free and in control of her life if she released her obsession. The skin rash would clear up when her nerves calmed down, and the desperate feeling would leave her. In time she would understand that this physical addiction was interfering with her development. She would also find comfort in not having to feel afraid for her physical safety.

I suggested that she get therapy. I am neither a therapist nor a medical doctor, so when my clients have a problem that can be resolved with the help of a doctor, I recommend it. But how she lived her life was her decision alone.

I never heard from Nadia again.

Addiction to Exercise

June exercised three to four hours per day. If she missed one day, she became hysterical. She stressed that she did not feel right unless she was jogging or doing some form of aerobics for at least three hours daily.

I asked, "How do you have the energy to do anything else?"

She insisted that her routine gave her a lot of energy, but she looked anorexic. Her bones were visible, and when you saw her, you wanted to feed her immediately. She had had many injuries, but these did not stop her from pursuing her routine. I asked June what she was running from.

Looking at me as if I were out of my mind, she asked, "What do you mean?"

I said, "Well, I think you're using exercise to escape from dealing with certain issues."

June has not had a personal relationship for a long time and says that she does not miss this aspect of life. Of course, one can be very happy and not be involved in a personal relationship, but I was concerned about her addiction to exercise. In June's case, her compulsion to exercise was as much an addiction as an alcohol or drug dependency.

There were days when June had to force herself to get out of bed in order to do her routine. She was so exhausted that she would fall asleep putting her running shoes on, but come rain or shine, she did her exercise. She started having a lot of trouble sleeping; she felt as if she were always running even while she was lying in bed trying to sleep.

"June," I said, "you are given only a certain amount of vital energy in a lifetime. If you use it all up in exercising, you will suffer from a loss of energy during the second half of your life." (She was thirty-five years old.)

"I didn't know that," she said. She was adamant that she did not feel well if she did not exercise.

"Have you ever had a weight problem, June?"

"I still do," she replied.

This, of course, was a fantasy. She couldn't have weighed more than 110 pounds, and she was five feet seven inches tall. Her friends were worried about her because she seemed totally consumed with exercise. She would often be late for work; her boss warned her that if she was late again, she would be fired. I spent two hours trying to get through to her. I was worried that she would totally collapse. She wouldn't listen; she just kept repeating that she felt terrible if she did not work out every day.

I stressed that it was fine to exercise but that she was taking it too far. What she was doing to herself was dangerous.

Six months later she came to see me again. She had passed out at work one day and had been taken to the hospital suffering from fatigue and malnutrition. She had been recommended to a therapist, and this had finally caused her to look at her compulsion. She seemed more relaxed on her second visit to me. She had forced herself to stop exercising compulsively. She now worked out for forty minutes, three times a week, and watched her diet to make certain that she was eating properly. She still had periods in which she found it difficult to control her desire to exercise more strenuously, but she was working on the problem.

"I must have been crazed," she said. "I could not stop working out. In the beginning I exercised normally, but then I began to feel a real high when I worked out for longer periods. I kept getting thinner, but I thought that I looked great. My mother tried to reach me, but I wouldn't listen to anyone. I now see that I was killing myself with exercise. The first time we met, you asked me what I was running from. At that time I thought you were silly, but now that I've been in therapy I can see I was running from my feminine side. I kept getting thinner and more muscular, then my period stopped. I realize now that I was afraid to relate to men, so I tried to look like a man. It is all still a bit confused and I haven't completely come to terms with everything, but I'm beginning to understand my compulsive addictive nature. I feel better now that I don't work out so much. I have time to do things I'd neglected because I was afraid to do anything that would interfere with my exercise routine. I think I would have killed myself if I hadn't stopped the compulsive exercise. It seems so silly now, but I just wasn't able to stop."

"Exercise is fine and healthy," I said. "It becomes unhealthy only if you use it to escape your problems. It shows a total consumption with the physical, whereas you should give yourself time to work on your spiritual nature. Your body is a sacred responsibility and you must not abuse it by overworking it."

June had learned a great deal since our first session. It was unfortunate that she had to be hospitalized in order to wake up. There is an easier way to learn. "Common sense in all things," my grandmother used to tell me. There's a great deal of wisdom in this simple advice that could save a person a lot of heartbreak in the long run.

Addiction to Metaphysics

Metaphysics can become a dangerous obsession for many people who get a "high" from delving into psychic phenomena and mysticism. Like alcohol or drug addiction, it can be an escape from reality, and like those addictions, it can creep up on a person; it starts out as an interest and gradually takes over one's life.

Pat started out by being curious about metaphysics. He went to a card reader and found it interesting. Next he had a past life reading done, and then went on to astrology. He sought out metaphysical groups that taught meditation exercises to "attract what the universe owes you." He thought of little else and read every book he could find on metaphysical subjects. He moved on to dietary practices that he felt would make him more receptive to psychic phenomena, including vegetarianism and fasting. His friends worried that he was becoming too involved and they warned him that he was becoming addicted to this study.

"I want to be a professional channeler" were his first words to me during our session. A channeler is a person who allows a soul from the astral plane to use his or her body to transmit messages to the physical world. Another name for channeler is medium.

"Why?" I asked.

"I feel that I am being directed to do this" was his reply.

"Who is directing you?" I asked next.

"Voices tell me that I was born to do something great for the world."

Pat went on to explain that his interest in metaphysics started with the death of his mother, one year before our meeting. He had desperately wanted to communicate with his mother, whom he sorely missed, so he had started seeking people with the ability to communicate with souls who have passed over to the other side.

I told Pat that it wasn't wise to try to communicate with those who have passed over. It keeps them attracted to the physical world because one's thought forms are transmitted to them. There are times when we receive messages from those who have gone over to the other side, and it is a beautiful and very sacred experience, but it happens only when they want to contact us.

"You mustn't keep trying to contact your mother," I cautioned. "You must let go and help her to release herself totally from the physical plane. You must consider what is best for your mother and not your personal desire to communicate. Your mother is fine, and you will see her when it is your time to pass over.

"I am very worried about your preoccupation with metaphysics," I went on. "It is dangerous to become overly involved with psychic phenomena. I fear that you are trying to escape life through your obsession with metaphysics."

Pat responded by defending his obsession. He informed me that a reader had told him he had been a great priest in Atlantis and that he had great powers at that time. He was now busy trying to regain that power.

I have always disliked the word power with its dangerous implication of control over other people. If you are seeking power, your motivation cannot be selfless. The drive to acquire power is always selfish and causes nothing but heartache.

I am very leery of readers who tell their clients that they have powers. People who seek psychic help are often in a vulnerable, suggestible state and are seeking affirmation of their own self-worth. It is very easy for an unscrupulous person to take advantage of these clients' susceptibility and to feed them ego-inflating nonsense that can do them great harm. This is a terrible abuse of the trust that the client places in the reader.

It is wonderful to read and study metaphysics, but it is danger-ous when it is used to escape life. Pat, who was an accountant, was very unhappy in his job and did not feel important. He was also frustrated in his personal life because he felt that nobody understood him. Everyone wants to feel important and needed, but we must not use metaphysics as a way of feeling more impor-tant than our neighbors.

"I don't think you were born to be a psychic healer, Pat," I said. "You could do yourself great harm and put yourself terribly out of balance if you pursue this course. You have more than enough to deal with here and now. The path to happiness lies in being responsible for your own life and work."

Pat explained that there were times when he felt he was losing his mind through grief over the loss of his mother. He had used his metaphysical studies to keep himself from dealing with these feelings.

We talked about issues relating to his job and how he could make his work situation more pleasant. I suggested that he stop all metaphysical pursuits for the time being and that he seek therapy. He needed to deal with his unresolved feelings about his mother's passing and his need for control. With obvious relief, he agreed to pursue this course of action.

After Pat left, I thought about this session for a long time. It was good that he had been seeking answers, but I knew he must learn to look within himself and not try to find the answers elsewhere. He had gone too far in his pursuit of knowledge of the "other side." Dealing with life on the Earth plane would be plenty for him to handle at this time.

In a single incarnation one is given more than enough lessons to learn; if a person should receive more, he will be given more. One does not have to go to the mountain to find one's spiritual teacher, for the God force lies within all of us.

Self-possessed "gurus" are dangerous people to follow, especially if you are the type of person who looks to others to make your decisions for you. Psychics and healers can give guidance and support, but one should not abdicate responsibility for one's obligations and life choices.

Addiction to Drugs

The number of people who are addicted to drugs is truly astounding. Our schools are overrun with students who are taking drugs, and parents are terrified that their children will succumb to peer pressure and take drugs in order to feel accepted.

Education must begin in the home! Children learn from the example of their parents. If parents drink to excess and take inappropriate drugs, their children are likely to follow their example. So let us set a positive example for our children.

Any drug that is used for recreational purposes or to escape the pressures of life is inappropriate. Drugs affect the emotional body and can be mind-altering and therefore dangerous. If you could psychically see the effect of drugs, you would have little trouble in avoiding their use. A crust is formed around the brain, and negative influences are brought into the astral body through the use of inappropriate drugs. The astral body is the spiritual body. It is a part of man that remains when the physical body is gone. The crust is a filmy coating that can be seen only by a psychic. It is not noticeable to the physical eye. It takes many years in the astral plane for this crust to be dissolved.

Thinking that these drugs are not harmful does not protect you from their negative influence. Drugs impart a false sense of power. This is fantasy, and when reality intrudes, it brings with it depression and despair.

Drugs have a place in the world but should not be used for entertainment. It is best to get through your troubles with a clear mind and a positive outlook; this will aid you spiritually.

It is difficult to stop any habit, but in the long run it is more difficult to continue doing something you know is wrong. If you stop doing something that is bad for you, there is a great feeling of relief; it is as if a great burden were lifted from your shoulders. You no longer worry that you cannot stop. You don't have to feel guilty when you wake up in a fog from the residue of drugs or alcohol. You have your dignity back. It is intolerable to live a life that is not free. Addictions steal our freedom from us by consuming our time and energy, and often our money. Think of all the extra time you will have when you are not using the time to escape from yourself by drinking or taking drugs. Think of all the things you have wanted to do but were not clear enough to do while under the influence of drugs or alcohol.

"I cannot imagine life without a glass of wine at dinner." This statement verges on self-pity. There are hundreds of ways to relax that do not involve drinking. Drinking is not really relaxing. Excessive drinking causes one to feel hyper and out of sorts. Dinner can be very enjoyable without drinking alcohol. You will be amazed at how differently you look at things and at people when you do so with a clear head. Keep your thoughts positive. Think of the great things that go along with your freedom from addiction. Take it one moment at a time. Do not keep rationalizing your addiction. Stop yourself from harming yourself. Once again, it is easier to stop than to keep worrying.

If your attitude is one of service, it will support you as you stop your addictive behavior. Stop thinking that you are being deprived of something; you are not being deprived of anything except your dignity. Your body is the vehicle that carries your soul, and you must not pollute it with drugs or alcohol. This is wrong, and you know it is wrong. Stop pretending that you are ignorant of this truth. As the Bible says, "Know the truth, and the truth shall make you free."

How does one overcome an addiction? First, accept that you

have a situation that is out of control for the time being. Second, replace the desire for the addiction with a desire to serve. When you are busy serving and thinking of the needs of others, you will not be consumed with the thoughts of your addiction. Third, be patient with yourself. You cannot overcome a serious problem overnight; it takes time, patience, and self-discipline. If you keep your thinking on a spiritual level, it will be much easier to conquer your problem. Do not think about deprivation; think about freedom. Find help, for there are people standing by to help you. Many people have experienced the feeling of withdrawal and they will help to guide you and support you in your efforts.

No matter how many times you have failed, try again. You will succeed if you keep trying. Every one of us is incarnated with something to overcome. You must handle your physical problems on the Earth plane. If you have been incarnated into a family with addictive problems, it is because your soul needs to go through the experience. Don't blame others for your problem. Each one of us has free choice. As an individual you choose to take a drink or drugs; no one forces you to do this. It is very important not to allow yourself to worry about what others will think of you if you quit your addiction. You must remain aware that if you stop, you may help others to do the same. Example is very powerful. Your example may save the life of another person.

The Angel on the Mountain

I received a note from Lawrence inviting me to join him for a day in the country. Arrangements were made for a driver to pick me up on Sunday morning, and I was driven to a large and impressive estate in the mountains. I've always loved the mountains and there is no place I'd rather go more. The mountains seem very much alive, with their great dignity and majesty. Lawrence greeted me at the front door of a beautiful Tudor-style mansion and showed me to the library. There were thousands of books on shelves that rose from floor to ceiling and covered all the walls, and the furniture was elegant and comfortable-looking. The home felt well looked after. The wood was highly polished, and the paintings on the walls were originals.

"This home belongs to a dear friend and a teacher of mine whom you will meet soon," Lawrence said. "His name is Sir William. The home has been in his family for years. I thought it would do you good to have a day away from the city. We now have the opportunity to talk, and later we will go for a walk in the mountains."

"Lawrence, I'm really grateful to be here. It is a wonderful home. I felt myself calming down as soon as I got in the car. The city is a great place, but it gives one balance to spend time with nature."

Lawrence showed me the artwork in the house and talked a bit about the various artists. Tea was brought in, and we sat down to relax. I told Lawrence that I had been dealing with many clients who had problems with addictions. I explained the method that I had used to help them and asked if he could give me any additional advice.

He was silent for a moment as he sipped his tea, then he raised his calm gaze to me and said, "Tell your clients this: A sense of humor will serve you. Laugh at yourself and this will calm you. Laughter can be a great healer. Prayer will also help. I do not mean prayer that asks an impersonal God for a special favor, but prayer that addresses our higher self, the God that is within, and asks for strength. This is true selfless prayer. Take a moment to quiet yourself and then recognize the God force that is within. This type of prayer will center you and help you to get through any trouble that is burdening you. If you want your freedom more than you want the substance to which you are addicted, freedom will come to you. It can be a joyous experience to let go and allow yourself to relinquish your addiction. The choice is yours: freedom or slavery."

The wind was blowing, and its sighing breath filled the room as Lawrence finished speaking. I could feel the power of the wind as it blew around the walls of the house.

I would pass this information on to others, for it would be a great help to many. To surrender to your higher self: yes, that was the answer. It would not be easy for a lot of people, but it was not impossible for anyone to overcome an addiction. I once met a man who had been addicted to heroin for many years. He was finally able to stop. No one who knew him thought that he had the inner strength to do it, but he surprised everyone and is a changed man. He told many about his experience, and his words served to help others to overcome their individual problems.

"Many are called, but few are chosen," Christ said. I remember someone using that phrase when talking about his ability to finally conquer his addiction to marijuana. I think that all of us are called and are given the choice to be free souls or to stay in the prison of our addictions. I remember a young girl of sixteen who was able to tell her peers, "No, I will not do drugs." She held firmly to her decision, and shortly some of the other kids followed her lead and also were able to say no.

"Lawrence," I said, "do you think religion can become an addiction?"

"Anything that becomes an obsession is a form of addiction. If you think you cannot live without something, you have a problem with it, whatever it is. Religion in its organized form forces people to live within a framework of prescribed beliefs. *If these dogmas interfere with your freedom of choice, then it is important to think about your relationship to religion. Anything that interferes with your personal freedom is a form of giving over your power to choose and thus can become an addiction." Law-rence smiled and said, "Let's go for a walk before it becomes too dark to enjoy the view."

We put on our coats and went outside. The view was breath-taking. The sun was just beginning to set behind the mountains, the air was fresh, and the scent of pine trees enveloped us. We walked together, silently feeling the beauty as well as looking at it.

"There is a great Deva, an angelic presence, that stands on top of the mountain. If you look closely, you will be able to see this force. You will certainly be able to feel it if you allow yourself a moment of silence." We continued on without making a sound. One can also feel this force by sitting quietly in a church. It is a presence that no words can adequately describe. It is a feeling that surrounds one.

I allowed my mind to rest and to take in the sunset. I did not need to speak. I was happy to be walking and to be next to Lawrence. As I looked at the mountains, the words of Jesus— "For thine is the kingdom and the power and the glory"—flowed through my mind. These mountains had great dignity. They stood tall and proud. I felt small and weak next to them. It was not an uncomfortable feeling but a realization of the power of nature.

There is so much beauty to experience on the planet. I wished I could share this view with everyone I knew. How can man deny that there is a God force when he looks at nature? How can man allow himself to miss so much by staying locked in the prison of his personal desires? We walked on for another few minutes, and then Lawrence said, "We had better return to the house. The driver will be waiting to drive you home." I felt a wave of sadness at the thought of leaving. Lawrence touched my shoulder gently. "Do not worry, my child, you will return soon. This is the first of many days we will spend in the country. I hope that my friend Sir William will be able to join us here one day. You will learn a great deal by spending time with him. He has been a great teacher to me." It had never occurred to me that Lawrence might have a teacher, but on reflection it made perfect sense.

We arrived back at the house where the car was waiting. We said good-bye, and I got into the car. The driver seemed to fly back to the city. As I entered my apartment, I felt the quiet exhaustion that comes from walking in the fresh air. I put the opera *Tosca* on the stereo and sat listening. The beauty of the music filled the room.

I thought of Lawrence's teacher, Sir William, and was excited at the prospect of meeting him. Lawrence's smiling face kept coming to mind. I thought about him as I listened to the opera. Music is a great comfort. Yes, it is true that life can seem very difficult. There are times when we feel we cannot go on, but then the sun comes up and it is a new day. With the dawn, we are given another opportunity to learn. It is all quite simple but rather remarkable. Life in the physical world presents us with many tests, but there is also great beauty to experience. If you live a life of service, you have few problems. If a problem comes up, you are fortified by your point of view. Yes, it is difficult to overcome addictions, but it is not impossible. If you love yourself and keep love at the forefront of your mind at all times, you will be able to retain your sense of humor and go on with courage and a sense of fun. Yes, life is supposed to be fun. There is no happier feeling than when you know that you have shed a great burden. Addictions are burdens; they lock us into an oppressive cycle of need and fulfillment.

The music stopped, and I sat for a while in silence. It was wonderful. All of life can be wonderful if we allow ourselves to enjoy every part of it. You are not really living when you wake up in a fog because of drugs and alcohol. I turned off the lights and got ready for bed.

I dreamed about the mountain, the Deva, that Lawrence had described. I saw myself climbing the mountain in my dream. Lawrence stood at the top, and I climbed to join him. The dream was of us standing on the mountaintop looking at the view. Everything was in vivid color. Standing together, we looked past the horizon and saw the limitlessness of everything.

∴ V I ∴
Ambition

Ambition is the desire for success or power, but with true love there is no desire. If you are truly a loving person, you cannot be an ambitious person. We have been taught that ambition is the prerequisite to success, and you may well think that in order to live a successful life you must strive to fulfill your ambitions. But ambition serves no one. A free person is not an ambitious person. Let me explain. To work hard and to enjoy doing a good job does not mean that you are ambitious; it means that you are a person who possesses character.

What does ambition gain us? Does it make us happy within ourselves? Are we ever good enough or rich enough or respected enough? It becomes a vicious cycle. As with an addiction, the more you get, the more you want. It is sad that people feel that their self-worth is derived from what others think of them and their success. There is only one great success, and that comes from living a life of service. Nothing can ever fill the essential emptiness of life on the material plane until we integrate this realization into our very being.

One may ask, "If I am not ambitious, how will I ever be really successful?" The answer lies in the universal law that we get what we earn. Some people work very hard and strive for success and wealth. Life goes on and they never fulfill these goals. Some people do little and yet earn great amounts of money and are respected by others. I think we should realize that individual karma is often at play. If in this life or in a previous one you have earned the right to be successful, then successful you will be. Hard work is fine, it is a person's duty to work. If you are given a respectful title and a good salary, that is wonderful. But if you are not given a title and a large salary, why should you think that your life is not worthwhile?

We are always trying to prove something to somebody, often our parents or our peers. But what are we trying to prove? We are trying to prove that we are important. In the eyes of the God force, each person is equally valuable. When you pass over to the other side, it will not matter whether you are the president or the doorman. The only thing that will matter is the quality of your life.

Making It

Cindy was obsessed with ambition. Determined that she would get an important promotion in her company, she was relentless in her pursuit of the higher title. She worked sixteen hours a day and had no life outside her job. She slept fitfully, was always worried that she had not done enough work, and was snappish and ill-natured. No one liked her. Like a robot she would work regardless of how she felt. She was sick for three months one winter but never took a day away from the office to rest. She lost touch with everyone she knew because she was too busy working to return phone calls. Finally, people stopped calling. I asked her about this, and her answer was that she was going to get the promotion no matter the price. Her father had told her she would never amount to anything, and she was going to prove him wrong even if it killed her. Her face was fixed in a scowl of total, unwavering determination. She listened to no one. She certainly did not listen to me. I warned her that if she did not slow down she could have a nervous breakdown. She had come to me to find out when her promotion would come through. She became very angry with me and stormed out after I told her honestly that I did not see a promotion, that I felt she might have some competition at the job and might remain in her current position for at least another year.

Time passed, and when the promotions were handed out, she did not receive one. Her boss told her that he appreciated her hard work but that she lacked the skills to get along with people. Recognizing that she needed a break, he suggested that she take a few weeks off and get some rest. "We'll reevaluate your progress next year," he said.

Cindy was devastated and sank into a deep depression. It was because of the depression that she returned to talk to me. I told her that her failure to receive the promotion was not the end of the world. "You must take more time to live and enjoy yourself," I said. "It's fine to work hard, but you're stressed to the breaking point. I'm sorry you didn't get the promotion. I know you must be very disappointed." I let this sink in, then went on, "Sometimes situations that seem devastating turn out in retrospect to be very helpful. You're being given an opportunity to reevaluate your job situation. Do you really want to continue living the way you have been? You're a nervous wreck, and you've forgotten how to have fun."

Cindy kept staring at me angrily, then said as though she hadn't heard me, "I cannot believe my boss said that I lacked skills in getting along with people. I just try to make everyone do the best job they can. What's so bad about that? If I can work hard, so can they!"

"Not everyone has the same abilities and the same capacities," I said. "You mustn't expect everyone to feel the same way you do about work. Yes, it's good to keep the work place professional, but it sounds to me as if you're too hard on people. One can be firm and kind at the same time."

"I was going to be general manager before I was twenty-eight years old, and now it's not going to happen," she said.

"Why twenty-eight?" I asked.

"I have always set time goals for myself. I finished college at the age of twenty-one, grad school at twenty-three. I always felt that I could do things faster than other people. It is important to me."

"That is unfortunate for you, Cindy. It certainly doesn't make you appear adaptable. You must not keep living within such strict guidelines. You will never have any peace in your life if you keep yourself totally goal-oriented. How about your spiritual development?"

"I don't know what you mean. I'm not interested in any particular church," she said.

I explained that I meant service and thinking of others. She half listened and seemed uninterested in this part of the discussion. When our time was up, Cindy left, saying angrily that she would get the promotion the next time. Nothing would stop her. She would work harder. I thought that ambition would never bring her any peace, and that was a tragedy!

There is a big difference between mature, professional behavior and ambition. Yes, it is important to do the best job you can, but then you must accept things as they are and not despair because they are not exactly the way you wanted them to be. Many people work very hard and never seem to "make it" in the eyes of the world.

"Making it" has nothing whatever to do with one's spiritual development. People equate making it with gaining the approval of others, but to work only to get approval is the wrong approach.

We must learn to do things because it is our duty to serve. This should be the motivation for all of our work. If you work solely to serve, you will not be bothered by what others think about you. It is liberating to do one's duty with no desire for gratification other than what comes from living with service on one's mind at all times.

Ambition Is a Killer

Nothing could stop Martin from working too hard. But as a result of overwork and no rest he suffered a slight stroke. He was hospitalized and firmly warned by his doctor that he must slow down. Martin's wife was very worried about him, but he wouldn't listen to her. She tried to persuade Martin to slow down, but he snapped at her to stop nagging him. Martin left the hospital and went right back to work. He wouldn't let anyone help him; he felt that he was the only one who could do his job properly. Martin stayed at work until late at night and did not eat properly or get any form of exercise. He kept repeating that he wanted to be a millionaire by the time he was forty. His wife didn't care about great wealth. They were very comfortable and she thought that Martin should be grateful and enjoy life more. But he wouldn't take a day off, no matter what. He felt that time was money.

At the age of thirty-nine Martin dropped dead from a heart attack. This great tragedy seemed so unnecessary. If Martin had heeded the doctor's warning and slowed down, he would probably be alive today. When I spoke to his wife after the funeral, she was very sad and felt that she should have been firmer with her husband. I assured her that she had done all she could to help him. This was a tragic case of a man who died an early death because of ambition.

"Ambition can be a terrible thing," Martin's wife said through tears of grief. "It's ridiculous when you think about it. Martin had everything to live for, but it never seemed to be enough."

"Workaholism" is chic nowadays, but it gains you nothing if you end up a statistic. You can do a very good job and make a fine living without killing yourself. I know a man who heads a large corporation. He never seems overloaded with concerns about work. If he has had a trying week, he leaves the office early on Friday. He doesn't neglect anything, but he refuses to kill himself because of his job. He has fine people working for him whom he trusts. He took a great deal of time choosing these people, and he picked an excellent staff. He once said that a good boss is a person who can delegate responsibility. He loves the outdoors, and he recharges himself by going to the country as often as possible. He lives a quality life. Temperance is a word he uses often. "I don't drink to excess, nor do I eat or exercise to excess. I live every day with a sense of moderation." It is possible for you to live a life like this man. It may seem difficult, but it isn't especially compared to the difficulty of living with constant anxiety.

There are times when we all feel overloaded with work. Things accelerate at certain points, and we feel that we must go on even when our energy is spent. Prepare for these times by relaxing when you can. This will give you the added "juice" you need to get through a particular deadline. But don't live each day as if there were always a deadline. This will shorten your life and make you ill-tempered. Your body will tell you in no uncertain terms if it is overloaded. Stress manifests itself through a wide range of physical symptoms, including digestive disorders, sleeplessness, nervous tremors, skin rashes, and heart problems. Pay attention to these and slow down. If you do take heed, you will save yourself from more serious problems. What is the use of driving oneself to the breaking point? You are not judged by your bank account or your title when you pass over to the other side but only by how well you have served others. This produces a quality life.

Don't Try to Run the World

On one occasion when I was feeling quite overworked, Lawrence commented that I looked tired and that I should take a break. When I told him that I was currently dealing with a number of very serious cases, he frowned slightly and shook his head. "This is not an excuse for overworking your vehicle," he said. "It will serve no one if you collapse."

"You're right, of course," I replied. "I'll slow down immediately. Perhaps I have been overambitious."

Again he shook his head, but this time he smiled and patted my hand. "No," he said, "this is not a case of ambition; you're not overworking to gain anything for yourself. But even people who are not motivated by wealth or titles must be careful not to overuse their energy. In each incarnation we are given only so much energy—some people more than others. You must use this energy sparingly, or your health will suffer. You have nothing but time. What's the hurry?" He shrugged, and I had to laugh.

"People are always rushing around frantically," he went on, "like those old vaudeville performers who used to spin plates on sticks, trying to keep everything going. And for what? It is seldom that something is so urgent we can't take a bit more time. None of us has been given the job of keeping the world running. Resting the body is just as important as any other part of life. People think they are wasting time by resting. This is foolish. A wise man is seldom tired. He spares himself the trauma of overused nerves. A master would not take an extra step to get from one point to another—he would not use the energy. He would arrive at his destination in the smoothest, most economical way possible. We use too much energy doing things that we feel are important, only to discover in retrospect that they were not important at all. Weigh your actions. Think before you act or react in a given situation. This will save you a great deal of stress and will promote health and longevity.

"You will hear people say that if they were not ambitious, they would have accomplished nothing in their lives. This is not the case. Remember, the law of karma is that we get what we earn. Should our attitude be one of stress and struggle, or one of calm resolution? You can work hard and focus your energies on doing a good job without becoming enslaved by ambition," Lawrence said.

"Ambition can cause depression. A person can feel that what he is doing now is never good enough or that he is not working hard enough. This can bring about feelings of hopelessness and inferiority. In the eyes of the God force, all men are equal. It is one's spiritual development that is judged by the higher self, the God within. Ambition can hurt others. In your involvement with your ambitious pursuits, you can forget the feelings of those around you. You have heard people say of someone, 'He would walk over dead bodies in order to get ahead.' This is alarming but not uncommon. Is it worth hurting another to get what you desire? Reflect on that for a moment. Isn't peace of mind more important than physical gratification? Let us hope so.

"Go forth with the proper attitude, an attitude of service, and you will feel a sense of well-being. Look at those around you and see what you can do to serve them. Self-involvement is a large problem on the planet today. People become so consumed with their desire to 'make it' that they pay little attention to the sufferings of those around them.

"You can be a caring, responsible human being and still have success in business. If it is your karmic right, you will do well. If there is something that the soul needs to learn through the experience of failure, then failure will happen. But what is failure? He who does his best with the proper attitude never fails. Failure must not be judged by what another man thinks of you or your accomplishments. Love what you are doing. Love your work, for that is your service. If you have been given financial security, enjoy it and help those who are less fortunate. Do not allow yourself to put your self-worth on the heading of your business stationery. Titles mean nothing; they die when the physical vehicle passes over.

"One of the greatest men I have ever known lived a life with no material comforts. He had nothing but the bare necessities. He was never stressed and had a wonderful sense of humor. Great leaders were drawn to this man because his peace gave them great comfort. He once told me that an incarnation was not very long, so why should he waste time trying to achieve fame or wealth? These things had no value in the life of the spirit. I learned a great deal by observing him. He performed no action without thinking first. He would not waste his energy on things that did not nourish the soul. He was always willing to listen to anyone who needed his fine ear. He lived a joyous life, a life of true service.

"Do not confuse ambition with the joy of doing a good job. It is always wise to apply yourself to whatever duty has been placed before you. It is the constant striving for more and more that creates inner havoc. Observe your actions, seeing what you are doing that is not necessary. Eliminate the superfluous and you will have much more time to devote to your spiritual development. Work for the good of all, not for your personal gratification. Each person is important, and your actions toward others should be carefully thought out. Hurtfulness is often the result of lack of forethought. You can save yourself and others great heartbreak by thinking before you act.

"Ambition poisons the spirit and causes restlessness. An ambitious person is a self-consumed person. A person who does his or her best with whatever is presented is a person of character. Never look for the result. Accept the result and go forth. If you are always focused tightly on the end, you will miss out on the moment.

"Indifference, which arises from unhappiness or anger, is not the answer. It is important to care about everything we do, and we must also care about everyone on this Earth. This is part of being connected to the whole, to the God force that suffuses everything. Think of others rather than your personal desires, and you will not have to fight the tendency to fall into the slavery of ambition."

• • •

After that meeting with Lawrence, I thought for a long while about what he had said. In our society everyone seems overly concerned with "making it," with achieving financial success and position. But these things never bring inner peace and happiness.

My friend Kathy who has been fighting cancer for years knows that she will not live long, but she is never negative or depressed. When she is overtaken by sadness, she gets busy helping someone and forgets herself. She fights hard to get well. She loves her husband and her two daughters and wants to be well for them, but the resources of modern medicine have been exhausted. Having had surgery for brain cancer twice, she has opted to spend the rest of her days with her family and friends, choosing not to undergo any more surgery. No one who meets Kathy is unaffected by her inner glow. Her laugh is infectious, and she can cheer anyone because she is totally interested in everything you are doing and how you are feeling. No matter how ill she is or how much pain she feels, she maintains her dignity and her humor.

I was with her one day when she was reflecting on her life. "I used to be very ambitious when I was young," she said. "I always worried about what other people thought of me and my work. But now I realize that the things that seemed important then really weren't."

"What things?" I asked.

"Well," she replied, "it doesn't matter what title you are given or what anyone says about you. It only matters that you are doing the best possible job of whatever you have been given to do. When you are seriously ill, you perceive life in a different light. I now live each day to the best of my ability."

Larry is a very successful artist. He works very hard and enjoys working, and is not in any way ambitious. He has never worked to achieve fame but for the love of doing a good job. He laughingly told me one day, "When I was a student, I dreamed of fame and fortune. I wanted to be discovered. My family wanted me to be a lawyer; they were afraid that I couldn't make a living at my art and that I wouldn't be respected by their friends. So I was determined to prove them wrong. I *would* make a big name for myself as an artist. As time went on, I learned that this was very silly and that I would never be happy if I spent my life seeking fame. I found that happiness lies in working for the love of the work itself and for the joy that people find through the work."

The "S" Word

A woman named Sonya strutted into my apartment and looked around as if she were sizing up the place and its owner. She was overdressed and wearing a great deal of makeup. Still standing, she said, "I have a few questions to ask you, darling."

"All right, Sonya, ask away," I said.

"Is my boyfriend involved with another woman? Do you think I should have a baby so that I will have someone to leave my money to? Should I sell one of my apartments because I want to get out before the market drops?" She shot these questions at me without taking a breath.

"Sonya, I don't know quite where to start," I said. "Why don't you sit down and relax for a minute while I organize my thoughts?"

Sonya sat down, and I looked at her for a moment and then said, "Why don't you tell me about the situation that involved your best friend's husband?"

Looking startled, she said, "You must be a good psychic if you picked up on that. I just wanted to prove to myself that I could get my friend's husband. I seduced him one night when my friend was out of town. He went wild for me and left his wife. I didn't want to have a relationship with him, I just wanted to know that I could have him if I wanted. I made it very clear that I didn't want to see him anymore. It's not my fault that the marriage was over."

I was amazed at her apparent callousness as she told me this story. "I always get what I want," she continued. "I wanted a good job on Wall Street so I slept with the boss. There was another man who already had the position I wanted, but I convinced the boss that this man was stealing from the company."

"Was that true, Sonya?" I asked.

"Of course not." She laughed. "But I knew I had to say something extreme or the boss wouldn't fire this man. I had no intention of working my way up the corporate ladder. I knew that if I was clever I could start at the top."

"What about the man you got fired? You lied about him. Doesn't that bother you?" I asked.

"Why? I got what I wanted, didn't I?"

"You are very ambitious," I said.

"Yes, I am," she agreed. "Nothing stops me from getting what I want. That is the secret of my success."

"I don't think you are successful, Sonya. Do you ever stop to think that these things which seem so important to you don't last?"

"Come on," she said contemptuously, "don't get spiritual on me."

"I was merely presenting you with a little food for thought. I would like you to take a moment to think of eternity. You'll never find true happiness from something you attain through the heartbreak of others. You're totally consumed with your own physical desires. Take a good look at yourself. I don't mean to be unkind, but I would like to help you as long as you're here."

"I don't need any help," she snapped.

"If you don't need any help, why are you here to see me?" I asked.

She learned forward, her lips a thin, tight line, and said, "Listen, Mary, I grew up with nothing. I swore that one day I would have everything I ever wanted, no matter how I got it. I would one day go back home and show everybody that I was a success. Everything I have I've gotten through using my wits. I made an appointment with you because I wanted some insights on selling some property, and I wanted to know about some personal matters. Isn't that what you do, give people insight?" She paused and waited for my reply.

"Yes," I said, "I do give my insight, but I also point out the things I feel are important for a person's spiritual growth. I hope I haven't offended you by bringing up the 'S' word."

She laughed, then sat back in her chair and looked around the room as I spoke about the importance of helping others. Watching her leave a little later, I saw a very sad little girl trying to prove that she was a worthwhile person.

I heard from her again a few months later. She asked for another appointment, and I agreed to see her. I felt a very deep sadness when I thought about her.

When I opened the door to let her in, I was astonished at the changes in her appearance and demeanor. She seemed a different person—calmer, happier, somehow softer. As she sank into a chair, she asked me for a glass of water. When I left the room to get it, I heard her sigh, and when I brought it to her, she thanked me, took a few sips, and began to speak.

"After our last appointment I was too busy to think about anything you had said to me. In any case I hadn't really listened. Life went on as usual and everything seemed in order. Then one afternoon I was walking down Fifth Avenue, and I saw the man I had gotten fired. He was staggering down the street, obviously quite drunk. I tried to avoid him but he saw me. He started screaming at me that I had ruined his life. His wife had left him, he had been unable to get another job, and it was all my fault. He said, 'I did a very good job, and you got me fired with your terrible lies. You ruined my reputation in the business world, and no one will hire me. Think about me when you go to your fancy lunches or on one of your shopping sprees. Think about the fact that you ruined my life and livelihood and destroyed my family.'

"I tried to get away from him, but he kept following me. His face was contorted with grief and anger, and tears were pouring from his eyes. I ducked into a hair salon, and he didn't follow me. When I peeked out the door a few minutes later, I saw that he was gone. Breathing a sigh of relief, I started walking down the street. Before I knew it, I was sobbing uncontrollably. I became totally unglued, so I stopped to sit on a park bench.

"I realized that what he had said was true. I was totally

immobile, in a state of shock. When I looked up from my tears, I saw a homeless man looking at me. Usually I would have been frightened, but feeling totally numb I just looked at the man. He smiled and asked me, 'Are you all right, miss? You look as if you are having a bad day.' Think of it: A man who looked as though he didn't have a dollar to his name was asking me how I was. I smiled and said I was fine. Reaching into my purse I offered him some money. This was the first time I had ever done that. He said, 'No, thank you, miss. I don't need your money. I just wanted to see if I could do anything to help you.' He smiled and walked away.

"These two incidents, one right after the other, really shook me. As I walked home I knew it was time to change. I wasn't certain how to start, but I knew I could no longer live a selfish, ambitious life. I went to my boss and told him I had lied in order to get the man fired. He listened to me, shocked, and promised that he would rehire the man if he would return. I resigned from the job and decided I would go back to school to learn a skill I could be proud of. I came today to tell you this story and to let you know that I now understand what you were trying to tell me in our first meeting. I'm now quite aware of others and do what I can to help them."

We talked for the next half hour. Sonya was no longer afraid of the word "spiritual."

Sonya's hunger for success stemmed from her childhood feelings of inferiority. It was unfortunate that she had an unhappy childhood, but this was no excuse for destroying other people to get what she wanted.

We all have incidents in our past that were upsetting. Many of these incidents shape our later lives. At some point, however, the past is a memory; it should never be an excuse for thoughtless, selfish behavior. It becomes tiresome to hear people go on about how terrible their childhood was and how misunderstood they are because of it. It is much better to use your experiences to try to make the lives of others better. You can learn a great deal from any experience, positive or negative. If your childhood was unhappy, it was because you had karmic problems to work through. You attracted your childhood with all its joys and sorrows.

Don't Become Ambitious about Your Personal Development

A few days after my second meeting with Sonya, I was out shopping. My arms were loaded with packages, and as I walked along the street, one of them fell. As I stopped to pick it up, another one dropped, and then another. When a shadow fell over me as I tried to juggle all the packages in my arms, I looked up to see the tall figure of Lawrence standing over me, his blue eyes twinkling. "May I assist you, young lady?" he asked.

"Thank you, kind sir," I replied with exaggerated courtesy.

"You look as if you could use a moment's rest," he said. "Let's have a cup of tea."

We went to a restaurant on the next corner, and as Lawrence arranged my packages on the seat in our booth, the entire pile toppled. He laughed and said, "It looks as though we're both all thumbs today." Leaning back in his seat, he regarded me silently for a moment, then observed, "You're looking a bit more rested. Have you slowed down a little?"

I nodded. "I can take a hint, Lawrence. I don't usually have to wait until a house falls on me."

"That is good sense," he said. "A wise person can feel the touch of a feather. He doesn't need to have a crisis on his hands in order to learn."

I told Lawrence the story of Sonya, and he seemed pleased to hear of her progress. "Where there is life, there is the opportunity to change and grow," he said. "We never know who will wake up spiritually. If a person reaches out one finger for help, we must stand by to take his hand. It takes patience, understanding, and tolerance to help others. It's a wonderful surprise when a person like Sonya has a spiritual realization. Never give up on anyone." He paused to take a sip of tea.

"How is your writing coming along?" Lawrence asked.

"Fairly well," I replied. "I'm trying to explain things in a simple, straightforward manner, and our discussions have been a great help to me. At times, though, I feel I'm not working fast enough."

"Do not put undue pressure on yourself," Lawrence cautioned. "It will cause you to feel anxious. All you can do is your best. Do your best with whatever situation is presented to you, and your life will be balanced. It is important to realize that in this world there can be no perfection, but one can always do a bit better. It will interfere with your spiritual development if you criticize yourself instead of focusing on the next lesson that has been placed before you. Yes, aspire to do the best you are capable of doing, but do not waste your energy in being upset because you feel you are not developing fast enough. This is your ego speaking, and such self-criticism is counterproductive to your growth. People who think they are never good enough are self-involved people." He took a sip of tea and then continued: "I knew a woman who felt that she lived a perfect life. She ate the perfect diet and slept the right number of hours. Each day she did the proper physical exercise and attended the best lectures and classes to broaden her knowledge. If someone asked her to go to lunch or the movies, she would become very upset and snap at the person, saying she had no time for such silliness because she was working on her development. She lived totally to perfect herself. This is actually an extreme form of narcissism.

"But one day she snapped under her self-imposed discipline. She just could not get up one morning. I called on her and told her to get up because we were going out to have some fun. 'Fun?' she said. 'But I haven't yet done my exercises or studied for my class.'

" 'Never mind,' I said, 'we'll spend the day together.'

"I took her to lunch and then to a funny movie. Afterward we took a walk in the park and stopped for a cup of cocoa. She hadn't done anything like this for years. Returning to her home she said that she felt ten years younger. 'I should think so,' I said.

'You gave your nervous system a good rest. Laughter is one of the greatest remedies for stress. You must spend more time living and laughing, and less time trying to perfect yourself. In this way you will achieve a healthy balance.' "

I laughed at this story. I knew countless people who were so consumed with their goals that they never took time to just be. They never gave themselves a break; they were always trying to be better and achieve more. This was a form of ambition that caused them to be short-tempered and anxious. Taking time for laughter and fun was the way to find one's balance. Lawrence continued.

"When your motivation is to be of service, you will never be bothered by worrying about the results of your actions. You will be doing your best, and your actions will speak for themselves. You defeat your purpose if you become ambitious about serving instead of serving for its own sake because the act of serving aids the planet. You are seeking ego gratification. Stop thinking about yourself, and you will have no problems."

As Lawrence finished speaking, I was thinking about a client of mine who was always saying she wanted to do more for the world. She felt that she had been born to do great things, but she just was not able to figure out exactly what those things were. I had told her that she should look at what was directly in front of her; there was more than enough to keep her busy. "I don't want to do little things to help people," she insisted. "I want to do great things. Why should I settle for doing little things when I feel born to greatness?" This woman's motivation was purely selfish and had nothing to do with helping others. Sadly, I was never able to persuade her of this. I suppose she is still seeking her place in the world's idea of greatness.

When I arrived home after my meeting with Lawrence, I put the packages down and went to get a glass of water. The phone rang. "Hello," I said.

"Mary," said a tearful, trembling voice on the line, "this is

Willa. I just got fired from my job. I don't know what to do. My
father will be very angry. He thinks I'm unable to hold down a
job, and I guess he's right. How will I tell him? He's held the same
job for the last thirty years, and this is my fourth in two years. He
has pounded into my head since I was a child that job security
is the most important thing in life. Now I will have to listen to
him tell me what a failure I am. I tried to keep this job, but I was
not fast enough with my typing. And I always felt that I was being
watched and judged."

"Calm down, Willa," I said. "It's very upsetting to lose your
job, but you mustn't allow yourself to be upset just because you're
not like your father. He doesn't understand your creative nature.
It is very difficult for creative people to hold down a nine-to-five
job, and it's obvious this was not the right job for you. Are you
going to spend the rest of your life trying to prove to your father
that you can hold down a job the way he has? Don't think that
you're a failure because a certain job doesn't suit your individual
temperament. Do you have enough money to pay your bills?"

"Yes, I can take care of things for a month," she answered.

"Good," I said, "then I think you need to take a break before
finding a job that doesn't make you feel pressured. You need to
figure out what you would be happy doing, and that should be
your work. It doesn't matter what the work is as long as you enjoy
it. Didn't you tell me that you had always wanted to be a de-
signer?"

"Yes but I thought it was a silly dream, and I was worried that
it wouldn't be financially stable. Do you think I'm a failure,
Mary?"

"Of course not, Willa. You're one of the kindest people I've
ever met. How could a person like you, who is always thinking of
others, think for one moment that she's a failure? You must stop
judging yourself by what your father thinks. You are not your
father, and he is not you. You must be true to yourself."

"You're right. I can't go on like this any longer. I'm going to
get a job at my friend's restaurant. That will pay the bills until
I can decide what's best for me. My father won't like my working

in a restaurant, but it isn't his life. I'll try again to explain my feelings to him."

"Fine," I said. "Just don't allow yourself to expect your father's opinion to change. You'll just become disappointed, and that will frustrate you. Talk to him, but not today; wait till you're calmer and don't expect a positive reaction. Maybe he will surprise you, but if he doesn't, you won't become unhappy when your expectations of him are not fulfilled."

After this conversation I felt that Willa would be much happier. Perhaps she wouldn't keep trying to live up to her father's ambitions for her and would begin to live her own life.

A Bit of Lawrence's History

I sat looking at Lawrence, realizing that I knew little about him. Having felt immediately comfortable with him at our first encounter, I had never asked him personal questions, but I was confident that he would tell me everything he felt I needed to know. He knew, I'm sure, that I would never dream of invading his privacy.

"What would you like to know about me?" he asked, the laugh lines deepening around his eyes.

By this time I'd known Lawrence long enough that his apparent ability to read my thoughts scarcely surprised me, so I asked, with hardly any hesitation. "How did you become so spiritually developed?" The corners of his mouth turned up a bit in a faint smile, and I continued, "I hope that doesn't seem a silly question, but you're so enigmatic. It might be disturbing if you weren't so warm, so human, so . . . open. I think it would be very interesting to hear a bit of your life's story."

He folded his slender fingers around his teacup, holding it in both hands and absorbing its heat, and gazed into its depth for a moment. Then he began: "I grew up in a very happy home in England. My mother was an extraordinarily kind person, very musical. She was also gifted with what used to be called second sight, psychic ability. My father, a physician, passed over when I was ten years old. He had a brilliant mind and taught me a great deal about medicine and philosophy before he passed on. I always had an unquenchable thirst for knowledge. Eventually this led me to the study of ancient wisdom and the body of metaphysical knowledge that has come down to us from the beginning of civilization. This knowledge has been passed along by certain teachers to students who were ready to accept it and, along with it, the responsibility to impart the wisdom when mankind was ready to hear it. I studied with a teacher first in France and later in Egypt. I had a great desire to serve humanity in any way I could. I am here to help students like you through listening and guiding." He looked up from his teacup and smiled again. "This is all I can tell you for now."

As I sat thinking this over, I knew there was a great deal more to learn and that, in time, I would be told whatever Lawrence felt was important.

Ambition Is Endless Slavery

I received a phone call from Cindy, the woman who was obsessed with her desire to get a promotion at her job. She sounded despondent. It seemed that once again she had been passed over for a promotion. I didn't know what to say. I didn't see eye to eye with Cindy, but I tried to be sympathetic to her feelings. She talked very quietly and sounded as if she had no energy at all. I asked her if she had tried to change the way she dealt with her co-workers.

"I thought I had," she replied, "but my boss said I still had a problem dealing with people. And he didn't feel that I could handle being in charge of the staff."

"Well, you can only go forward and try to do better next time," I said.

"I am quitting my job," she said firmly. "I won't stay and work for another boss. I couldn't handle being told what to do by someone who has the job that should have been mine. I'm going to Europe for a month to think things over."

"That's good news," I said. "It must be the first vacation you've had in years."

"Yes. I don't know how I'll handle the free time. It will be so strange not to be working sixteen hours a day."

"You will be surprised at how quickly you adapt to rest and having fun," I told her. "Enjoy every minute of the trip. There is a lot to see in Europe, and you're bound to meet fascinating people. Stay interested in everything, and you will have a wonderful time."

Cindy was one of those people who had to learn everything the hard way. Now she needed some time to look at herself and her life. I hoped she would see that her ambition had brought her no happiness.

If you allow yourself to fall into the maya of ambition, you will have a life with little peace. Ambition is not the same as hard work and dedication. Ambition is selfish and self-serving.

You have nothing to gain by being ambitious, and everything to lose. You will lose your sense of humor. You will lose your perspective. You will lose your free time. You will lose your ability to think of anything but yourself because you are constantly struggling to be the best or the richest. An ambitious person often becomes nasty and embittered; because he is so tired from struggling to gain his desires, he has no time for rest and no energy to help anyone else. But remember, with true love we cease to struggle.

As H. W. Shaw said, "Common sense is instinct, and enough of it is genius." If you use your common sense, you will see clearly that all that is yours will come to you. Most important, keep your sense of humor and enjoy life to its fullest. That attitude will bring you balance and peace of mind, the most precious jewels of this life.

∴ V I I ∴
Relationships

Many people are preoccupied with, even consumed by, their desire to find the perfect personal relationship. They are constantly seeking Mr. or Miss Right, and over and over I hear about the despair that people feel because they have not succeeded in finding the one person they think will make their lives complete.

Personal relationships are wonderful when they enhance one's spiritual development. Such a relationship can be the vehicle for us to work through a particular psychological issue. In such a case the relationship often ends once we resolve the issue. There is nothing wrong with this; it is as it should be. We attract people into our lives because there is something we need to learn. This is as true of our personal interactions as it is of any other aspect of our existence. We attract what we need in order to learn and grow. When one lesson has been learned, we are presented with the next one. Think about this for a moment. If you look back on your past relationships, you can see just what you learned. Your goal should be to avoid repeating past mistakes and to work toward spiritual freedom. This is all part of growth and is quite marvelous when we look at it from the proper point of view. Most personal relationships are unsuccessful because people think too much about what they feel they should have rather than about what they can do to serve their partners. They are constantly asking themselves, "What am I getting from this relationship?" The proper question is, "What am I giving to this relationship?" Universally speaking, a personal relationship is an opportunity to serve another human being.

It is impossible to have a happy, loving, and lasting relationship if you are thinking about getting instead of giving. When you love someone in the true spiritual sense, you cease to struggle with your personal desires—you simply love that person. You do not try constantly to manipulate that person according to some fixed idea of the "perfect couple" or perfect family but accept them the way they are. Certainly, people can grow and change through their relationships if they choose to do so. We function as a sort of mirror for the one with whom we are involved and thereby immeasurably aid in each other's self-understanding, but only as long as we do not become judgmental during this "mirroring."

Everything Is Relationships

We first relate in the womb of our mother. We are dependent and completely focused on the person who feeds us. As we grow, we have relationships with our toys, our siblings, our friends, our teachers and other authority figures. We relate to ourselves on many levels, and as the years go by we start to relate to other people on a one-to-one personal, romantic level. The most fulfilling relationship possible is the one between ourselves and the God force that lives within us. As we grow to relate to the God within, we are not afraid of relating to others, for we are thinking only of loving and of serving.

Family Relationships

How many times have you said, "I am this way because my mother never approved of me" or "My father never felt that anything I did was good enough"? I have heard this type of statement countless times. If one did not have good parenting, the soul often keeps looking for the "good mother" or the "good father" in its personal relationships. This causes many people a great deal of heartbreak; they are constantly being disappointed as they try to turn other people into perfect parents in order to fill this lack in their lives.

It is essential for us to understand that the individual chooses his or her family. There is no chance involved. We are incarnated into our family because of the soul's need to learn and grow through these particular relationships. Karma is involved; we have known all our family members in previous lives.

You and you alone choose your family. Many of us might say that is impossible, but it is the law of karma. Realizing and accepting this fact will help you to understand why many relationships are very difficult and psychologically complex. If you have been given a particularly difficult family situation to deal with, it is for the purpose of having your soul learn and thereby balance a karmic bond or debt.

Your parents create your body; they do not create your soul. The soul is eternal and enters into a succession of mortal bodies. Every conception is an immaculate conception in the spiritual sense: You cannot conceive a soul.

You can, however, choose the way you react to a given situation, regardless of your upbringing. This is very important. It plays a large part in our ability to have healthy, loving relationships. Throughout our lives we carry experiences and feelings from the past. At a certain point in our development, character should take over and free us from the burden of holding on to the past. The past is merely a memory, and the choice of how to deal with this memory is yours.

Searching for Approval

Rebecca keeps trying to gain approval from her mother. She even married a man she did not love because her mother thought he was wonderful. She had wanted to be a singer but chose to be an attorney because her mother did not approve of the theater. She has spent her whole life trying to please her mother.

Rebecca was very depressed when she came to see me and could not figure out why. I asked her if she had ever talked to a therapist about the depression. "My mother does not approve of therapy" was her reply.

"But what do *you* think about therapy?" I asked. "What difference does it make if your mother agrees or not? It is you who needs to come to terms with your unhappiness."

Rebecca was vehement—she could not do something that would upset her mother. Her father had died when she was very young, and her mother had raised her alone. Her mother lost no opportunity to tell Rebecca that she had given up everything for her and that Rebecca was all she had in the world.

As Rebecca spoke I realized that here was a very complicated karmic relationship between mother and daughter. I felt psychically that in a past life these two souls had been married. This would explain the overinvolvement and the desperation Rebecca felt as she tried to please her mother on one level. Yes, there were psychological issues, but there was more. I told Rebecca what I thought about the karmic relationship between her and her mother. This seemed to make sense to her. I also stressed that this was not an excuse to ignore the problem; she must deal with the relationship as it is manifested in this life.

She agreed to go into therapy to try to learn to detach herself from her mother. It was wonderful that she loved and appreciated her mother, but she must learn to live her own life and free herself from the fear of not living up to her mother's expectations.

Our souls learn a great deal through our relationships with the members of our families. We should try to get along with the members of our families, but if this is still impossible after much hard work, we must learn to detach ourselves. This is very difficult for many people because we are programmed from the cradle that we must get along with our families, that we must seek approval from these souls. But as we have seen before in these pages, the only approval that matters is the approval that comes from within ourselves.

Loving Relationships

A common factor among many of my clients, as well as among most of humanity today, is a high level of anger, expressed in such questions as: "Why me?" "Why is everything so difficult for me?" "Why am I not having a loving relationship?"

We must learn to love in order to attract a loving relationship. We must understand the law of karma and not look upon it as our adversary. The law is our teacher. The human soul, in passing from one incarnation to the next, learns new lessons all the time. A key lesson is that the right action brings happiness, and the wrong action causes great pain.

Why is it that certain people seem to attract healthy, loving relationships while others are always involved in totally unhealthy situations? The reasons are not necessarily psychological. Clearly, psychology has its part to play in the nature of relationships, but in no way is it the total picture. There is karma involved. If you have dealt satisfactorily with the issues that have caused you to attract unhealthy relationships and have freed yourself from the tendency to become involved in such situations, this will change the pattern of attraction around you, and you will be more inclined to attract a relationship that is loving and supportive. In other words, you will, as always, get what you earn according to the law of karma.

Understand that you are given the opportunity to grow and to serve with each relationship presented to you. If you can hold that point of view, you will save yourself great heartbreak and serve mankind at the same time. Once again, we attract personal relationships in order to grow spiritually. If you spend all your time trying to force relationships to fit into your desired fantasy, you will always be unhappy. If you operate with a true loving motivation, however, you will never have an unhappy moment. You will be free to love selflessly. Only when we learn to be selfless can we have a true, spiritually developed personal relationship. This is not easy for most of us because we are so much the product of our own wrong thinking. People think that a relationship should fulfill all their personal needs and desires. Learn to have no desires, and you will not be disappointed.

There is nothing more beautiful than a true, spiritually developed relationship between two people. It is the personification of love in action. The merging of two souls in harmony is truly sacred.

Two clients of mine have this type of relationship. Ben and Rose have been married for seven years. Prior to this they had both been involved in very unhappy relationships. Ben's first wife had been very possessive and insanely jealous. She called him at his office constantly just to make sure he was there. Ben never cheated on his first wife; in fact, he did everything in his power to make her feel secure, but after trying for nine years, he could no longer stay in the marriage.

Rose's first husband had been totally obsessed with money and power. He had no time for his wife, never leaving work before ten at night. Rose devoted herself to the marriage. She was also very involved with church work, and she taught art to underprivileged children, which helped her to stay in balance. Then, in the fifth year of their marriage, Rose's husband had a serious car accident. He never recovered, and after eighteen months of struggling he passed over. Rose took care of him this whole time.

When Rose and Ben first met they were both still recovering from their first marriages. First they became great friends, and then they married. Two of the happiest people I have ever met, they are grateful to have found each other, are totally supportive of each other's needs, and are always busy helping other people.

Passion and the Karmic Bond

Love has been misconstrued throughout the ages. Passion is not love, but passion between two souls who love each other brings us back to a feeling akin to unity with the God force. Passion without love creates feelings of emptiness and causes people to behave in outrageous ways. People kill in fits of passion. This is not to say that passion is bad; on the contrary, it is wonderful. A great artist must have passion to produce great art. Without passion, a work of art is static, dead.

Passion, in the spiritual sense of the word, is one of the ingredients of greatness, but it is essential to avoid confusing passion with love. When there is deep spiritual love between two souls, there is often great passion as well, but great passion does not mean there is deep love.

How many times have we thought when we met someone that we could hear the "Hallelujah Chorus"? We vow our deep love and are certain that this relationship will last forever. Then a few weeks pass and we begin to feel as though the bloom is off the rose. The attraction has faded and not much is left. Successful relationships are built on a firm foundation of truth and respect. The absence of this foundation is why many relationships are short-lived. A firm foundation based on love must be built in order to have a spiritually developed relationship.

Client after client has asked me, "Why did I do it again? I should have known better than to jump into this relationship before I had time to know the person and his (or her) character."

"Never say never" is also a rule of spiritual development. There are cases of karmic meetings in which two people connect and feel totally familiar with each other. This is rare, though, and one must be careful not to confuse a karmic meeting with sexual attraction, a dangerous situation.

Personal relationships are wonderful when they enhance our spiritual development and are not just neurotic playgrounds for working through one's personal complexes. We attract people into our lives so that we may come to terms with psychological issues that inhibit our spiritual growth. Once such an issue has been dealt with, it is time to get on with one's life. We must not make our personal life too important, for that will never give us inner happiness. The only true happiness comes through living a life of service. We must try to dispel the fantasy that we can be happy only when we are firmly embraced by the arms of our loved one. This is a trap and will cause us nothing but constant worry.

If there is something we need to learn, a situation will be presented to us. Our only hope of having a healthy, happy, spiritually developed relationship lies in learning to be selfless. We must be thinking constantly of the needs of the person with whom we are involved. If we are thinking of that person's needs, and he or she is thinking of our needs, balance will be maintained. This may seem a strange notion, but think about it. We are free when we are able to look at life from a selfless, universal point of view, but we have been programmed to think of life in terms of goals. We try to be the best and to get the most. *I* is almost always the first word one hears from another person, and people are always asking, "What about me?"

As I've stated several times, this book merely presents another way to look at life. If we were all constantly thinking about the needs of those we meet, there would be few problems on the planet. In our personal lives we are allowed to learn many valuable lessons, to work through many karmic ties, and to experience getting back to wholeness through relationships.

Why do we suffer through our personal lives as we do? Often, where there is great pain, there is growth. Pain, whether emotional or physical, is a great teacher, and we are on the Earth to learn. Everything is presented to us as an opportunity to learn.

Marriage

Marriage is a bonding of souls and is not to be entered into lightly. Because it is so serious, we should be certain that we are marrying for love and not for passion. Passion is often the motivation, and when it begins to fade, the marriage falls apart.

When you are in a marriage, it is essential for your spiritual development that you do everything humanly possible to keep the relationship whole. If, after trying everything possible, you can't keep the relationship alive, then it is your spiritual responsibility to end it with love and dignity. We've all heard accounts of the types of behavior exhibited by those participating in a breakup or divorce. It is amazing how the behavior of people can change drastically when one person in a relationship decides that he or she can no longer continue. The battles can become so outrageous that we wonder if there was ever any real love in the relationship.

People tend to leave their marriages too easily these days. Divorce, as difficult and traumatic a process as it is, seems to have become preferable to working through conflicts and problems, although there are many people who stay much too long in destructive marriages and relationships. But whether one leaves a relationship or remains in it, the object should be to do so in a way that shows spiritual development and character. Marriage can teach great spiritual lessons; it is one of the highest tests of selflessness.

If you have been presented with a particularly difficult situation, then consider that you have been given an opportunity to grow, learn, and serve. You have to work against being so self-consumed that you become unaware of your partner's discomfort. And when you have done your best, that is all you can do.

Marriage in its highest form is sacred and should be entered into with the sacredness of attitude that it deserves. I have heard hundreds of reasons why people decide to marry: "My mother wanted me to marry him." "I married him because I wanted to get away from home." "I was on the rebound from a past relationship, so I married her." "My biological clock was ticking, and I wanted to have a baby; I chose the first person who would marry me." None of these is an adequate reason for marrying, and most often marriages based on these reasons will end in divorce.

Working on Relationships

Yes, there is passion with true love. The feeling of connection to the person you love is a vital part of marriage. If the passion has died, other problems are often operating because the death of passion is a symptom, not a cause. If we are not thinking of the needs and the feelings of our partner, we can feel passionless. If your mate feels the need for physical attention and you are not in the mood, think about his or her feelings, and you will not be burdened by your own desires. If both parties are thinking of the needs of the other first, before their own personal desires, balance will be achieved. This is love in action.

In a situation where a person no longer feels a physical attraction to his or her mate, the test is to love the partner in a more mature and developed manner. Leaving someone because of a loss of physical attraction is not a loving reason. If you truly love someone, you want to feel close to that person and to fulfill his or her needs. Otherwise you become burdened by your own desires.

Unquestionably, we have issues from the past that must be

worked through. A marriage or close personal relationship is a wonderful vehicle for us to do this. We let down our guard with people we are close to, and this is good.

People often treat their mates or members of their family in ways they would never treat their friends. People think they can be abusive or do or say anything to their partners, but manners, courtesy, and kindness are essential ingredients in all our relationships. Never take your partner for granted; that could be the death of your relationship.

Personal relationships are terrific if they enhance one's spiritual development. Our personal life is only a small part of our existence, and we tend to concentrate on it at the expense of more important aspects. We are devastated if we are not with our true love. In searching for the one true love, a person may block out the rest of the world and make the quest for romance his or her primary concern. This can be disastrous. We are only happy and fulfilled if we are serving in some way, and we can learn through a romantic, emotional, physical relationship—but we must not make it the sole focus of our life.

Love creates harmony. Discord is not an aspect of true love. When we act in a loving manner, we are not burdened with unhappiness. Easier said than done, you might say. But we all tend to make things more difficult than necessary. When you are not thinking about yourself, you are joyous. Try it and experience how freeing it can be.

It has often been said, especially since the pop psychology boom of the 1960s and 1970s, that maintaining a relationship is hard work, but if you have to work too hard at it, you are probably in the wrong relationship.

Willie and Linda were always "working on their relationship." Each went to a therapist once a week. "I do everything for him, and he does nothing for me," Linda stated on her first appointment with me. "What about my feelings? I am not getting my needs fulfilled."

I listened to Linda talk on about how miserable she felt in the relationship. Not one happy word came out of her mouth.

Finally, I said, "It is tragic the way you're living. It is totally joyless and self-consuming. It's also exhausting, and the energy could be better channeled."

"Better channeled into what?" she asked.

"You could use the energy to enjoy each other and stop criticizing each other's every action. Must you analyze every aspect of your lives? Where is the bliss, the joy that comes when you love another person completely?"

I heard from Linda two months later. She and Willie were getting along much better; they had cut back on their therapy sessions and were spending more time together. Each had decided to let the other be. She sounded much happier and I was delighted.

The Selfless Ideal

Sarah and Martin felt that their marriage was on the rocks. They were constantly quarreling about whose turn it was to do specific chores. Sarah would say, "I always do the cleaning. Martin never picks up his clothes." Martin would retort, "I pay all the bills. Why should I have to do anything around the house?" "He is never romantic," Sarah would complain. "He never even brings me a single rose." To which Martin would reply, "She's always nagging me. She sounds just like my mother." They went on and on complaining about the other's failure to fulfill their needs.

I asked them both, "Where does love come into your relationship? All I am hearing is selfish bickering. I think the two of you are oil and water." They protested that in fact they loved each other very much. I discussed the issue of selflessness with them and asked them to try for one week to think of nothing but the needs of the other.

At first they argued with me, each of them saying in effect, "I cannot live without my needs being fulfilled." I went on to explain love in the selfless ideal. I stressed that they must learn to forget themselves and concentrate on the needs of the other. Ultimately they decided to try it.

A few days later Sarah called, delighted to say that Martin had noticed she was very tired and had done the dishes without being asked. This was the first time Sarah had become aware of the stress Martin was going through, and she had been very patient with him. The concept of selflessness put into practice worked for them.

A dear friend of mine asked me once, "How does the giving not become a burden on the receiving person?" If the receiving person learns as well, through example, how to give, harmony and balance will be achieved. Also, if the giving person is giving with no expectation, no desire, there is no possibility of his or her feeling burdened. We are only burdened if we are looking for reward. People have been programmed to seek rewards: If I give to you, you owe me. We should give for the pure pleasure of giving. That is the essence of happiness. That is freedom.

I was standing and watching children play in front of Abingdon Square in Manhattan one day when I turned around and bumped right into Lawrence. Laughing, he led me to a bench and joined me in watching the children, and it was here that I expressed the difficulty I was having in clearly explaining to people the need to be selfless in their relationships.

"The selfless ideal is difficult to comprehend if you are a materialist," Lawrence answered. "The materialist desires some tangible evidence that he is being selfless. This is a contradiction. If your motivation is one of giving and serving, you will not be burdened by your own ego. You will not have to worry about how you feel, for you will not be thinking about yourself. To be of service will make life joyful, loving, and fun. If you are always worrying about how you feel and about how people are reacting to you, the fun will be eliminated. Life should not be perceived as merely a series of traumas. When one integrates the viewpoint of selflessness into one's very being, there is no place for unhappiness. It is really rather simple, isn't it?"

"Yes, Lawrence, but sometimes the simplest things appear to be the most complicated to put into motion."

Children

"It is unfortunate that often children have not been taught how to share," Lawrence said as we witnessed a scene between two little ones fighting over a toy. He went on: "Children should be taught consideration for all things. They should be taught proper manners. Many children have never even been taught common courtesy. This will ultimately cause the children to be uncomfortable and unwelcome in the homes of others. It is the duty of the parents to educate their child. The first schoolroom is the home. Children should be taught at a very young age the dangers of drugs and alcohol. A parent should not wait until they try things at school or in the playground to tell them that they are courting disaster.

"Children must be taught how to relate to others. They will not know if they are not taught. Balance is also important. Some parents are too strict; others are too permissive. All children cannot be treated alike because they possess different temperaments and sensitivities. Just because two children are born into the same family does not mean they are alike; the parents create the body of the child but not the soul. Children bring in traits from previous lifetimes. How is it that a single family can produce a doctor, a teacher, a deep-sea diver, and a criminal? Did they not all attend the same schools and have the same food for dinner? Did they not receive the same amount of attention from their parents? As a parent you must do your best but then accept that there is also karma at play.

"There are many 'problem children' on the planet today. It is alarming that so many of them seem to need psychological help at a very young age. Parents must be responsible for the development of their children, but they are not totally to blame for the problems with which the children are incarnated. The fact that many souls are incarnating with very deep problems brought over from prior lives is playing a large part in the problems we see with our children. There is no other adequate way to explain the problems children are having today."

"Lawrence," I said, "one of my clients has a six-year-old daughter who is constantly telling her mother stories of times when she has lived before. Her mother is confused as to how to handle this situation. What is your advice?"

"Many times a child remembers past life experiences. This usually happens before the child is seven years old. After that age, the child becomes involved with the physical circumstances and closes off the memories of past lives. Young children are often psychic. Parents should listen to these stories and let the child know that they are truly interested and that it is all right to tell of such things. Children also tell their parents about imaginary friends. An adult may think this sort of thing is sheer fantasy, but often the child is able to see entities such as nature spirits that adults cannot. Remember that fairy tales were based on the truth, and do not allow children to think you do not believe them. This is all a normal part of the soul's development."

"One more question, Lawrence," I said. "How should parents handle a child who is a genius?"

"Genius in a child can cause imbalance if it is improperly handled. Parents become very impressed when they think they have produced a genius. They send the child to advanced schools or force the child to spend hours in the study of music or science. The child's physical vehicle is not capable of sustaining the amount of energy that goes through his body when there is this much mental activity. It is wise to acknowledge the child's talents, but it is necessary that the child have adequate playtime. Do not force the development of the genius, for this will cause an imbalance within the glandular system of the child. Balance the mental and physical energy of the child, and he or she will have a much happier and healthier soul."

I asked Lawrence what the key was to a happy relationship with one's children, parents, and mate.

"To love with detachment in all our relationships is yet another key to the door of freedom. Possessiveness is not love. It is impossible to possess another soul. Even if you give life, you cannot possess the person to whom you gave it. You are responsible only to teach, to raise, and to nurture the soul. Beyond that, no one can choose the destiny of another. If you marry someone, that person is not your possession, although, sadly, many people treat marriage as a certificate of ownership. This is not love, it is control.

"If we learn to love with detachment, we will not be bound by our own desire, we will be loving for the total joy of doing so. If you love without desiring anything in return, you are never upset, for you are not thinking about yourself.

"Detachment does not mean not caring; it means not expecting. Expectation causes disappointment when things do not turn out the way we wish. The person who loves with detachment deals with what is and not with what if.

"Personal relationships are only a small part of our lives. To consume ourselves with the desire to have the perfect personal life limits our development. Only through selfless living can we be truly loving individuals. Our relationships are presented to us so that we can grow spiritually. They are important because they serve us on the road toward living a life of service."

Lawrence offered to walk me home, and as we walked he added, "Love means to be totally free, free from the bondage of any thought of yourself or of your personal desires. It is only through selfless living that we can ever be truly loving individuals. Our relationships are opportunities to grow and to learn the true meaning of love. They are an important aspect of our development."

When we reached my apartment, Lawrence bowed to me and said, "Until later." As I watched him walk away I felt privileged to have spent the afternoon conversing with one who was living the "selfless ideal."

∴ VIII ∴

Adaptability: Accepting Change

We are often too rigid in our attitudes. We see things as black or white and will not acknowledge that there are shades in between those two extremes. We must learn to accept that with spiritual growth our views sometimes change. As we move forward in our development we must learn to let things flow. Rigidity denies us the opportunity to grow and experience. In spiritual life things often seem to be going in one direction one day and in a completely different direction the next. This can be distressing, but we must not become frustrated and angry. We must accept day-to-day change as a part of development.

Certain people, because of their early childhood training, are naturally more adaptable than others. The father of a client of mine was a career officer in the air force. The family moved to a new place every three or four years. My client was always adapting to new schools and new friends, so frequent change became totally natural for her.

Other people find change very difficult. Peter was raised by his grandmother in a small town. He was trained to wake up every morning at five o'clock to do the farm chores. Because of this schedule he learned to go to bed by ten in the evening. Peter now lives in New York, but no matter what is happening, he excuses himself at ten o'clock, saying he must go to sleep. This has greatly affected his social life and appears rude to others. I told Peter he needed to adapt to life in the city, but he refused to change his pattern.

If you are interested in spiritual growth, you must learn to "turn on a dime," to adapt rapidly to changing conditions. You must not fuss and fume and have a negative attitude if things do not happen the way you expect. The situation is probably necessary for your development. You must deal with what is, not what you desire.

Surely you have met people who are so rigid that you think it is unwise to even have a discussion with them. Why waste the energy, you think, for it will serve no purpose except to get everyone upset. Observe this type of person and see how unbalanced it really is to be close-minded. If you do not open yourself to change, you will lose much. Keep yourself open to the views of others. You may not agree with those views, but it is important to listen and not to judge. Just keep yourself available to the possibility of change, for those who can adapt themselves have a much fuller life and learn great things. Even positive change frightens people. This is something we must work on if our lives are to be happy and free of stress.

For instance, let's say you choose to attend a certain film. You arrive at the theater to find that the projector is broken and the film has been canceled. What do you do? Do you fume and stamp your feet, or do you find something else to do?

Plans change, situations change, and people change. Learn to accept this and not to live with expectation or the desire that things will remain a certain way. We all spend too much time and energy being disturbed by external situations. This is sheer waste-fulness. Just deal with whatever happens and you will feel fine. If you are driving your car and you come to a place where the road is closed, you must take another road. You will still reach your destination; it does not serve you to stop your car and fret that the road is closed. Find another route and get on with your travels. Maybe you will find that the new road is more beautiful than the one you were driving on in the first place.

Always keep yourself prepared in case something disturbing happens in your life. If you keep yourself psychologically sound, you will be capable of handling whatever comes your way. People often feel unable to cope when they are surprised by situations that come "out of the blue." We frequently are asked to deal with situations for which we did not have an opportunity to prepare, but this is not a problem if we have already made our own inner preparation. Keep aware at all times that external circumstances can change without a moment's notice. Adaptability is the an-swer; if you can "go with the flow," you will have a much easier time. Know that the worst can happen. This does not mean you should be negative; just try not to be naive. Be happy when things are going well but do not fret or become paralyzed when you must deal with adversity or surprise. This is life and we cannot stop disturbing things from happening. There will always be problems, plenty of them, and they will crop up when we least expect them. Know that this is a possibility and do not allow yourself to become shocked or terrified when you must deal with the unexpected. Work on your inner balance when things are going well and be aware that at any time things on the physical plane can change. Prepare yourself ahead of time so that your nervous system will be strong enough to handle anything that comes your way.

This is not pessimism but sheer common sense. For example, people become distraught when a mate says, "I am unhappy so I am leaving." The other party is shocked and reacts with total disbelief, saying, "I can't deal with this situation. I wasn't pre-pared." But one should always be spiritually prepared in some way. Situations of this nature happen to people every day. Do not

take things for granted in your personal life. Know that everything
will be all right, no matter what happens. Do your best with the
given situation, for you can do no more. Don't think that things
will never change; always be aware that circumstances can and do
change constantly. How could there be growth if we experienced
no change? How would we ever grow spiritually if we were not
asked to deal with situations that surprised us? Once again, this
does not imply that we should live negatively, full of paranoia and
fears of gloom and doom. I am merely saying that if you always
prepare yourself for the possibility of trouble, you will not become
devastated by adversity. Be flexible and stay aware, and you will
save yourself great heartache in the long run. Try to prepare each
day to deal with whatever comes your way. This is growth and will
aid you in your quest for spiritual freedom.

Harriet had been referred to me by another client, a friend of hers
who was worried about her. Harriet's friend did not know how to
help her out of a deep depression. It seems that after twenty years
of marriage, Harriet's husband had asked for a divorce. Harriet
was totally shocked, feeling that she had had no warning. She had
thought everything was going well in the relationship.

Harriet arrived looking very well dressed. Perfect, in fact. Not
a hair was out of place and everything was perfectly coordinated,
including the gems in her earrings that matched the color of her
suit. Harriet said she had never spoken to a person like me before
and felt a bit uncomfortable. She had made the appointment
because she respected her friend's opinion and she was desperate.
Thinking about her comment, I asked her what exactly "a person
like me" meant?

She said, "Well, you know, I was expecting a gypsy, and I'm
a bit surprised to see someone who doesn't look the way I expected."

"Harriet," I said, "do you always have preconceived notions
about people and things? Don't you think that's a bit limiting?"

"Well," she said, "I'm very used to living a certain way and

I'm also used to being around things that are familiar. My husband and I had a very orderly life, and I don't know how to live any other way. My father always insisted that his household be orderly and controlled, and as a child I always knew what was going to happen. There were no surprises; each moment was totally planned. Our summer vacations were always the same. Dinner was always at the same time, and we went to bed and got up at the same time. In my marriage I tried to maintain the same kind of order, keeping everything on a schedule and always aware of what was to be done at any given time. Now that my husband has left me, I don't know what to do. For the last twenty years I've arranged my life around his needs and his work schedule. Now I have time on my hands, and I just don't know how to cope."

She started to cry. "I am so embarrassed," she said. "I should have better control over my emotions. I don't see how I can possibly adapt to living without my husband. It's all I know. I've never worked for a living and have only a few friends because I was always busy with my husband. I felt secure in knowing exactly what I was going to do each day."

I thought it sounded as if she were running a military camp instead of a marriage, but I didn't say so. I waited to hear her say one word that indicated she loved her husband. She seemed more concerned that her orderly life had been disrupted—living in boxes, I thought. There is a little box for everything, and all the boxes are placed neatly on her shelf. What a sad way to live.

"Harriet," I said, "of course this is very upsetting to you. You haven't had enough time to adjust to the situation. Have you considered talking to a therapist to help you through this difficult time?"

"Oh, I couldn't do that," she exclaimed. Obviously she was not open to this idea. It was amazing, in fact, that she had even come to see me.

"Isn't it possible that your husband became tired of living a life with such routine?" I asked. "I believe he left because he felt a desperate need for change. It would serve you to learn a bit of adaptability. There is much ahead for you in life if you allow yourself to grow. Change often precedes growth. You must find new ways of spending your time. I think you have artistic abilities that you have neglected."

She looked a bit startled and said, "I did paint when I was in school, but after I got married there never seemed to be time. I was always so busy."

"Well, you have time now. I think you should take a class to sharpen your skills and start painting again. It will help you to get through this crisis, and you may enjoy yourself. You don't have to worry about money, so why not volunteer some time to help others? You may be very pleased when you see that there is a lot to do out there. You just have to be adaptable, go out and do things. Possibly, when you get more involved with life and with others, your husband will see life with you as more interesting. I think that in your case this separation from your husband can be a very positive thing. It won't necessarily be as terrible as you think. You're still on relatively good terms with him, aren't you?"

"Well, yes," she said. "In fact, he asked me to have dinner with him in the city tomorrow evening."

"You said yes, didn't you?"

"I told him I would have to think about it because I don't like to go to the city at night and I don't like to eat in restaurants."

"Well, then, this is a good time for you to try changing your routine a bit. Are you nervous about seeing your husband?"

"Nervous? No, I don't think so. I guess I'm a bit nervous about being in the city after dark."

She ultimately agreed to see her husband and to try to have a pleasant evening. I did not perceive that this separation would end in divorce. If Harriet could learn to change her set way of living, she and her husband could enter into a much more positive relationship. We continued talking for another half hour and discussed other possibilities for change. We also talked about her fear of letting go of her routine. I told her that it was all right to be afraid; the important thing was for her to go ahead and do things anyway. In time the fear would pass. She would be too busy living her life to be burdened by the fear of living it. When leaving, she promised to call and let me know how she was doing.

After Harriet left, I thought about the many people I had met who lived their lives in an orderly, regimented fashion. These people never wanted to take any risks. Only when a tragedy occurred did they realize that things in life do change, and it is wise to prepare for it. Preparing for change is a mental process. You learn that in life change is inevitable, and you tell yourself to be prepared for it. This does not imply that you must worry constantly about the future; it means that you know circumstances may change at any given moment, which is fine. The thought of change should not cause panic because it can be exhilarating; it is all in the point of view. To develop into a truly spiritual person you must know and accept that circumstances will change when it is necessary for your soul's development. It is really all right in the long run.

I have seen people go to pieces because they planned a dinner party for eight and at the last minute one person canceled. "It will ruin my seating arrangement, and the table will not look right. Whatever shall I do?" The answer, of course, is a simple one when we are not blinded by panic: Rearrange the place settings and set the table for seven people. Change the seating!

One of the greatest tests we can undergo is the loss of a spouse or partner. This event causes the most massive changes in one's life. It is not uncommon for the surviving partner to become despondent and feel unable to go on. You don't have your companion to do things with any longer, so all your actions seem empty; you don't know how to get through dinner alone, you can't sleep without your partner next to you.

It is fairly rare that both members of a couple leave the Earth plane at the same time; one partner almost always passes over before the other. Inner preparation for this situation is absolutely necessary. You should not deliberately avoid thinking that one day you will no longer have your spouse or your lover or your parents, superstitiously believing that if you don't think about it, it won't happen. It's not necessary to dwell on the possibility of such a loss, but you should be aware that this event, no less than any other, is a part of life and therefore a lesson for your growth. Remember that there is no death but only a change from physical to spirit life. If no one really dies, then no one is left behind; it is only because we don't understand that we think we have been left.

When such a loss happens, talking to a friend or a professional counselor is helpful. You need support to help you through this difficult time. Eventually you will be able to replace the deep feeling of loss with positive changes. Specialists in grief counseling are available, as are support groups for the bereaved. Also, in addition to the above—and most important of all in such painful times—you should keep busy doing other things. Fill the time with positive actions, and the pain will not seem so unbearable. The feeling of loss will not go away entirely, but in time the pain will lessen and be offset by positive changes. And if you prepare yourself for the possibility that one day you may be going on without someone you love, you will be better able to handle the change. If you educate yourself to understand that there is no death and that loss is a part of your growth, this along with service to others will help most of all.

Roberta lost her husband after a three-year illness. She had done a wonderful job taking care of him. They had been married for fourteen years, and Roberta could not deal with the thought of life without him. Her husband had been a very spiritual man and was not afraid of passing over. Aware of her dependence on him, he had always worried about how his wife would manage without him.

"Roberta will not accept the possibility that I will be leaving very soon," he told me from his hospital bed a few weeks before he passed over. "I have tried to talk to her and to help her prepare, but she will not listen to me. The doctors have told her the truth about how serious my condition is, but she won't listen to them either. She keeps repeating to me, 'Everything will be all right. Nothing is going to change. You'll be coming home soon and life will be back to normal.' " He stopped to get his breath, then continued, "Try to talk to her. I'm afraid she'll have a nervous breakdown when I do pass over. If she would only prepare herself a little, it would be much easier for her when it does happen."

He had no strength to talk any longer so I left the room and went to find Roberta. She was standing at the nurses' station, talking with one of the nurses. I was not looking forward to the conversation I was about to have because it is very difficult to find the right words to help someone living in a state of denial. "Roberta," I said, "your husband is asleep. Let's go get a cup of coffee. You could use a little food, too."

At the hospital coffee shop, Roberta seemed very nervous, and she looked very thin and drawn. I took a deep breath and began, "Roberta, your husband is very worried about you. He feels that you're not accepting the seriousness of his condition."

"Yes, I am," she snapped, "but I know he will be all right. I'm taking care of him, I'm going to make certain that he gets well." She looked away from me, her lips trembling.

The food arrived, and Roberta picked at her sandwich. I wasn't sure I knew how to proceed, so I sat quietly and drank my coffee, struggling with myself to find the right words. "Please don't be angry with me," I finally began, "but I must tell you as your friend that your husband may not live much longer, and you must try to prepare yourself for this. I realize that you love him very much, and the idea of life without him seems unbearable. But you are worrying him because he is afraid you aren't facing the severity of the situation and that you won't be able to cope when he is no longer here with you."

"Why should I try to cope with a situation that I will not have to deal with? I refuse to accept the possibility that he might die. If you were really my friend, you wouldn't be talking to me in this way."

"Roberta," I said, taking her hand, "you must stop this. You are making the situation much more difficult than it has to be, and you are upsetting your husband, who loves you and is deeply worried about you. He has been suffering for three years, and he's afraid to pass over because he thinks you won't be able to deal with it. You must be strong and let him know you'll be all right. This is the help he needs most from you now. He knows you love him, and you know he loves you. None of us ever wants to lose someone we love—there is nothing worse for a person to deal with—but we must forget ourselves and think of what is needed. It is necessary that you try to make your husband comfortable."

She stared at me, looking very angry. I thought she was going to tell me to shut up and stop interfering. Instead she started to sob. "I can't go on without him. What will I do? I don't know how to take care of myself. He took care of things for me. Even during his illness I always felt safe, knowing he was with me. What will happen to me? How can I live without him?" Her sobs deepened, and I put my arms around her.

"You'll be all right, Roberta. We're all here to help you. You will not be alone. Change is very hard, but it is not impossible. You will see your husband on the other side when it is your time to pass over. Now the important person is him."

"I know he can't go on much longer and his case is hopeless," Roberta responded. "My mother has been trying to prepare me, but I just wasn't ready to face it."

She was quiet for a moment, then she sighed deeply and said, "Let's go back and see him. I'll let him know I will be all right. Yes, I am terrified of the change, but I will think about that later. You're right—now I must try to make him happy. I've been acting a bit selfish, I'm afraid, and I'm sorry, but I couldn't help it. The thought of his leaving was too much for me to bear. I thought that if I did not think about that possibility, maybe it wouldn't happen. I've been childish, and I must go back to him acting grown-up so he won't feel that I'm a child who can't face life."

Roberta spent the next few weeks making her husband comfortable. No longer did she live in denial. She was facing the probability that he would not live much longer and began to think about life without her husband. When he passed over, he seemed very much at peace.

Roberta is doing well now. She went through a period of mourning but kept herself busy. She became active in a group that supports people who have experienced similar losses and also became a Big Sister one day a week to a young girl who had lost both her parents. The change has not been easy, but it became easier as soon as she prepared herself for it. When I hear from her now, she tells me of all the things she is doing that are helpful to others. She speaks of her husband with great love but feels that he is doing fine and one day they will see each other again. Roberta has surprised all of us who know her by her ability to accept change and to be useful after her great loss. No one needs to worry about Roberta; she is doing just fine. Certainly she has moments of great sadness and she misses her husband, but she is not afraid of life and is living it to its fullest.

I remember discussing adaptability with Lawrence. We were together admiring a Victorian brownstone on a tree-lined street in Greenwich Village. Looking at the brownstone I said, "I hope they don't change this building too much. I think it's wonderful the way it is. It reminds me of a time in history when the world seemed much more elegant."

"This building needed to be adapted to modern times," Lawrence said. "Possibly it had electrical wiring that was too old and therefore dangerous. The external building may remain much the same with a bit of a facelift, but there is probably much work needed on the interior."

"Much like us," I added.

Lawrence laughed, and taking my arm, he walked with me. "A point well made, my dear. Change must come from within. People think that if they redo their hair or their wardrobe, they will be changed. Not so. These things make us feel a bit better in the short term, but they are not lasting. Only when one works on the inner self does one feel the effects of change. I knew a very unhappy woman who made great changes in her person: She lost a great deal of weight, changed her hair color, even changed her residence. On speaking to her, though, I realized that she still acted and reacted the same way she always had. She was a great complainer and continued to be a complainer. She was a much thinner complainer in a much improved home, but a complainer nonetheless. She had done nothing inside herself to resolve her unhappiness, and so she remained unhappy.

"I knew a second woman who had been just as unhappy as the first but who had done nothing to change her outward appearance. Nevertheless, many people remarked on the changes that seemed to have taken place within her. Her disposition was much kinder than it had been, and she was much more pleasant to be with. When I asked her about the new person who seemed to have emerged, she said she had been working very hard at changing her way of looking at life. She had resolved many psychological issues that had been keeping her living in a way which represented only half a life. But she found a new inner freedom through the changes in her character."

I smiled at the story and thought about Harriet, the woman who had come to see me a few days before. I hoped she was adapting well and had been able to change her life for the better.

As Lawrence and I continued walking, I asked him, "How do you think I can best help people to become more open to change? I believe many people would suffer less if they were able to prepare better for upset and disruption. I don't want them to feel paranoid. I just want them to be able to deal with whatever happens. Inner preparation seems to be a necessary ingredient."

Lawrence nodded. "Education is necessary in order to be able to adapt. People do not know they can have a better life. They become locked in the familiar, and anything out of the ordinary seems intimidating. I once spoke to a man who spent most of his life in a bar. He finally came to the realization that it was not wise for him to live in a blur of alcohol, so he stopped drinking. Prior to this, though, he could not imagine life without a drink in his hand. In time he adapted to his new life of abstinence from liquor. He remarked that he had never thought life without drinking could be so wonderful. He had been afraid to stop drinking because it was a large part of his life. Now he was much happier and could scarcely believe he had waited so long to stop. He was enjoying his new life and was helping others by his example.

"It takes courage to change. One has to be willing to try and not give up! In time the change seems normal, and the old life becomes a memory. People react violently at times when they feel that they are not ready for change. There are times when we are forced to change, to adapt. It is rare that life waits until we feel totally ready, but if you are ready, you will not be thrown out of balance when change occurs. You become ready by not thinking of your desires but accepting whatever happens and realizing that an opportunity has been given to you to learn something. Once the lesson has been learned and digested, you will be presented with something else.

"It is a never-ending process. To think of the words, 'Not my will but thine be done,' can be very helpful. In so doing we address our higher self, which knows more than we do. Allow this part of yourself to be your guide. Do not rebel against this guide, for you will stifle your growth. How many times have you heard someone say, 'I cannot believe I held on for so long. My life is totally different and much better than anything I ever expected. What if I had allowed myself to refuse to let go? I would have remained miserable. But my life is wonderful'? Habits do indeed die hard. People think they would prefer to stay miserable because at least they know what to expect. It is rather silly but not uncommon."

I thought about clients of mine who were involved in very unhappy personal relationships. They complained all the time and lived with great anxiety. If I suggested to them that it might be wise to separate, they would panic. Most of them would say, "But what if I don't meet someone else? At least I have someone in my life. Maybe it isn't a very good relationship, but there aren't any other possibilities." These people stay in unhappy situations because they are afraid they cannot adapt to the change. When people have the courage to end dysfunctional relationships, they are often much happier and are amazed at how long they stayed in the relationship. If they had seen before how wonderful change can be and that it was nothing to fear, it would have saved them a lot of pain.

To grow spiritually you must be prepared for change at all times. If you become locked in your own routine, you will not be open for growth. People say, "What can I do? I feel as if I am in a rut." "I say," Lawrence said, "you need only open your eyes to see opportunities to change and grow. How can you allow yourself to stay in a rut when there is so much to do and to learn? Do not allow yourself to become lethargic in your development. Do not fear change—welcome it with open arms."

My friend Kathy adapted to having cancer. It was a terrible shock, of course, when she first received the news, but she went on to deal with it. She didn't pretend she didn't have cancer, but she learned to live with it. She considered the love she had for her husband, family, and friends and decided that she would do her best to live each day to its fullest. She once remarked to me that many of the things which seemed important in the past had turned out to be not so important at all.

We must all adapt, as Kathy did. The moment we are born, we all begin to pass over. Death should not be viewed as the grim reaper but as the natural progression of the life process. Everyone leaves the Earth when the time comes.

Growing older is often difficult for us to accept. People become upset at the changes they see in their bodies as time goes on. No one enjoys knowing that the body deteriorates with age. I knew a woman who tried to hide the fact that she had a son in his twenties. She lived in terror that someone might see her passport and discover her age. Each year as her birthday approached, she went into a depression. I have never met a person who had so much plastic surgery. She went to nightclubs to see if she could attract young men, not to be involved with them but to be reassured that she could still attract them.

There can be great comfort in growing older. As I think back to my own teens and early twenties, I realize that life is much easier after one grows up. The older we become, the more we are given to increase our wisdom.

How does one learn to grow old gracefully? I think the answer lies in adaptability. One must see this process as the natural evolution of the physical. You can take good care of yourself through proper diet, exercise, and right thinking. A sense of humor helps, too. If you don't allow yourself to be consumed with the physical, you won't tend to be so frightened of natural changes. Think of growth and of the spirit. You are not alone. We are all here together, going through many similar experiences. Be the best you can be during each period of your life and do not dwell on the changes that occur in the physical body. Accept them and you will be free.

Giorgio was a very talented violinist who started performing in public at the age of seven. Hard work and constant practice served to bring him rave reviews throughout his career. Then, when he was thirty years old, he injured his hand and could no longer play. I met him one year after the accident. He came to me because he felt I might be able to help him understand why this had happened to him. He felt that he had been punished. He sought therapy but was unable to release his depression. He could not bear to listen to any of his recordings or to attend the performances of other musicians, but he did have a wonderfully supportive family that tried to help him see his life was not over.

It broke my heart to see him so tortured. We discussed the laws of karma, and I suggested possible alternatives for him. He remained depressed after the first appointment but was quite open. He returned to see me three more times and in time started to study psychology. He received his degree in psychology three years after we first met.

Giorgio is now working with students, teaching the violin and helping them to understand and use their gifts. His degree in psychology has given him greater understanding of the nature of the creative artist. He is sharing his brilliance and doing a great service for others. It was not easy for Giorgio. He suffered and struggled to make some major life changes, but he accepts his new life and seems happy. He has moments when he truly misses performing, but he doesn't allow this longing to depress and paralyze him. He is using his great gift in the best way that he can at this time.

Giorgio is comforted by the fact that he made many recordings before losing the use of his hand. Many people were privileged to learn through his work and to find peace and enjoyment from listening to him. Giorgio could have chosen to remain locked in the past and refused to continue to be productive, but he didn't. He is able to tell stories of his days as a musician, and his memories give him great pleasure. I have much respect for him. Acceptance of change does not happen overnight; it is a process that includes education and adaptability.

Lydia could not adapt to the changes she saw in her relationship with Philip. She told me she had expected things always to remain the same. In the early days of their relationship Philip had been very attentive, bringing Lydia flowers and gifts, and being very romantic. He called her on the phone constantly, telling her that he adored her. As time went on, though, he no longer brought her flowers, and there were times when he seemed consumed with work. Lydia was in a panic; she felt that he no longer loved her because if he did, how could he have changed? I told Lydia that relationships always change and seldom does the intensely romantic aspect of a relationship continue past the early stages. I felt that she needed to accept the natural progression of a relationship and perhaps should try harder to keep the romance alive.

"Is it possible Philip is simply comfortable with you and feels that you don't need constant physical reminders of his love?" I asked her. "It takes enormous energy to continue to be romantic. People get very busy with other aspects of their lives. Aren't you being a bit selfish in not understanding that Philip has many responsibilities with his career? Accept things as they are, Lydia, or leave the relationship if you are terribly unhappy. It will make you ill if you continue to be so upset."

Don't expect that you will stay lost in the euphoria of being in love with your beloved throughout the course of a relationship. Keep the love alive by being able to adapt to your mate's needs, and you will not succumb to despair. Don't feel that you must be shown you're loved every minute of the day. Remain loving, and take the relationship as it is. With true love there is great passion, but passion does not guarantee true love.

If You Have Difficulty Adapting

Adaptability depends on our having a strong sense that the circumstances of our lives are presented to us for our growth. If we attract a situation, karmically speaking, it is because we need to learn something. No matter how bad the problem seems, it will pass. Time is a great healer as well as an intelligent teacher. More than anything else, it takes time to integrate change into our lives. Try to let go and see what is waiting for you around the corner.

It is a great adjustment for many mothers when their children grow up and leave the nest. Their lives have been totally involved with the day-to-day needs of their children, and now they feel empty and lost. They must adapt to the fact that their children are now adults. I would tell them to be relieved that the stereo is not blaring rock music anymore. They might then say, "I miss the noise level." It does get easier with time, and it helps to keep yourself busy with things you had always planned to do when you had more time. Didn't you always want to join the art club or go to the symphony? What about taking a class to learn something that has always interested you? How about volunteer work? Perhaps you've always felt that you wanted to be involved in helping others, but you've just never had the time before. Keep yourself interested in everything, and you will adapt to the change and be very happy with your new life.

Let us get on with our lives. As Lawrence said, "To grow spiritually, you must be prepared for change at all times." I cannot stress that too often in referring to the spiritual.

True spirituality consists of the knowledge that life—every part of life, without exception—is sacred and of behavior based on that knowledge. We are here to grow and to learn to serve our fellow beings in whatever way is possible for us. The purpose of life is the soul's development. No set rules or dogmas are necessary; we don't have to believe anything. We must only try to be good people who are interested in the needs of others.

The philosophy of service and selflessness is universal and excludes no one on the basis of his or her religious beliefs. We need to work together for the good of the whole. Each of us can serve in his or her own way, using different talents. Let us not fight one another because we do not share the same religious beliefs. In this way we also have to be adaptable. Let us think only of service and selflessness! We often have to adapt our viewpoint to that of our neighbor. Listen and do not judge. Who are we to stand in judgment of another?

Acceptance of change will help us to have a life that has constant growth. Rigidity is antithetical to growth. If we keep our bodies totally rigid for a long period, our bodies will start to lose their flexibility. If we keep our minds and hearts rigid, the same thing will happen to them.

Take a deep breath and be grateful for the changes you have been given, for they are given to serve you on the road toward freedom of the spirit. Free yourself.

∴ IX ∴
Patience

True love brings great patience, whereas impatience has its roots in selfishness. If you are impatient with someone, you are thinking only of your own feelings. Our individual problems with impatience are encouraged by the fact that we live in an impatient society. People are always in a hurry and become short-tempered when they feel that things are not being done fast enough. We often don't allow others or ourselves the time we need. We speak before we think and find ourselves making mistakes because we didn't think before acting. More often we react. Slow down and relax. Things will still get done if you do them with a bit of kindness and patience.

I was privileged to meet a very great man who never seemed to be in a hurry. I never saw him become anxious or impatient. He never rushed anyone and always listened intently to whatever anyone said to him. I once asked him, "Don't you ever get impatient with people or situations?" He smiled and replied, "Why should I when I know I have eternity in front of me?" I often think of the beauty and magnitude of that idea. We have eternity in front of us!

Each person has different capabilities. We are not all capable of executing every action in the same amount of time. We must not fault others if they are not as quick as we are; this is being judgmental, and who are we to stand in judgment of anyone?

Some children walk at eight months; some don't walk until they are eighteen months old. Is either child less of a person because he didn't move at the same speed as the other? We bring with us different sets of circumstances from past lives, and some have lived many more lives than others. Is it fair to judge one soul against another? Let's say you have practiced the piano for twenty years and have become a master of that instrument. Are you selfish enough to become angry with a pupil who has been learning music for only the last four months?

Patience is indeed a virtue, and though many of us say that we don't have it, we can achieve it with practice. It is worth working for because we cannot act in a loving manner if we become impatient with others.

We are all used to measuring time by the hour or by the minute. An entire lifetime is a drop of water in the ocean of time, but eternity seems beyond comprehension. People think that life ends with passing out of the physical world. Nothing ends, everything merely changes form. If you can accept this notion, then patience can become a reasonable goal. Live one moment at a time and make it the best moment it can be. Your best today may not be your best tomorrow; don't waste sacred energy by being overly self-critical. Don't castigate yourself for your mistakes. Go forward and try to do better when the next opportunity arises.

People are often self-critical so that they can escape feeling vulnerable, the idea being that if you criticize yourself first, you will not be upset by someone else's criticism. But this is not being loving toward yourself. Love in action means to love yourself as well as others. You can't belabor your every imperfection; this will serve no purpose except to make you ill. Be mindful, though, that there is a great difference between loving yourself and narcissism. In Greek mythology, Narcissus was a beautiful youth who fell in love with his unattainable reflection in a pool and pined away. Narcissism is love of the physical, nonspiritual part of oneself. From the viewpoint of love in action, self-love implies loving the inner being who is striving to connect with the higher self. You must love yourself for the beauty of the spirit that lives within you. It can take great patience to learn to love in this manner.

The physical person is not one's being because the physical does not last. The spirit is real because it is eternal and lives on after our bodies die. If you were given a wonderful physical vehicle (that is, body), be grateful; karmically speaking, you have earned it. It is your responsibility to take care of all that has been given to you. This often takes great patience, for time and thoroughness are needed to take care of physical needs as well as spiritual needs. Many people, for example, are overly self-critical about their weight. The body maintains balance when it is nourished properly, but often we don't nourish it properly. It is easy to reach for the fast food or the candy bar, but time is required to prepare salads and vegetables. Patience is needed to tend to the body as we should. Most people are unsuccessful in their dieting because they lose patience. If the results don't happen fast enough, they give up.

Instant gratification is the cry of the world of advertising. There are instant breakfasts, instant coffee, instant weight-loss products, and on and on. People feel they should be able to transform themselves instantly. This is usually not possible, but with patience and tolerance most problems can be solved and depression and self-torture avoided.

Think Before You Speak

Many tragic mistakes and heartbreaking thoughtless acts are produced by impatience. How many times have you heard someone

say, "I'm sorry, I wasn't thinking"? How many times have you
been embarrassed because you put your foot in your mouth? You
can avoid this by thinking before you act or react to a given
situation. Don't say just anything that comes to mind but take a
deep breath and have a little patience before you speak. It will
save you from living your life as one big apology. Sometimes we
could save the feelings of another person if we just took a little
more time. Words are things, just as thoughts are things. Once
they are said, they cannot be taken back—they are set in motion.
Think about that: Stop, look, and listen. Have patience, and you
will save yourself and others a great deal of pain. If you hurt
someone by your thoughtlessness, he will probably say that he
forgives you, but the damage will have been done. To live a life
with love in action, you must learn to conserve your language.
Toward that end it is necessary to judge carefully when and how
to speak, and when to keep silent.

The gift of listening is a great art, and as with all great arts,
skilled practitioners are rare. We are all drawn to people who
listen well, and we find it frustrating to talk to someone who
always interrupts when we are trying to explain our views on a
given subject. Many people seem to be reluctant to listen; they
appear to want to be talking all the time. Learn to listen, and it
will serve you well and teach you a great deal.

Every act that we perform is important. The way one closes
a door is important. You can learn to be patient through each and
every action you perform throughout the day.

A Bitter Lesson

In a state of near nervous collapse, a woman named Joy came to
see me. It seems she had met a young European man who was
visiting America and fell madly in love. After knowing him for
three weeks she left the States and moved to France to be with
her beloved. Everyone who loved her tried to tell her she should

take more time before changing her life so drastically, but she allowed her passion to rule her judgment and flew off to be with her lover. Within a few days she began to see that he had a rather unusual behavior pattern. He disappeared for hours with no explanation, and when he finally returned, he acted very cold and heartless.

Joy had taken all her savings with her, and aware that she didn't speak French, her beloved offered to open a bank account for her. After two days he never returned. She waited and finally became hysterical, thinking he must have had a terrible accident or was perhaps murdered. She finally went to a small bar they had visited a few times. She approached the owner and told him that her dear one had disappeared. The owner began to laugh. He said, "I hope you didn't give him any money." Suddenly she realized that she had been betrayed. She was left with nothing to do but call her family and ask them to send her money to buy a ticket home.

If Joy had only waited to get to know this man, she could have avoided the whole terrible situation. She came to me because she wanted me to tell her that she was the victim of karma. I told her that I was afraid her misfortune was a definite case of bad judgment and that she must not try to use karma as an excuse for her own foolishness. I told her that if she had exercised a bit of patience and self-discipline, she would not have had to suffer like that. I then suggested that she talk with someone who could help her work through the emotional trauma. "In the long run, Joy, it is all a part of experience, and it is all right," I said. "Learn from this situation and get on with your life. Time is a great healer, and it will serve you well."

Criticizing and Judging

If you are a truly patient person, you will not be judgmental. Too many people spend their time and energy judging their neighbors and criticizing the deeds of their fellow man. If everyone would take the time to understand the nature and circumstances of those with whom they come in contact, there would be no time for judging. One cannot understand another human being until one takes the time to come to know that person. This takes great patience!

Each of us has free choice to do whatever we decide is best. Often, upon viewing the actions of those we know, we feel that we could advise them to make a better decision, and we become angry when someone does something we think is wrong. By all means observe and advise when you are called upon to do so, but be aware that ultimately it is the individual's choice to do what he or she feels is right. Try to understand the individual's motivation. You may not agree with someone's decision—you may even be shocked—but you must remember that every person has free choice. It may take great patience for you to keep quiet and not stand in judgment of another's action, but try to spend your time helping rather than judging. Helping, in the true sense, is not interfering. Only in cases where you feel that someone is in danger should you take the chance of acting in a manner that might appear to be interfering. It is not wise to allow tragedy to happen because you waited too long to assist someone; this is not a case of being impatient or judgmental but of using good sense.

None of us can totally understand another human being, but we can develop the ability to see people for who they are and not for whom we would like them to be. Too often we are disappointed because people do not fulfill our expectations. It is selfish to expect another person to please us; it is judgmental to demand that one's personal expectations be fulfilled. Look closely at the people with whom you come in contact and respect them for who they are. If you find that you do not want to associate with someone because of his or her behavior, then detach yourself from that person. It is better to do that than to stand in judgment.

Each person has the right to develop at his or her own rate. Some people decide that they should seek therapy or counseling; others decide to leave things as they are. Some choose not to deal with anything but just get through life the only way they feel they can. Who are we to judge what is the right way?

Learning Patience

Intelligence consists largely in the ability to learn from one's mistakes. Be tenacious and do not give up. How many times in your life have you been faced with a situation you felt you could not handle? Perhaps you thought it was impossible to perform some action or to reach a particular goal, but you kept at it and then saw that you could do a lot more than you ever felt possible. Let's say, for example, that you thought you would never be able to use a word processor or computer. You sat in front of it and could not figure the darn thing out. But you kept at it, and in a month's time you were doing quite well. In three months you found that you even enjoyed sitting in front of the screen. Ask any actor how many auditions he had to go through before he got his first part. He will more often than not say it was a difficult process, but he kept at it and the part finally came. Often he will tell you just how close he came to giving up before perseverance paid off. A stockbroker will tell you the problems he had when he was "cold calling" clients at the beginning of his career. Beginnings are difficult and attempting something new can be embarrassing, but time and patience are the cure.

I am amazed at the patience my friend Louise has with her children. No matter how many times they ask her questions, she takes time to answer them. When her little boy Kevin was trying to learn to tie his shoes, I watched Louise show him eleven times how to do it.

I said, "Louise, you're amazing. Not once did you lose your patience while you were showing Kevin the same thing over and over."

She answered, "It didn't take any patience. I love him, and I remember what it was like when I was little, trying to learn to tie my shoe. It seemed like an impossible task. My mother had no patience at all. She felt that I should be able to do anything the first time she showed me. I often couldn't, so she made me feel inadequate. I swore that if I was ever a mother, I would never allow my children to feel the way my mother made me feel. It's a pleasure to show the children how to do something." Once Kevin finally accomplished tying his shoe, he tried to teach his little sister.

I thought how admirable it was that Louise didn't allow herself to treat her children as her mother had treated her but was able to learn a positive lesson from her own situation. Too often I hear the excuse that "I'm impatient because my mother [or father] was." It is not necessary to pass your own experiences on to others.

If you love truly, you will not have to work at being patient; you will automatically be so because that is the kind way to be. You will do whatever is needed, for that is a large part of love in action: doing what is needed. In Louise's case, she needed to show her son Kevin something eleven times, but she found it a pleasure to do this for her child. This is a sign of a good mother. People often remark that they have a wonderful mother, and they usually go on to speak of the patience their mother showed toward them. When I was little, I used to watch my grandmother work on her quilts. She sat by the hour sewing the tiniest stitches. She never seemed to be impatient or in a hurry to finish the quilt. She enjoyed every tiny stitch. She enjoyed the process of quilting as much as she enjoyed looking at the finished product. She promised to teach me how to quilt, but at the time I felt that I had better things to do than learn quilting. It seemed to me that it would take forever. I realize now that it would be a wonderful thing to know how to do, but of course there is still much time!

When we are in too much of a hurry, we miss a lot. If you read a book too quickly, you may not remember it well. If you don't take the time to proofread something you have written, later you may find many mistakes. When you don't take the time to help another person, you may regret it. Have you ever been abrupt with someone on the phone and afterward realized that the person really needed you? It would have taken only a few minutes of your time to help.

Harris is an architect. He is always making mistakes because he never completely finishes a project. He forgets to check some final detail and as a result has to defend himself in lawsuits when clients sue him. It amazes me that this keeps happening to him. He always calls in complete despair and total panic. I have repeatedly told him that he lacks patience and that his mistakes could be avoided if he would only take the time to check things thoroughly. But he is always in a great hurry to get the job done so that he can be paid.

Enjoy Yourself!

A sense of humor is very important for all of us, and most often we can discover something humorous in every situation in which we find ourselves. Laughter helps the nervous system relax so that it is better able to handle the stressful situations.

Take a deep breath before you react to anything. The old trick of counting to ten doesn't hurt either. If you have an action to perform, do it to the best of your ability. Don't just rush through it in order to get it done but enjoy all aspects of it. If you do, you will be a lot more comfortable with whatever you have to deal with. We are all given the ability to teach in some way; there are always things one person can do better than another. If you are called upon to teach, do it with love. If your motivation is one of truly helping, how can you lack patience? Have you ever watched a gifted teacher? I had a wonderful music teacher who would allow me to go over and over the same passage, never rushing me or making me feel that I was slow or stupid. Of course, she could easily play things that were very difficult for me, but she never made me feel inferior; she just let me practice a piece until I was able to do it correctly. She seemed to enjoy teaching people like me.

Music itself is a good teacher because it is only through practice and patience that one can become proficient at it. The same is true of any art. By all means be inspired by the work of those you admire, but try not to judge your own progress against that of anyone else. Enjoy learning for its own sake.

Loving Yourself: Taking Care of Your Body

Illness is a great teacher of patience. Many of us have suffered a relapse of the flu or a cold because we weren't patient enough to stay in bed and get well. We seem to think we have no time to be sick because we have too many important things to do. Consequently, it isn't unusual for us to feel miserable for weeks instead of a few days because we refuse to take the time to recuperate properly. If you are sick, stay in bed. Other things can wait. Your health is a sacred trust and must be preserved at all costs. If you have a cold, your body is telling you clearly that it needs a rest. To continue a strenuous regimen of activity when your resistance is lowered by illness could easily lead to your contracting a more serious disease. You are also being inconsiderate of others who are exposed to your sickness. It is selfish not to take care of your health. We always have things that need to be done, but think of the needs of your body rather than of the pressures of your daily routine. If you are patient at the onset of a physical problem, you will preserve yourself in the long run.

Many people exercise too strenuously and injure themselves. If this happens to you, stop your exercise routine. The pain of an injury is telling you to slow down. To keep exercising regardless of an injury can be very dangerous. The philosophy of "no pain, no gain" can end up causing you a great deal of pain, and a permanent crippling injury can hardly be considered a gain.

Lawrence said, "If you love your body as the divine instrument that it is, you will not be plagued with feelings of despair. If you love your body, you will treat it in a loving way. Do not dwell on the physical. Too much time is consumed in *thinking* of food and exercise. The key is balance, and if you are plagued with *ideas* about diet, you will be out of balance. Health is attained through a combination of proper feeding and proper thinking."

Take time to think about the total person. Spend a few quiet moments each day, not moments of meditation but of contemplation. Think about what you must do, and it will help you to get through the day with less stress and worry. If your body is out of balance, take time to think about the best way to put it back into a balanced state. All actions you perform are of equal importance; each is connected to the whole. When brushing your teeth, do it well. When preparing food, do it with care and thought. Even in a small action such as closing a door, think about it and realize that it is important. Nothing is important and everything is important. There is no conflict here, for both parts of the statement are true. Don't be anxious or in too much of a hurry. Do the best you can with everything that has been given to you and treat the body with reverence.

Eat to maintain life. You must use common sense in your dietary practices. Common sense tells us what the best foods are for feelings of well-being. If you are not aware of the needs of your body, take the time to study this subject, about which many excellent books have been written. Once again, be patient with yourself, for it takes time to learn and you have plenty of time.

Measure Twice, Cut Once

Have you ever noticed how often you must redo something because you did not take the time to do it correctly the first time? There is a great feeling of accomplishment when we do something correctly. The carpenter's adage, "Measure twice, cut once," contains an essential truth: If you are building a bookshelf and you take the time to measure the wood properly, it will all fit together nicely, you won't waste wood, and you'll be pleased with the finished product. If you rush to get the job completed, you'll experience frustration and may have to redo the whole thing, which is wasteful of time, energy, and materials. How often we find ourselves running in a circle when we could have walked a straight path!

You must not pressure yourself to be "spiritual." A person who becomes a bit enlightened often wants to be able to do things immediately. The emotions do not always follow the intellect as quickly as we wish they would. There are times when we understand something intellectually but cannot integrate this intellectual understanding with our emotions. For instance, we know that to desire nothing is the free way to live, but to learn to desire nothing is not easy. If you try to pressure yourself, it will bring feelings of self-defeat. I would like to explain this concept to you in more detail because I feel it is important to understand.

Through my discussions with Lawrence's teacher, Sir William, I was able to understand this concept more clearly. I first met Sir William in the fall. Lawrence invited me to a gathering at a beautiful town house on the upper East Side of Manhattan. He explained that his teacher wanted to meet me. When I arrived at the address Lawrence gave me, I was ushered into a beautiful, quietly elegant home. There was an enormous stained-glass window in the entryway that contributed to the feeling one has when entering a church. I was introduced to a charming older man who projected an indescribable feeling of warmth to which I was instantly drawn. He told me that he was very interested in the work I was doing, about which Lawrence kept him informed. He introduced me to the others, we all sat down, and Sir William began to speak:

"It is important to try not to pressure yourself to become more spiritual. This will cause you to become upset with yourself and possibly to be defeated. You must not make your spiritual development a goal like finishing a marathon race. If you put too much pressure on yourself, you will surely fail and give up. You will think it is no use.

"Spiritual development must never be goal-oriented; such an attitude is purely physical, not spiritual. You must not think you will receive a gold star each time you do a right action; you must not expect to be patted on the back for your selflessness. Also, you must not expect that because you are living your life in a spiritual manner, all will go well. Do not expect. Be patient. If you pressure yourself and castigate yourself for your mistakes, you will become depressed, and this will cause you to be negative. It takes time to establish a new way of thinking. It is not done overnight, and it is not done without a certain number of failures. *Failure is not important.* The important thing is to examine what you have learned and then to move onward. Balance is the key to a healthy life. If you put yourself under pressure, you will upset the balance of your nature. Try to guard against going to extremes. If you go too far in one direction, you will probably have to go equally far in the opposite direction.

"I must emphasize the point: *Do not pressure yourself to be more spiritual.* This will defeat the whole purpose of your growth. It will steal your feeling of freedom. It will lock you in a cell of your personal desires. Just *be!* Aspire to do your best with any given situation. A sense of humor will serve you unfailingly. You are learning to be selfless. You are learning to be grateful for all that you have been given. You are learning to think positively instead of negatively. You are learning to do whatever you can for whomever you meet. It takes time, of which you have plenty. Take your life one day at a time and do the best you can with what is given to you. You can do no more than your best. Remember, your best today may not be your best tomorrow. So be it!

"Self-defeat serves no one. If we are constantly asking 'What's the use?' we will never move forward. There is always much to learn, and we are seldom presented with a situation that, looking at it in retrospect, we could not have handled better. Once again, your best at a specific time is all that you can do. Often, our best changes as we grow spiritually. Some situations are handled better after we have worked out problems that have hindered us. This will always be the case throughout our lives. Examine your reaction to any given situation and see whether you could have handled things better. When another such situation arises, use what you have learned and try to deal with it in a more selfless manner. The key is the word *selfless*. If you are thinking of what is best for those around you, your decisions will be much easier.

"We spend so much precious time going around and around on a carousel, becoming dizzy and unable to cope. Slow down a bit; take your time to look over a given situation, and then move ahead. Self-defeat and self-pity go hand in hand. If you feel defeated, you also feel sorry for yourself. If you feel sorry for yourself, you become paralyzed with fear and stop your development. Only a fool is never afraid, but a wise man does not let fear stop him from moving forward and taking positive action. Laugh at yourself and accept your shortcomings, for we all have them. We are here to work out our problems and to learn to conduct ourselves with spiritual development and character. Each person carries excess baggage from his past experiences; that is human. Each person has free choice to decide how he or she will deal with this load. Do you keep carrying this extra burden with you, or do you learn to lighten your load? The choice is up to you. Self-defeat will not serve you in any way at all.

"A positive attitude can be developed to help you through any given situation. You must always look for the light at the end of the tunnel and not just sit in the dark because you are unsure of exactly where the light is. Have you ever met someone who was sincerely positive? A person who always has a nice disposition? Don't you desire to spend time with a person who is light and happy? This is the type of person you should aspire to emulate. We can learn much by example. A child learns all he knows by watching and imitating those around him. In the beginning we are all children on the road toward spiritual freedom.

"Try to surround yourself with people who are positive and supportive. If you are constantly surrounded by negative people, you will pick up their negativity. Certainly, you must try to be a positive example to these people, but you must also have the courage to remove yourself if that is necessary.

"The motivation for your spiritual development should be one of growth and service. You must not do things in order to get something in return. It should not be your desire to move to the head of the class. You will not be graded on your spiritual development. Take time and grow. There is no rush. All happens as it should in the time that is given to the individual soul; this is the law. The Almighty does not judge anyone. Each person controls his or her own destiny. No diplomas are given to us for completed course work in our spiritual development, and we are not graded on the swiftness of our progress. One can always do better. It is a never-ending process. That is well and as it should be. Be patient with yourself and with all those you meet. Do not judge. Take each moment as it comes and live that moment to its fullest. If you do, you will have a productive life. Each person chooses his own path. It is for us to assist if called upon and to remain silent if that is needed. If your goal is only to be of service to mankind, in whatever capacity you are able, you will not be concerned with thoughts of the result. The action and your performance of that action are all that is necessary to consider at any given moment. Look beyond yourself to the needs of others, and you won't have to look further. All is right in front of you. Be joyous in all that you do, and your actions will be pleasurable. Be aware of your shortcomings and aspire to be a better person, but do not dwell on what you cannot do. Use your time to the best of your ability; in this way you will not be struggling constantly. Your life will flow, and you will positively affect the lives of all with whom you come in contact. This is the key to living a blessed life. All life is sacred. Each of us strives in his own way and in his own time to feel connected to the God force that lives within each of us. Let us not allow our lives to be a struggle to reach the goal line. Let us live to serve, and all will be well."

Sir William paused for a moment and then asked if there were any questions. The group was silent. No one seemed to feel the need to question. He laughed and said, "I did not realize I had such clarity. If there are no questions, then let us enjoy some tea together."

A tea trolley was brought in. The mood was one of good humor. We all moved about and got to know one another a bit better. Sir William seemed a bit tired. His dog, a beautiful collie, sat at attention by his feet, and he stroked the dog as he spoke to us. It was a wonderful evening.

Lawrence walked around, speaking to everyone individually. He came over to me, and I said, "Lawrence, thank you so much for including me tonight. I learned so much that will be useful not only to me personally but to my work. Sometimes I find it difficult to find the right language to explain things to people."

"Simplicity takes time and patience to achieve. You are doing fine. Remember, you can only do your best at any given moment." He laughed.

Sir William rose and bade us all good night. His driver was waiting to drive us home. "Until we meet again," Sir William said and left the room.

The car seemed almost to fly, for I was home in a few minutes, feeling totally relaxed and ready to sleep. Indeed, I thought as I drifted into slumber, we do have eternity in front of us. We don't have to be confined within the framework of a clock. Life is eternal. Knowledge is freedom. Each moment we are given the opportunity to learn and to grow through what we learn. It is all rather wonderful. Patience is a great virtue. Things pass, but the God within remains constant.

∴ X ∴
Gratitude

Many of my clients are terminally ill, and people often ask me, "How are you able to go to hospitals to visit people who are very ill or even dying? Don't you become depressed?"

My answer is that I'm very grateful I'm a visitor and not a patient. After the visit is over, I'm able to walk out into the sunshine. I'm not being flippant. It *is* upsetting to see people who are suffering, but my concern must be for the sufferer and not for my own discomfort. If I am focused on helping another person and am grateful for the opportunity to be of service, any uneasiness I may feel will fade into the background.

As I've mentioned before, one's energy and physical well-being should never be taken for granted; they are very special gifts. When you don't feel well, life becomes much more difficult; therefore, you must take care of yourself and treat your body with respect. In the course of their lives, people spend endless accumulated hours in front of the mirror, looking at what is wrong with themselves instead of thinking how wonderful it is to have a healthy, energetic body. Unfortunately, we often have to lose our health before we become grateful for it. Countless times I've heard people who were ill say, "I never realized before that the most important thing in life is health. I can't believe the amount of time I spent complaining about things that weren't important at all!" There are indeed great lessons to be learned through illness, but one doesn't have to get sick to learn gratitude.

Having It All

Tara, a beautiful woman with a very successful business, came to see me and began by saying that she wanted to "have it all."

I asked, "What exactly does 'having it all' mean to you?"

"It means money and a beautiful home and a great relationship," she said.

"What about peace of mind? Aren't you grateful for all you have been given?" I asked.

"Of course I'm grateful," she replied a bit impatiently, "but I think you can have it all in life if you go for it."

"You get what you earn, Tara. If you are to have something in life, you will get it. It seems to me that you have a lot right now. Why are you worried about the things you don't have?"

"I want a fulfilling relationship with a man who is very successful, and I don't have that yet. I came to see you because I thought you could tell me what was going to happen."

"You're healthy, aren't you?"

"Yes," she replied, "I've always been healthy."

"You have plenty of money and some good friends, as well as a supportive family?"

"I do," she answered.

"If you are to have a good personal relationship, it will be presented to you," I told her. "It's a waste of your sacred energy to be consumed with this issue. You will only make yourself unhappy. Can't you spend your time being a bit more grateful?"

"I am grateful," she snapped. "I told you that! I just don't understand why I can't have everything. There's no reason why I shouldn't get what I want."

"Tara, you are thinking totally about the physical. Aren't you at all interested in your spiritual development?"

"What do you mean?" she asked.

"I mean that you are thinking only about your desires and not about how fortunate you are. You should try to change your point of view before you attract a situation that will force a change on you which may be much more difficult."

She looked rather annoyed. I felt that I wasn't reaching her; a sterner approach seemed needed. "Stop thinking about yourself and what you don't have," I said. "It is outrageous to see a person like you, who has everything, complain about the one thing she doesn't have. I think you should go home and make a list of all the things you have been given."

When she left, she was obviously far from delighted. She hadn't come to me expecting to be told to do something that clearly had nothing to do with achieving the goal on which she was fixated.

A few weeks later, Tara phoned me. She sounded far calmer and happier, and as we talked she told me she had left our session feeling angry and frustrated. I asked her if she had done as I'd suggested, and she said she had made the list even though she thought it was silly. Then she went on, "The list kept getting longer and longer as I thought of more things. I was shocked. It really made me aware that I should try to be more grateful. I guess I get impatient and don't take time to be happy about the things that are right in front of my nose. I decided to try to let things happen instead of insisting on having everything right now."

I told her I was glad to hear that she was attempting to live for the moment rather than becoming obsessed with her desires and being resentful that she didn't have everything to which she thought she was entitled. I suggested that she keep looking at the list and adding to it.

I have met many people like Tara. They have so much but keep looking for more. *Things* will not make anyone happy. It is nice to be surrounded by precious possessions, but then what? The need to possess things becomes a never-ending cycle.

Living Gratitude

I have a dear friend who is the most unmaterialistic person I have ever met. She has very little, wants nothing, but is always in a good mood. She has told me many times how grateful she is that she has food and a roof over her head.

Her family was once very wealthy but lost everything in the stock market crash of 1929. My friend grew up during the Depression and vividly remembers hard times when her family had little or no food. Like many others who were children during that time, she has never forgotten how bad things were, but instead of being embittered and fearful that such times might return, she lives each day with intense gratitude for even the smallest things. Other people often misunderstand her and think she is a bit eccentric; for example, they can't comprehend the pleasure she derives from simply sitting outdoors and watching people stroll by her apartment house. She is interested in everything and everyone. If she has ten extra dollars, she will give it to someone who needs it. I have learned a great deal from her. Her struggles have been great, but her happy disposition gives no clue of this. She laughs at things that other people think are great tragedies. This lady *lives* her gratitude.

One must aspire to make one's life a living, breathing hymn of gratitude. People are always talking about how grateful they are, while in the next breath they are complaining about everything. One must carry gratitude in one's heart. If you are truly grateful, you won't feel the need to tell everyone how grateful you are; it will be obvious from your actions. Everyone has experienced relief when he or she thought something bad was going to happen and then things turned out all right. You may go to the doctor, for instance, because you are worried that something is wrong with you, only to find that you are healthy. You feel a great sense of well-being and vow that you will never take your health for granted. Then, by the next day, you forget about your scare. Almost everyone who has spent time traveling by air has been in an airplane that encountered turbulence, an anxiety-producing experience. You begin to worry that the plane is going to crash, and then you start making deals with God: "If this plane makes it, I'll never complain about anything again! I'll never be nasty to another person." After the plane has landed safely, you forget your resolutions. You go off on your merry way, continuing to complain about things.

"Gratitude is the primary requirement for spiritual development," Lawrence said. "You must be grateful for the life force that pervades your very being. If you are grateful, you will send forth a positive vibration. All who come in contact with you will be affected by this vibration. *Notice everything that is around you.* Be grateful to Mother Earth, for she supplies all your physical needs. Respect her, and she will continue to feed you. Respect your body, and it will serve you well. If you live a life of gratitude, you will feel that it is a privilege to serve and to give.

"How many times have you been admonished to 'count your blessings'? You probably heard it as a child from your parents or your minister. Think about it. Look around you and see just how many things you have been given that are truly wonderful. Do not turn away and pretend not to see the suffering that is around you. Do not walk through the world wearing rose-tinted glasses. Take a good, long look and be grateful for all you have been given.

"Make a list of the things you have to be thankful for. Lists can be very helpful, for they remind us to be aware. Take your time doing this and do not forget the little things. Running water, warmth and a roof over one's head are too often taken for granted. *Take nothing for granted.* The world is full of people who don't possess these comforts. If you look closely at your list, you will see that you have little to complain about.

"This is a time of great suffering on the planet. Appalling numbers of people are homeless amid great prosperity. Illness and depression are so widespread as to be completely overwhelming. The world is full of despair. Ask yourself what you can do to help those who are less fortunate. If you are blessed not to be among those who are suffering, do not delude yourself into believing you are untouched. We are all connected. The Golden Rule implies that what affects one of us affects all of us."

Many people tell me that they refuse to read, watch, or listen to the news. They find it too depressing. They do not want to hear about the problems in the world because they feel helpless to do anything about them. But it is important to do something, anything, no matter how seemingly small. Every action has an effect upon the whole; no action is a small action.

Lee was in a terrible automobile accident. He lay in a semi-coma for eleven days. His survival seemed almost hopeless, and even then, the doctors were not sure he would ever walk again. The family was devastated. Lee was a brilliant young man of twenty-seven, first in his class at the Massachusetts Institute of Technology. Everyone who knew him loved him, and he seemed to lead a charmed life. His family was very wealthy. He had a lovely girlfriend who had been with him since they were teenagers. Everyone assumed they would marry and have a great life together.

At the request of Lee's sister, a good friend of mine, I went to the hospital to visit him. His family was seated outside the room, in shock, suffering greatly. Lee's mother was praying, begging God to save her son. I sat with her, and she said she had never taken the time to be really grateful that she had such a wonderful son, and feared that she had taken too much for granted.

"If I could only have another chance to tell him how much

I love him and how grateful I am that he is my son," she said, and she began to cry. "Our family has never experienced anything like this. Everything has always gone smoothly. I got used to things being totally comfortable. I know I'm being punished for taking life for granted. I should have been more helpful to others and not stayed so involved in my own protected world."

"You aren't being punished," I said. "These things happen in life, and it's difficult to be prepared. You mustn't give up hope. Where there is life, there is always hope."

"Lee was always trying to help someone. He would even bring home stray cats and dogs. I wouldn't let him keep the animals, and he cried. I wish now that I had let him keep them."

Lee's father sat down beside us, his face gray and drawn. I could feel his pain. "I wish I were in that bed instead of my son." He took a deep breath and continued, "I have lived a good life, and he has a whole life in front of him. I was always so busy when Lee was a boy. He'd wait for me to come home from work—I can still see him running out to the car to say hello. He wanted me to attend his baseball games, but I always told him I was too busy at work. Even as a little fellow he tried to hide his disappointment and said he understood. I never told him how proud I was of him. Isn't it amazing that something like this has to happen to make us think about the things we should have done?"

I later found Lee's sister in the hospital chapel, kneeling in front of the altar. I knelt beside her and put my arms around her shoulders. She sobbed for a few minutes, and then as we rose to leave, she said, "I don't know how my parents will survive if my brother doesn't pull through. They always made me feel that Lee was the most important person in the family—you know, he was the only son and would carry on the family name. I love my brother, but I was a bit envious of him. He never did anything to make me feel that way; I just always thought my parents loved him more than me. There were times when I was very mean to him, and he couldn't understand what he had done to upset me. My parents always loved me, but I never thought it was enough. What am I going to do?" She started to cry again.

"If we had the benefit of retrospect, we would all do things differently," I said. "It's not unusual for us to feel competitive with our siblings, but you mustn't punish yourself. Learn from this and go forward."

A few days later I received a phone call from Lee's sister. He had come out of the coma, and it looked as though with therapy he would eventually be all right. The doctors weren't certain that he would be able to walk, but their outlook was quite optimistic. Lee smiled at his family, whispered that he was happy to see everyone, and thanked them for being there. He asked where his girlfriend was and if she was all right.

Lee's mother thanked me for my support and told me, "As soon as Lee is better, I'm going to do more to help others. I'll start by giving some time each week to help people. I was a teacher before I got married, and I think I could help others to learn to read and write. I'm so grateful my son has survived that I don't think anything will ever really upset me again. I feel as if I have been reborn!"

In time, Lee was able to walk. He still has a slight limp, but he says this just reminds him how lucky he was. The family has been doing a great deal to help others. Lee's father spends more time with his family and has also given a great deal of money and time to an organization that helps to educate underprivileged children.

Rita has an inheritance that allows her not to work. She is good looking and has an excellent figure she can maintain without dieting. Her main form of exercise is going from Saks Fifth Avenue to Bergdorf Goodman to shop, but Rita chronically complains. She seems to have no trouble attracting men, probably because she is bright and has a witty side that some people find amusing. It seems she wanted to see me as some form of entertainment, but she found the session less than amusing and spent a great deal of the time with me fussing with her fingernails, quite distressed that she had broken one.

She was like a character in a novel—the spoiled rich girl who looks at life as one long series of parties. Everything about her was chic: the clothes she was wearing, her hairstyle, her address. She told me, though, that she was "bored, bored, bored!" While she didn't feel like traipsing off to Europe, she felt the need to get away. She hated to go to the south of France out of season, and Italy had become just too "common" these days. She complained about the drabness and lack of charm of the city, and no man she met was interesting enough to keep her entertained. She had been bored at every party of the season and just could not deal with the stupidity of her friends. I thought, How could a person like this have any friends?

I found myself fascinated by her, though. Certainly she aroused my curiosity. "What do you think I can do for you?" I asked.

"I want you to tell me about my future," she replied. "Isn't that what you're supposed to do? I want to be astonished by your ability to know things about me without my telling you anything."

"Rita, this isn't a parlor game," I said. "I'm too busy to waste my time trying to pull rabbits out of a hat for your entertainment."

She seemed stunned. "Well, darling, I didn't mean to ruffle your feathers, but I needed something new and different and I thought you could supply that for me."

I suggested that a better cure for her boredom would be for her to use some of her abundant wealth and time in trying to help others. "Why should I do that? This is America. Can't people help themselves?"

Now it was my turn to be stunned. Her blindness to the suffering around her left me speechless as she went on complaining about everything and wondering why people were so stupid and lacked "class." She perceived herself as more intelligent than anyone else. She thought her parents were stupid, her neighbors were low-class, and her friends were becoming tiresome. I asked her if she ever read. "No one is writing anything worth reading" was her reply.

"Rita," I said as the session neared its end, "you must realize that this one life you are living is only a drop of water in the sea of eternity. If you don't wake up and try to do something for someone else, you will have a very unhappy time in your next life. If you don't stop complaining and learn to have a bit of gratitude, you will be incarnated in your next life with nothing. How can you live with yourself? You do nothing but go on and on about how awful everything is and how boring all people are. If you would stop and take a good look at yourself and the emptiness of your life, you might become at least a little frightened. Wake up before it's too late! You have been given everything, and the only lesson you've learned is that the planet owes all this to you. I've never met anyone so self-consumed."

I stopped, feeling that I might have gone a bit too far. I only hoped the shock treatment might wake her up a bit.

But Rita just batted her eyelashes and sighed. "Well, I had better be off. I want to get to Saks before closing. I need some night cream." She got up and said it had been marvelous to meet me. I could just as well have been talking to my refrigerator, I thought. I'd as much as told her that her life was a worthless wasteland, and she'd shown no reaction at all! As she left she complimented me on my "homey" apartment.

Feeling only relief, I closed the door behind her and started to laugh. You can't reach everyone. Ultimately, people have to decide for themselves how to live their lives. I could only do my best. Rita must enjoy this state of negativity, or she would do something to change. She might be shocked when she leaves the physical world and finds out that there is no Saks Fifth Avenue on the other side. It is likely that on this side she will continue living with this negative, bored attitude. Maybe something will happen to jar her awake, but she could well go on living the rest of her life as she has been.

I was completely surprised a few months later when Rita called to make another appointment with me.

"Why do you want to see me again, Rita?" I asked. "I don't feel there is anything I can do for you."

"Oh, I just felt that it was time for another checkup," she said.

"Rita," I said, "I'm not your dentist."

As usual she was unfazed and just pressed on: "Well, darling, I have thought about the things you told me, and I think your idea of trying to be grateful is rather interesting. I don't really understand it, but I thought we might chat about it again if you could find a little time for me."

I hesitated for a moment, wondering whether there would be any point to another session, but I gave her an appointment.

She arrived at the scheduled time, loaded with shopping bags and out of breath. "I hope I'm not late," she said. "I was having lunch with my girlfriend, and she was so newsy that the time just sped by."

"Did you have a nice lunch?" I asked.

"The food was positively dreadful," she replied. "And the atmosphere! My dear, I thought I had lost my way and ended up in a greasy spoon. You just cannot get good service anymore!"

I thought this would be a very long hour as Rita chatted on and on, not giving me much of an opportunity to say anything.

Finally I managed to interject a question: "You said on the phone that you wanted to hear more about the subject of gratitude."

"Yes, I do. I've never heard anyone speak about it in the way you did. Is it part of a new type of psychology?"

Trying to conceal my astonishment, I said, "Haven't you ever been thankful for anything?"

"Of course," she laughed. "Thanking people is a sign of proper breeding."

"That's not exactly what I meant," I said. "Have you ever felt grateful for all the good things you've been given in your life?"

She looked at me blankly, as though this was an alien concept to her. I'd actually managed to say something to which she had no reply. I used the opportunity to explain to her that all of the advantages she enjoyed and took for granted—her appearance, her health, her material possessions, her family and friends—were really great gifts, and she should be deeply grateful for all of these things and more.

I could see that she still didn't understand, so I suggested she try the exercise I had given Tara and make a list of everything positive in her life.

Her face lit up, and I thought for a moment I'd made a connection, that at last she understood. But then she began to babble excitedly about what a wonderful idea this was for a new party game: a kind of scavenger hunt in which everyone would be required to compile a list of this sort, and the person who composed the longest list of things to be grateful for, in the shortest time, would be the winner.

I started to object, but then I thought, Who knows, maybe one guest at the party would learn something from this; if so, it would be worthwhile.

Leaving at the end of the session, she thanked me for coming up with an idea that she thought would be the "new rage." Wouldn't it be wonderful, I thought, if that were so—if gratitude became "the new rage"? Certainly it would help to make the planet a happier place.

Simple Gifts

Think about the people who are involved in your life and be grateful for these people: the mailman who brings your letters, the janitor of your building, the counterman who pours your coffee at the diner. None of these people or the services they perform should be taken for granted.

Simple actions can show your gratitude. Pick up the discarded wrapper that is lying at your feet. If everyone did this instead of leaving it for the next person, we would have a much cleaner environment. Just reach down and do this small act. We all have very short memories! This is a tragedy. We forget the kindnesses shown us in times of need. We forget the things our parents did for us and remember all the ways in which we feel they neglected us. We forgot the good times that we had with a former lover and remember only the heartbreak. If you have never gone hungry, you probably have not felt the gratitude of a starving person upon receiving a meal. If you have always had plenty of money, you have not experienced the relief of having all your debts cleared.

Why is it that many people who have little or nothing seem so grateful for everything? If your life is going well, that is wonderful, but don't become one of those people who forget others whose paths are not so smooth.

Carole was hysterical because she felt that her whole world was coming apart. She had lost her largest account at the advertising firm where she worked and was on probation. Her boyfriend had left her for another woman, and she had broken her foot while running to catch a bus for work. I felt that her boyfriend had done her a favor; he was lazy and had been quite abusive to Carole. She had never been happy with him but had been afraid to end the relationship. I tried to joke with her, feeling that this might help to lighten her mood, but she didn't see humor in anything. Certainly, things were bad, but they would not stay that way. In any case, she still had a job, and there are worse things one can break than a foot. When one is worried and in pain, it's difficult to see the positive side of things, but it's good to try to do so. I told Carole I would be there if she needed me.

Time passed and things did turn around for her. She was able to secure an even better account than the one she had lost, and her job was once again secure. While Carole was at the doctor's office, having her foot examined, she met a wonderful man. Her foot healed nicely, and one would never know it had been broken. When she told me all this, I said, "Isn't it amazing, Carole, how things have gotten better for you?"

"Yes, they are better," she said, "but they're still not perfect."

"But a month ago, Carole, you were in despair, and now things are flowing in a positive direction," I said.

"I wasn't *that* upset!" she exclaimed.

Carole had better wake up, I thought, or she will attract a whole new set of problems. "Aren't you grateful now that your boyfriend left you?" I asked. "Just think—if he hadn't, you probably wouldn't be dating such a fine man."

She didn't comment on this but just went on complaining about the imperfections in her life. I repeated that she should be more grateful and stop complaining. Couldn't she see the banquet that had been placed before her? Couldn't she remember how distressed she was one month ago?

"You're right—I do have a short memory. Things are really going well now. I should take more time to be happy about my life. I guess I have a tendency to become too self-absorbed. By the way, how are you doing?"

"Just fine," I replied, smiling a bit. Carole was obviously feeling a little guilty about being so self-absorbed. My intent was not to make her feel guilty; I was merely trying to help her become more aware of the goodness surrounding her. If we are able to feel real gratitude, we will not do things out of guilt. Guilt is not a proper motivation because it has its basis in selfishness. If you act from guilt, you are once again thinking about yourself. You are not acting selflessly but only to assuage your own feelings of guilt. This is very important for us to realize; too many of our actions are motivated by guilt.

The Gift of Talent

It has been my privilege to meet many extraordinarily talented people—artists, dancers, actors, and musicians—who have worked very hard to perfect their craft. Unfortunately, many such people take their talent for granted, forgetting that it is a sacred gift for which they should be constantly grateful. Great artists are

the means of bringing beauty into the world. It takes many incarnations to perfect any art, and the artist does nothing alone.
Artistic work is inspired by souls who have passed over to the
other side. Artists who understand this don't feel the kind of
intense pressure so many artists do. Their brilliance does not
begin or end with them; it is a gift to them in order to serve
others.

A well-known and quite successful writer came to see me. He
was afraid that one day he would no longer be able to produce,
and this feeling caused him to be in a constant state of anxiety.
He published his first novel when he was seventeen and had not
had a failure since then. I explained to him that he was not writing
alone, that he was merely a vehicle for the work that came
through him. "Don't you see the great gift you've been given?"
I asked. "If you can be truly grateful for being allowed to write,
you will never be burdened with this fear. You will be too involved
with serving others through your work to spend any time worrying
about yourself. You were able to write so well at such an early age
because you were incarnated with this gift. It's clear that you have
had other lives as a writer; such a gift as yours is never acquired
in a single lifetime. I don't mean to be overly metaphysical about
it, but there's much to be learned by understanding the nature
of a gift such as yours. You've worked very hard and served many
people through your talent. Don't allow yourself to become too
involved with your own ego. If you keep thinking it is all you
instead of being thankful for the gift, you will never have a
moment of inner calm."

He began to cry and said, "I've always felt the presence of
something larger than myself in my work. Sometimes, when I've
finished writing for the day, I don't remember having written the
pages in front of me. It is as if something takes over and writes
through me. I never really thought there was anything remarkable
about this; I just became used to it. Is it really possible to learn
to think in a totally new way? It seems so difficult."

"It really isn't," I told him. "Take time each day just to feel
gratitude. It can be five minutes or five seconds, but just be sure

you do it every day. When you sit down at your typewriter, before you start writing, take a moment to become calm and say a word to yourself that shows you are thankful for all you have been given. Then proceed with your writing. When feelings of anxiety start to take over, replace these thoughts with thoughts of gratitude. It won't happen overnight, but in time you will be amazed at the change within you. Your anxiety and self-doubt will diminish and finally disappear. Realize that you are greatly blessed with the talent you have been given, and treat your gift with dignity and respect."

I paused. He nodded slowly and thoughtfully, and left the session in a reflective mood. When I heard from him two weeks later, he told me he had been consciously working on changing his point of view and thanked me for my insights. He sounded quite calm and seemed thrilled with the progress he was making with his new novel. I knew that his best writing was yet to come!

Marcie called to tell me that she had just earned a part in a Broadway play. She had been auditioning for seven years, and this was her first big break. She would finally be able to quit her job waiting tables and work as a full-time actress. She was ecstatic, and I was thrilled for her. When I had first met her five years before, she was working very hard, acting for little or no pay, and like many other actors, earning her living at any kind of job she could find. But she never complained. She always remained confident that one day she would be a working actress. Marcie had loved the theater all her life and had a university degree in theater arts. She was always very happy when a friend of hers got a professional job, and never once did I know her to be envious of another's good fortune. She used to say to me, "I have been given talent, and I would like to use it to entertain people. I always feel so happy when people tell me that they enjoyed a performance of mine. I just feel good that I was able to make someone happy." She understood innately that she had been given talent and that this talent was to be used to help others. Her attitude allowed her to live each day to its fullest and keep on going no matter how many disappointments she experienced, secure in the knowledge that when she was to have a part, it would come to her. She said that she always did her best and knew that she could do no more.

If more performers viewed their work as Marcie did, they would be much happier. It's not an uncommon experience in New York City to be treated in a rude, surly manner by an actor or dancer working as a waiter in a restaurant in order to make ends meet. Such people may be taking out their frustration, disappointment, and feelings of rejection on the easiest available target, entirely forgetting how fortunate they are to have a job that keeps them fed and housed while allowing them to study and audition. If you are in such a position, remember that if you are to have work in your chosen field, it will come to you. Meanwhile, keep yourself in the vibration of your work by studying, auditioning, and doing the best you can in *all* aspects of your life, including the day-to-day job that provides for your basic needs.

Many times I have heard complaints such as the following: "I don't understand. My friend arrived in town, and three days later she landed a role in film. It's not fair! I've been auditioning for two years and haven't gotten anything."

My reply is always the same: "Your friend earned this part, or it would not have come to her. It's a matter of karma. It takes many incarnations to perfect any art. You can't know how many lifetimes your friend has been polishing her craft. Be grateful for the talent *you* have been given and don't worry about the success of others. It's foolish and dangerous to judge your life against anyone else's; you will only poison yourself with jealousy. All that you have earned will come to you. How does it serve you to spend your time being angry and envious? Let go of your anger and work on your craft. Enjoy your work and don't worry about the result. Just keep working because you have been given talent and are thankful for the gift!"

There's no such thing as perfection in this world. We can always do better. The quest for perfection can only cause us anxiety. All we can do is our best, and we should be grateful for the opportunity to be creative and serve others through our gift. Success by another's standards is unimportant. If you are to be successful in the material sense, this will happen. But real success, lasting success, is reflected only in a happy, fulfilling life—a life of service!

Jerry had been extremely poor as a child. He tells stories of reinforcing his shoes with cardboard because the soles were worn out and his parents could not afford to buy him another pair. He remembers the time he was given a new suit to wear to a school function; it was the first time he had any clothes that weren't hand-me-downs from his older brother, and he treated the suit as if it were a precious treasure. Now a very successful businessman, he has not forgotten his childhood. He is a generous man who is always doing something to help those who are less fortunate. He has taken great care of his parents and is very kind to the people who work for him. He lives with gratitude and, looking around at all that he has, feels blessed. He takes nothing for granted. He has worked hard for what he has but knows that many others have worked just as hard without achieving the same material success. "I know I've been very lucky," he says. "I only hope I can continue doing things to show my gratitude." He is very quiet about the ways in which he helps and never looks for reward. Often he does things anonymously.

Lenny, too, was a poor child, but now he is totally miserable. He puts all his money in the bank and makes his family beg for things. He lives in constant fear that he might be poor again. He is not having any fun with his success. He is also not helping anyone. Lenny has no gratitude for what he has been given. When his daughter became ill, he did not want to pay for her to see a doctor; his wife had to force him to take the girl to the hospital, where the doctor who examined her said that if they had waited any longer, the girl would have died. One would think this would have awakened him, but he continues to be the same miserly person.

Lenny's wife is a lovely, patient woman who tries hard to understand her husband's fear and continues to hope that one day he will change. Lenny, of course, doesn't see how fortunate he is in having her at his side. Like everything else in his life, he takes her for granted. Unfortunately, her patience and forbearance, while they seem admirable, support him in his selfish, oblivious behavior. She will disagree with him openly only when things get so bad that it is almost too late, as in the case of their daughter's illness. She would serve herself and her family far better by taking a firmer stand with him. Lenny has no reason to change when everyone around him continues to accept his behavior. If you find yourself living in a situation that you know is wrong, it is your responsibility to take some corrective measures. The actions you take need not be large; enough small actions over time can work real change. There's great truth in the ancient Chinese saying, "A journey of a thousand miles begins with a single step."

Molly lived with a man who physically abused her. She had very low self-esteem and felt that she deserved this ill treatment. As in many such cases, her mate was inconsistent in his behavior; one day he would be abusive, and the next he would be tender and loving, full of regrets and apologies for having hurt her. Time and time again Molly fooled herself into thinking that he had changed. Her friends constantly begged her to seek professional help.

After years of this treatment, Molly one day entered a hospital emergency room, her nose broken and one eye swollen shut. Here, by great good fortune, she finally received the help she needed. The nurse who attended her had also been an abused woman; she talked to Molly for a long time and took her home with her that night. The next morning she arranged for Molly to join a support group. It took a great deal of hard work and courage, but Molly was finally able to end her abusive relationship. She is very grateful she is no longer a prisoner and has helped to organize shelters and support groups for other abused women. Molly has never forgotten the help she received that night in the hospital; she feels that she was given a whole new life. She is never too busy or too tired to give aid to women in need, and it is through this work that she expresses her profound gratitude.

When I met her, I was deeply impressed by her dedication to a life of service. "I wake up every day full of energy, and I feel terrific!" she told me. "I only hope I can continue to help others. Nothing else is important. When I remember the way my life used to be and see the way it is now, I'm overwhelmed with happiness. My one desire is to show other women that they too can be this happy."

I received an invitation from Laura to have lunch at her home. She called one morning, sounding quite excited. She reported that she had started taking my advice to work on her music, only thirty minutes a day. At first this had been very difficult for her, but she had persevered; soon it had become easier, and she had actually begun to enjoy playing the piano again. Laura had been talking to a therapist about the feelings that had kept her from being able to work on her music. She was finally able to forgive her father, and she felt good about that. It was still difficult for her to think about Brian without crying, but she was at peace with the thought that he was fine on the other side. She was able to attend concerts and felt that soon she would be strong enough to perform publicly. I told her I would be delighted to have lunch with her and that I was pleased to hear she was doing so well. "I'm very grateful to have my sanity," she said. "There were times when I felt as if I had lost my mind. The pain was too much to bear. I now see that I'm all right, and I feel very happy about that. I realize that I have been given a great gift, and I intend to go forward and serve through it."

When I arrived at her home, I was thrilled to see that Lawrence was there. Laura laughed and said she had wanted to surprise me, so she hadn't mentioned him. She looked lovely, possessing a quiet elegance, an Old World charm. We all talked for a few minutes, and then Laura said she had something to share with us. She went to the piano and started to play. Lawrence turned his head toward me and smiled. He closed his eyes. Feeling moved almost to tears, I sat quietly and listened. Laura played with brilliance and total concentration. Her hands danced over the keys, and I was transported to a very special place. Here was a woman who, a short time ago, had been in such total despair that it seemed impossible she would ever be able to play the piano again. Now this lovely creature played with heart and soul. After finishing the piece, she sat quietly for a moment at the piano. When she turned to us, I saw that she too had tears in her eyes. She leaned over the piano and cried silently. I stood and went to her, putting my arms around her slight body. "I'm so grateful, so very grateful," she kept repeating. "It's as if I had been in a dark tunnel, and the light finally came through. I know now that I have been given a job to do, and I intend to do my best to prove myself worthy."

Lawrence said, "Often a person who is given great talent will be tested. Laura, you have shown that you have great character as well as great talent. You have suffered much, but through this suffering you have become spiritually stronger, an even finer vehicle for the talent that flows through you. Remember always that you are not alone. All of the adversity that has been given to you is part of your karmic destiny. Your music will be heard all over the world, and you will give great happiness to many people. It is indeed a great privilege to have helped you. Many people are given great talent, but the important thing is what they do with it. With gratitude for your gift and service as your goal, you can transcend any personal pain. You have worked hard and diligently to release the fear that was paralyzing you. 'Many are called, but few are chosen,' the Bible says. You have been chosen to help through your talent; you have chosen to do so. I am humbled by your gift."

Lawrence took Laura's hand and smiled at her. "This is a wonderful day," he said. "A day to be grateful for."

∴ XI ∴
Service

The central message of this book, one that it is impossible to repeat too many times, is that love in action *is* service. It is a message that has been delivered by every spiritual teacher through the ages. The way the concept is taught may vary, but the message is clearly the same: If you can learn to live your life as a constant prayer of service, you will never be truly unhappy. If service is your unwavering goal, you will be free from the burden of desire for self-gratification. Service, in that sense, is freedom from yourself.

Do Your Best!

You are given the privilege to serve in all aspects of your life. Your work is service. You may think that to be in a service profession you must be a priest or a rabbi or a yogi, but in fact, all work should be service. If you are waiting tables, driving a bus, sweeping floors, or writing for a magazine, you are serving. Ambition to "get ahead" in your profession or to be "the best" at what you do will interfere with your ability to do this. If you are doing a job halfheartedly, you will never feel a sense of well-being, but if your motivation is to give your best, you will find joy in your work. You won't be concerned with recognition or fame; you will be too busy doing the best you can, whatever the job at hand.

Each of us is incarnated with different abilities. We are not all writers, painters, or great scientists. Each of us has his or her own tools to be used in the service of humanity. It does not matter *what* you are doing; it matters only that you are doing it *in order to help.* This is service. Service is love.

Many people say they feel useless and not needed, that they would like to be doing more. If you are busy doing the best you possibly can, you will not have time to think about your needs. The desire to feel needed is selfish because it is another form of self-gratification. Just do your best!

If you are meant to do more, the means to do more will be presented to you. Does this sound too simple? We have been programmed to think we must actively go after the things we feel we need. This is not true; the things we need will be given to us if we can simply *be* where we are *at this moment.*

Work takes up a great deal of our time. How sad to go through life hating what we do. Many people are unhappy each morning of their work life because they hate their jobs. They just go through their day waiting for the clock to strike so that they can go home. If you are doing your job because it is your service, you will not feel as though you have to drag yourself through the day. If you stop thinking about yourself and start thinking about how you may help, you will have a great deal of energy. Haven't you known people who love their jobs? Such people always seem to have abundant energy. We are all capable of feeling this way.

Take pride in what you do! If you don't like your job, examine this. Is it because you need to find a different occupation or is it because you are not thinking of what you can do to help someone else? If you are not in the right profession, so be it. Until you are able to make a change, do the best you can at your present job. Don't spread your negativity to those who work with you; this will make the environment intolerable for everyone.

I enjoy going to my neighborhood grocery store. Grocery shopping is not usually an enjoyable thing to do; the lines are too long, and everyone in the store is usually in a bad mood. But the checkers at my neighborhood store are special. They seem to get along together, and they keep each other's spirits up. If you have a question about something, they take time to help you. The young men who stock the shelves always seem pleased to get something for you if you can't reach it. The attitude throughout the store is one of service. This is how it should be, of course, but how rare it is that people work in such a positive way! It makes one's whole shopping trip pleasant.

I'm sure these people aren't paid a high wage, but they don't seem to be angry or hostile about it, and they don't project negativity on their customers.

It's unfortunate that we find it surprising when people are pleasant in this type of situation. We have become used to rudeness, so we are surprised by kindness! If you are doing a job, *do* it. Don't inflict your unhappiness on others. Think about how the other person feels, and you will not be spending your time dwelling on your unhappiness. Your unhappiness will vanish when you are busy serving!

Hospitals are notorious for their surly, unhelpful, negative personnel. This is not always the case, but all too often it is. No one wants to be in a hospital; it is a frightening place. I was visiting a friend in the hospital, and my friend had a nurse who was lovely. She cheered up the room every time she entered it. Because my friend was hospitalized for several weeks, I got to know this wonderful woman whom I will call Jean. One day I said, "Jean, you're terrific, you make everyone feel well cared for."

"I just wish I could do more for them," she answered. "I think about how I would feel if I were in their place, and I act toward them as I would like to be treated. I love my job. It's wonderful to be able to help. Sometimes I feel a bit blue because these people are having such trouble, but I don't let myself dwell on it, I just go on and do the best I can to make them feel better."

A kind word or gesture makes all the difference in the world to someone who is ill. And it is so easy! It's much more difficult to be negative than it is to be kind. Negativity uses a great deal of energy and unbalances one's entire body and mind. The flow of energy through your body is smooth if you are acting in a kindly fashion. Notice the vibration that surrounds a person who is sending out positive energy. You just feel good to be around such a person.

You can serve through any action. In a marriage you can serve your mate. If you have children, you are constantly given the opportunity to serve. In a happy family each member should be concerned with the needs of the other members. If this were true of all families, there would be much less strife in the world.

Some people actually seem to feel that being selfless will somehow make them less of a person. Just talk to people about service and selflessness, and listen to some of the reactions: "What about me?" "What will happen to me if I do not take care of myself?"

Well, what *about* you?

People who came of age in the seventies and eighties have been labeled the "me" generation, and self-centeredness has been marketed as a virtue. Someone should publish a magazine called *Selfless*. I wonder if it would sell. Think of it—a complete magazine full of articles about ways to serve others! Some of the articles could be titled "Exercise Your Desire to Be Selfless"; "The Diet Revelation: Stop Thinking about Yourself"; "Walk Your Way to Your Volunteer Job"; "Eat Less, Serve More."

How did we become so self-consumed? It is a bad habit that we must break if we want to live a happier, more productive life. Replace thoughts of yourself with the desire to do something for someone else. Breathe a sigh of relief. It is tiring to be self-consumed and energizing to think of ways to help others. Your whole nervous system will relax when you are not constantly thinking of all the things that are wrong with your life. Think for a moment: Aren't you happy and balanced when you are concerned with the needs of another? Aren't you constantly in a tizzy when you are consumed with your own desires?

Consideration

One day a client came in who had just broken up with her lover of four years. Going on and on about how terrible the relationship had been, she kept repeating, "I did everything for him, and he did nothing for me." She said that now she was going to think about herself for a change; she'd had enough of thinking about others. "All I did was think about him all the time. Now it's my turn." I asked her why she stayed with him so long if she was so unhappy.

"Well," she said, "he had a rent-stabilized apartment in a good, safe neighborhood. I just didn't want to move into some dive that would cost me a fortune! Apartments are really hard to find."

"Hold on," I said. "You stayed in the situation because of his *apartment?* Isn't that a bit selfish?"

She took a moment to think about that. Then she said quietly, "I never looked at it that way."

"Well, think about it," I said. "You were living with him because he had something *you* wanted. You've just gone on and on about how unhappy you were. If you were so miserable, do you think your boyfriend could possibly have been happy in the relationship?"

"I did love him, in my way," she said. "It was just that it seemed everything always had to be the way he wanted. Whenever I let him know that I needed something from him, maybe just a little attention, he became quiet and started to watch TV or sat in front of his computer."

"Then what did you do?" I asked.

"I became upset and called my mother."

"What did your mother usually say?" I asked.

"Oh, not much. My mother has never understood me, either. She usually started telling me about my sister, who is married, and then I would feel frustrated because I am still single and living in a situation that is less than perfect. I would also feel angry that my mother wasn't thinking about me. I needed to talk to her; I didn't want to hear about my sister. I always felt that my mother liked my sister better."

"Why did you call your mother if you knew her response wouldn't be helpful?"

"She's my mother. Aren't you supposed to call your mother when you want to complain?"

"That depends on whether you have a mother who is capable of handling your dilemma. If you aren't expecting a certain reaction from someone, you won't be disappointed when you don't get it. Possibly you should have sought help from a professional counselor. You were locked in a situation you couldn't release yourself from easily. It's not necessary to keep yourself in this type of relationship. You didn't seem to understand his point of view. If the two of you had more understanding for each other, you wouldn't have been so unfulfilled. If he was thinking about you and your feelings and you were doing the same for him, there would have been a lot more harmony and a lot less anger. When you call your mother, do you think about how she is feeling and what you can do for her? Or do you think only about what she can do for you?" I stopped to let this sink in.

The room was quiet as she thought over my question. Then she said, "I thought I was not being good to myself if I was always doing something for someone else. Now I see that maybe I was a bit selfish in my behavior."

"That's good," I said, "but don't berate yourself for what's past, just work on changing your viewpoint. It will serve you well as you enter into a new relationship."

∙ ∙ ∙

Being of service does not imply losing one's own identity. On the contrary, one's spiritual identity becomes stronger, and one's desire for self-gratification diminishes. It is rather glorious. A life uncluttered by thoughts of the imperfection of things is a life that is fulfilled! This does not mean you should stay in a relationship that is damaging. Examine it carefully, with an eye toward determining what is needed. If, having done this, you decide that what is needed is for you to leave the relationship, do so. This decision may take some time. If it does, try to treat your partner in the relationship with kindness and consideration; there is no need to make someone else miserable while you are arriving at your decision. Remember, every experience is presented to us so that we may learn from it. This includes all of our relationships. However negative we may feel toward our partner in a relationship, that person has been an instrument for our own learning, as we have been an instrument for his or hers, and for that reason each partner is deserving of the other's gratitude.

Always think of how you are affecting another person by your actions or reactions. This is an important aspect of service! Once again, do not think that you are less of a person because you are not shouting your needs from the rooftops! We have become too used to indulging our "feelings," doing and saying anything we feel like and not considering how this may be hurting another person. To thine own self be true indeed, but please think before you act. Think of the way you are projecting your feelings to the rest of the world. Think of how you may help another by conducting yourself properly in any given situation. Yes, we need to be able to express our feelings to others, but we should never forget good manners no matter how upset we may be. Think about the needs of those around you when you are upset. How are they feeling? Are you affecting someone else with your discomfort? These guidelines will help you deal with your emotions without disrupting all those who come in contact with you.

This is not to say one should suppress one's feelings, for that will cause reactions from the subconscious; feelings must be acknowledged and often expressed, but always with consideration for others. There is a kind way to perform any action. Every action is important. No action is more important than another in terms of the care that one should take in performing it. Something worth doing is worth doing well, whether the action is large or small.

A waitress in my neighborhood coffee shop, Millie, is always chipper and makes one feel comfortable and at home. All the regular customers are happy to see her; she knows all their names and occupations, and remembers what they usually order. No matter how hectic the shop becomes, Millie has a pleasant disposition, and her attitude is infectious. If there is edible food left over at the end of the day, she gives it to the homeless people. Far from leading a carefree life, Millie works hard to support a daughter, and her legs cause her some pain and make her work difficult at times. But she takes pleasure in her work, and it is enjoyable to be served by her.

Lila is a receptionist at a doctor's office. If you call with a problem, she listens to what you have to say and makes you feel that the problem is being handled. The office is always busy, but Lila never seems rushed or impatient. If the doctor is not available at the moment, Lila will call you back as soon as possible. No trouble seems too small for her to take time to give comfort, and she makes you feel as though you are in competent hands. She is very understanding and has a great sense of humor. It's obvious that Lila loves her job and truly loves to help people.

Gary, a psychotherapist, has enormous patience with all his clients. He is very caring but can be firm when necessary. His directness is refreshing. He is always thrilled when a client doesn't need his services any longer. He has told me that his greatest desire is for people to go on with their lives and use whatever insight he has given them. He leaves the door open for his patients to return if they ever feel the need, but he lets them go without pressure. When he thinks someone is not ready to be without his support, he points this out in a way that allows the patient to make up his or her own mind. Because he knows that each patient's needs and personality are unique, he is capable of treating his patients as individuals and adjusting his approach accordingly.

Twice a week Gary gives his time to help teenagers who have drug problems. He receives no fee for this service and has opened his home to the teenagers as well, giving them a place where they can feel loved, understood, and useful; if they are going to have dinner at his place, everyone pitches in to help with the preparations. He gets them involved in games and sports, and shows them the joy of being drug-free and the peace that comes with helping others through one's good example. He is making a great difference in their lives.

Your help is needed wherever you turn. Give your time to a church or a hospital. One hour a week will make a big difference. No help goes unused. No time given to someone else is too short. If we all work together, much can be accomplished for the good of mankind. Never forget that each person on this planet is a spark of the Divine. Each individual is important. If you do whatever you can to make someone's life feel a little better, you will be living a life full of love in action.

Learning Selflessness

One afternoon, while walking through Greenwich Village, I went into a bookstore that specializes in antique books; it's something I love to do. While browsing through a shelf of books, I looked up and there was Lawrence. He pointed to a book I hadn't noticed and told me it might be of interest to me. He then asked if I would like to join him for coffee. I bought the book, and then we went to a corner cafe.

Lawrence was in his usual good spirits and asked how my work was going. I told him about my clients and about my progress with the book I was writing. Then I said, "Once again, you've shown up when a question was nagging at me." I took a sip of my coffee, then went on: "To many people, selflessness doesn't seem to come easily. We're all taught the Golden Rule as children, and people who behave selflessly are held up to us as ideals—Albert Schweitzer and Mother Teresa, for example. But that's the problem. Selflessness is presented as an attribute of extraordinary people, of saints, not as something we can practice in everyday life. In fact, what we see in everyday life is exactly the opposite— people concerned only with themselves, with heaping up as many material goods as they can and trampling anyone who gets in their way. And we're taught that ambition is a good thing, that it's important to 'get ahead in the world.' Since children and most adults are attracted to glamour and excitement, to the pretty things that material wealth can buy, the idea of selflessness is lost. I guess my question is, how do we learn to be selfless if we've never been taught it and it isn't apparently in our nature?"

Lawrence's calm, steady gaze had been fixed on me as I spoke. Now he looked away for a moment, as if in thought. When he turned back he said, "I think we have to ask what it *means* to be selfless. People often feel that selfless means giving up their rights. This may seem strange, but it's true. They feel that if they act in a selfless manner, they will somehow lose themselves or be taken advantage of. In fact, they have already lost themselves because they've lost their most important connection with the rest of mankind. Only through reestablishing that lost connection can people find their true selves, their spiritual selves once again.

"People must learn that we all have it within our power to be selfless, that selflessness isn't restricted to saints, that we don't have to give up all our worldly goods, that a selfless act is not necessarily a grand gesture—in fact, it is the small efforts of all of us that are important. We can start each day by thinking, What can I do to better the life of those I meet? What act of kindness am I being given the opportunity to perform? In what small way may I serve? It is not a gigantic undertaking; all we have to do is relax our grip on our own concerns and look around us!

"Do not confuse serving with interfering, however. Nothing

is more upsetting to others than trying to force your help on them. Don't dwell on how you feel in a certain situation; think about how those around you are feeling. If you are out of sorts, don't allow yourself to act in a negative manner. Be aware of how your mood is affecting those around you. This will help you as you learn to be of service to others. Selfish people live lives of self-imposed misery. Observe how many times each hour you use the word 'I.' You will probably be shocked by the self-absorption. It is a good exercise in self-discipline to observe your actions, reactions, and motivations. We seldom take time to observe ourselves. You were born in order to serve. It is your birthright to be of use to others. Strive to become selfless and discover the freedom this gives you. Live one moment at a time, and make it your *best* moment. Do your best with any situation that is presented. As you work to free yourself from yourself, your efforts will get better. This is evolution. It is an ongoing process from one life to the next. As in anything we undertake, we must exercise self-discipline if we are to achieve any degree of perfection. Enjoy the journey into a world of selflessness, a world that is truly blessed by your service!"

Death as a Part of Life

The waiter came by to refill our coffee cups. Lawrence got up and went over to another table to speak to a woman who was crying. I could not hear what was being said. I saw her listening intently, and then she took Lawrence's hand and held it. Her tears had stopped and she looked at peace. I waited to hear what he had to say.

"That woman lost her husband a few weeks ago. Pain can often be dissolved with understanding. A few words of comfort can be a great tonic to a grieving person. I explained to her that her husband was not really dead, that he had indeed gone on but she would see him again on the other side. Death is actually the easiest part of the life process to deal with if one is given a bit of insight. It takes so little to help another."

Lawrence is always totally aware of those around him. I learn as much by watching him as by listening to him. He is always serving, no matter where he is. His sensitivity is highly developed; he is a master of knowing when to say something, and how. Acutely aware of others' feelings, he never intrudes or interferes but simply does what is needed, tactfully and with great compassion. Some people help others because it gives them a feeling of power. That is always the wrong motivation and serves no one in the long run. We can learn a great deal through observation, as Lawrence has stressed. I feel that any time I spend with Lawrence is sacred.

My mind drifted toward my friend Kathy, whom I had recently visited in the hospital. I thought it would be good if Lawrence could speak to her; her death was imminent, and I felt he could be of service to her. As he often does, Lawrence seemed to read my thoughts.

He reached across the table and took my hand. "Your friend does not have much time left on the Earth plane. A remarkable woman, she has served others throughout her long illness. You, my child, have given her the tools to prepare her to go to the other side. What a privilege you have been given! Not often is one given the opportunity to help someone release the fear of passing over. Your friend has no fear whatsoever. Her fearlessness has helped all those who are suffering because of her illness to witness great courage and true spirituality. She has been a great educator for all those who have been honored to know her. I have sent her many loving thought patterns, to help support her through her illness. It would not be wise for me to visit her because my vibration would pull a great deal of force from her body and she needs all the strength she has left to help her make the transition from Earth to spirit. Just as it takes great energy to give life, it takes great energy to pass over. My vehicle is finely tuned, and my physical presence would not be helpful to your friend. You are doing her a great service, and I am pleased. I will continue to send loving thoughts toward her. This is how I can be of the greatest service in this particular case. She will go to her next life in perfect health because she has released the karma that caused her illness.

"Illness is often freeing, and we can learn a great deal through it. It is a blessing when one looks at it from the proper viewpoint. What an amazing way to serve! We learn much through an illness, and so many people are given the opportunity to serve and to grow through the pain of another. It is not as tragic as it may seem. The body finally ceases to struggle, and the spirit passes on freely to the next world. Pain is a willing servant when we allow it to serve and not destroy us. Growth is often preceded by pain. Pain calls our attention to something we need to know. If you broke your leg and felt no pain, you would probably lose your leg, for gangrene would set in. The purpose of pain is to alert us to problems. In this way it serves us well."

Pain

"Do not go through life trying to avoid any situation that causes you pain," Lawrence continued. "This will hamper your growth and interfere with your ability to be of service. Do not treat only the symptoms by taking a tonic to feel better. Examine the total problem, and the relief will be long-lasting instead of temporary. Treat pain as a teacher. We have all heard stories of people who lived better, more useful lives as a result of pain. To be released from pain—physical, emotional, or spiritual—should make us grateful. How easily we forget pain, once it has been removed. Mothers will tell you they forget the pain of childbirth once they hold the little soul in their arms; pain is a small price for the joy that comes with the birth of a child. The pain of separation from a loved one allows us to explore the goodness of feeling love and loving. This is, of course, different from masochism, the seeking of pain for sensual pleasure or as punishment for one's imagined transgressions. There are people who seem to enjoy the attention pain often brings. This is not using pain to serve but to avoid going forward, and it is counterproductive. Accept pain, for with pain comes great lessons. Release the pain through understanding and through thoughts of others. You will not be able to dwell on your pain if you are thinking of those around you. When you have physical pain, your body is telling you that you have something to look into. It serves us to find out from where pain stems.

"You serve the physical vehicle by taking proper care of it; you serve your emotional vehicle by observing what circumstances are causing you to feel discomfort. If you arc busy helping and serving with true love, your pain will often disappear easily and with little struggle. Remember, with true love one ceases to struggle. It is important to have compassion for those who are suffering, but this is different from pity, which places us above others. We must try to alleviate pain as we alleviate the problems it draws attention to; that is why we have doctors and healers. Understand that pain is not negative, and your response to others' pain and their problems should be compassionate, direct, clear, and unsentimental.

"The good doctor is direct and firm but not cruel. The good healer teaches that one must heal oneself in order to stay balanced. We can assist in the healing, but we cannot always fix things so that people are comfortable.

"Concentrate on how you may serve, even when you are in pain. Accept this experience as part of life. You need not repeat a painful experience in order to grow. Learn from it and understand. When people fear pain, they become very upset, but this shows that a person needs to grow. People frequently experience emotional pain when their desires are not being fulfilled, as in the case of so-called unrequited love. One feels that one has been rejected and that the pain of the rejection is unbearable. But isn't the thought of rejection selfish? You are thinking about your own desires and are experiencing pain because the one you desire is not fulfilling them. The God force within rejects no one. There is really no such thing as rejection. People are free to feel however they wish, and not everyone will feel the same as you do. This is not a tragedy but a test. Will you conduct yourself with spiritual development and character, or will you take off into a fantasy and destroy yourself over what you call a rejection? Will you aspire to be selfless and serve with dignity, allowing your loved one to be free as he or she chooses? Will you look at the emotional pain you feel and grow from it? Or will you choose to become hysterical and force the person you love to refuse to speak to you at all? This is a very common situation. Who among us has not felt unrequited love?

"Desire nothing but to be of service. Serve in all that you do. This includes your personal life. Do not expect—just serve! There are opportunities to serve at all times; you need not seek these opportunities, for they are right in front of you. Do not run from discomfort, for you will find no peace in constantly trying to avoid pain. Your peace will come through serving in any way that is presented to you."

Lawrence smiled and asked if I had any other questions. I answered that I didn't. I told him I felt that he had been very clear in his message and that it would be helpful. At that moment the woman with whom Lawrence had spoken earlier came to our table. She took Lawrence's hand and, with tears in her eyes, thanked him again. She told him that she was going to help a friend of hers who had also lost a mate recently. She said she felt that she had been given a purpose: to help others who had experienced the loss of a loved one, to comfort them as she had been comforted.

Lawrence spoke to her again for a few minutes, then she left. I told Lawrence I thought it was remarkable to witness a transformation of that depth in such a short time.

"A person who is ready is able to integrate information immediately," Lawrence said. "This dear woman was seeking help; that is why she was here today. She was able to listen to all I told her and to accept the information without fear or resistance. She wanted to be helped, so she was ready to hear. She did not challenge everything I said. Her higher self knew that what I was saying was true and was intended to help her. She is a remarkable woman and will do much good for those around her. It is a great privilege to help one with her character."

Lawrence told me that he had to leave because he had some

business to attend to. I told him I was grateful for this time with him. He asked for the check, but the owner of the restaurant just smiled and shook his head. We walked into the evening air.

My mind was buzzing as I walked home. At one point I looked at my watch and was startled to see that Lawrence and I had been together for almost three hours; it seemed like minutes.

My mind drifted to Kathy, lying in the hospital, close to passing over. Her family was constantly at her bedside. Everyone was heartbroken that here lay this remarkable woman from whose courage and sense of humor we had all benefited. Her mind had been affected by the cancer, and she was sleeping most of the time. When she was awake, she greeted us and made some little joke that would make everyone feel better for a moment. The last five years had been a time of great suffering for her, broken only by a few periods of remission, but during even the final stages of her life, she was serving all who came in contact with her. To my mind she was a heroine, and I feel greatly honored to have been able to help her through her illness; she helped me through her fine example.

Kathy was fascinated by the possibilities she saw in a combination of medicine and metaphysics. I knew it was likely that in her next life she would be granted the opportunity to explore this subject further. Her soul would retain the memories of all that she had been through in this life, and she would use these memories to serve others. During our discussions she had told me that she felt it was important to let people know how frightened she had been when she first fell ill. Education had released her fear. I often received phone calls from her in the early hours of the morning. Kathy would be having a sleepless night, and she knew that I was always awake very late. We discussed life after death, and she asked questions about life on the other side. She talked about her fears and felt better when she was able to face them and fight to free herself from them. She had been a very willing student, using books to aid her in her quest for understanding. The Bible as well as books on metaphysical subjects—such as Manly Palmer Hall's book *Questions and Answers: Fundamentals of the Esoteric Sciences* (Los Angeles, California: Philosophical Research Society)—were a great support for her.

Her example was a great teacher, and people were fascinated that she could deal with all she faced. Friends of hers called me to ask whether she was really all right or was only pretending to be. People always have a difficult time understanding how someone can be so peaceful while confronting a personal life-or-death situation. I told them she was acting just as she felt. "Observe her, and you will learn a great deal" was my message to these people.

Kathy worried about the depression she saw in many who came to visit her. "Mary, how can I comfort these people?" she asked me once.

"Just keep doing what you're doing, and your example will serve to help everyone," I told her.

"But why do people expect me to be frightened and depressed? I am not at all! If they only understood my beliefs in life after death and reincarnation, they would see there is nothing to fear."

"People fear the unknown," I said. "They can't imagine how they would handle an illness such as yours. They project their own fear and find it difficult to accept that anyone in your position could be as fearless as you are. Look at it this way: You're really helping these people, and that's a great privilege."

She always smiled when she heard that she was helping. "I wish I could do more, but sometimes I get so tired," she said.

You've earned the right to be tired, I thought.

Most of my clients never met Kathy, but I've told them of her great courage. They called me to ask how she was doing. Many wanted to know what they could do to help her. They remarked how her courage made them feel grateful for their own good health. She was serving even those she had never met!

I laughed as I thought of the way she was always using jargon from the 1960s, especially the words "groovy" and "cool." Once in a while as she lay dying she became conscious and whispered that something was "cool." When I had good news to share with her, she said, "Mary, that's the greatest." All I could think was that Kathy was "the greatest."

I found myself in front of my apartment building. I had been so lost in thought, I did not remember walking home. Reaching the front door of my apartment, I hurried to answer the ringing phone.

The female voice on the line sounded cheerful. It was the client I mentioned earlier who stayed in her relationship with her lover because of his rent-stabilized apartment. She informed me that she was doing well and had a long conversation with her ex-beau. She felt they were at peace with each other. She had found a small studio apartment to live in; it was more expensive than she would have liked, but she felt she could handle the rent. She also told me that she had surprised her mother with a call. She now felt able to accept her mother and not expect anything in return, which was an enormous positive step for her.

I said I was proud of her and was happy that she was able to be so mature and selfless. It was a wonderful beginning for her. Great changes often take a great deal of time, but she was doing just fine for now. Now is the important thing, just do your best for now!

The phone rang again a few minutes later. It was Gary, the therapist. He wanted to know how Kathy was doing and if I needed anything. Gary is always asking if there is something he can do. I reported on Kathy and thanked him for his concern. He told me a few humorous tales about the kids he was working with. He is so proud of his teenagers and their success at overcoming their drug problems. He told me to call if I needed him for anything and said he wanted me to know he was always available, no matter what time of day or night. We finished our conversation and agreed to talk the following day.

I suddenly felt very tired and lay down on the couch to rest. I drifted off into a reverie, my mind touching on past events in my own life. I thought about Lawrence, Kathy, and many of the other advanced souls I had known through the years, stretching all the way back to my early childhood.

Brought up by my grandmother, I was taught the importance of independence and was grateful to her for that. My childhood was difficult, but my grandmother did not allow me to dwell on the difficulties. Instead, she inspired me to go forward and deal with problems as they arose. There were times when I thought she was too stern, but these were balanced by her great love, which she was always showing through her patience and concern. Lawrence also seems stern sometimes, stressing as he does the need for self-discipline, but he is never harsh or judgmental. He and many others have shown me the value of tools I was given to work with in this life. Each of us has tools, and it is our responsibility to use them well and keep them polished and cared for.

I wondered how Jesus felt when he tried to teach people to live a life of service. He wanted his followers to let go of the physical world and reach toward their spiritual selves. He was the ultimate storyteller, using parables as instructional devices, as pointers to the spiritual life. As a child I was fascinated by these stories; as an adult I have found them more beautiful and instructive.

The message of all great teachers through the ages has been the same: To serve is the only reason to draw a breath on this planet. To serve is to live a life of spiritual greatness. Listen to the great musicians; read the great poets; enjoy the great works of literature and art. These magnificent artists have given you the fruits of their service to learn from and enjoy!

As I came slowly out of my reverie, I realized I was famished, so I went to the neighborhood coffee shop. As I sat down, Millie came to take my order. She asked me how my work was going. I had told her about Kathy before, and when I mentioned her now, Millie asked me to give Kathy her best wishes. I told her I would be happy to do so, and I asked how her legs were feeling. She laughed and said that as long as they were holding her up, she thought she was doing all right.

We talked until other customers came in, and she went to serve them. I love to watch her work; she is so aware of her customers' needs and preferences. In a way she had made this coffee shop her own little church. She enjoyed serving others, and as a result the shop was an oasis of calm in the noise and rush of the city. When I was younger I worked as a waitress, and it was tiring. Customers were often very difficult for me to deal with, and if I had been more like Millie, it would have made the job much more pleasant.

Millie came back with my order and poured me a fresh cup of coffee. She told me that one of her regular customers had to go to the hospital. She had taken him some food because she worried that he would not be fed properly in the hospital. "Mack never could take care of himself," she said. "I was afraid he would just give up if I didn't go over to see him."

"How is he, Millie?" I asked.

"Oh, just as feisty as ever." She laughed. "He should be back here having breakfast by next week. I was glad to be able to help him. He's been coming here for as long as I can remember. He's always bringing me something he feels might help my legs. He's up on all the latest natural remedies. I sure would miss him if he stopped coming in."

There are many Millies on the planet, serving in many ways. They are not interested in greatness but are merely doing their jobs with love and selflessness. They do not expect to be rewarded; they are too busy. These are truly spiritual people. Each of us knows some of them. Reflect on the attitude of these souls, and you will learn as much from them as I have. Observe, as Lawrence would say, and much will be presented to you. To live a life of service is to live a life of the spirit. One would merely exist if one consumed only what was desired. To desire nothing is freedom. This is not impossible, so do not view it as an impossibility. You can accomplish this if you truly believe that selflessness and service are the highest principle on which to build one's life. Be grateful for whatever has been given to you, for it has been given to you so that you may learn and grow.

As the beautiful flower grows from a tiny seed, you grow from the seeds that have been planted in your garden of circumstances. Not all of us will have to deal with problems as serious as those that my friend Kathy faced. We are each given our own set of circumstances to handle. Can you handle them with selflessness and humor? I hope so, for indeed we would all be the better for it. Each of us affects the good of the whole; never lose sight of that reality. We are all part of a single great being. The fantasy of separateness can be dispelled if we become aware of the unity that connects us all. We must serve all others in our own individual ways. Never feel that your life is less important than another's, and never allow yourself to feel useless. You can always do something to help. This is love in action! The act of loving is service. To truly serve we must work on becoming more and more selfless. Get yourself out of the way! Give up thoughts of your personal desires because these will only hold you back. Start in little ways, for everything is important. You are only responsible for doing your best. Think of being free from the torture of selfish thoughts, and you will be thinking of service. Change your point of view from that of acquiring to that of serving. Aspire to live your life as a life of service. If you do so, I guarantee that you will never have a moment of despair.

∴ XII ∴
Right Thinking

Like a wonderful dessert that is served at the end of a meal, it is good sometime to save the best for last. I have chosen this chapter to close my book because its message is the most important and is to be savored and remembered.

Your whole life and all aspects of your being are direct outcomes of your thinking. Thought is everything; there is nothing without it. If you doubt the truth of this assertion, try a little experiment: Observe your thinking for a few days and see what happens. As you do this, consider that music is thought, art is thought, writing is thought. It is perhaps a bit more obvious that science and mathematics are thought, but in fact everything that one does is the physical realization of thought. A painting is the thought of an image that is put on canvas. A musical composition is a thought turned into structured sound. The book you hold in your hand is a thought turned into language and then into the symbols that express that language. Language is perhaps the most powerful vehicle for thought because it provides us with a common ground for communication.

To develop into a spiritual being, you must learn to think properly. You must learn to guard your thoughts as the sentinel guards his post. Do not allow yourself to become lax in your thinking; you must learn to discipline your thoughts until you are able to think positively with no effort. Negative thinking causes one to live a life that is out of balance. What is negative thinking? It is any thought of ill will or greed, any thought of defeat or despair. Angry thoughts are negative when turned upon oneself or upon another person. Any thoughts that arise from self-pity are negative. Positive thoughts are those that are loving and kind. Positive thought is love in action; it is how one becomes a loving person. Have you ever injured yourself while thinking negatively? This is dramatic and painful proof that thought finds immediate expression in action; your own negativity is turned against you. This is a good lesson, and it serves us best if it is not repeated over and over.

We have all encountered people we would call negative. Such people are never satisfied. If the sky is blue, it is not blue enough. If they earn ten thousand dollars, it should have been twenty thousand. If they are given a compliment, they feel they are not worthy. Instead of expressing thanks gracefully, they belittle themselves and their accomplishments. These souls are often not even aware that they are being negative. It is the normal way for them to react, so they keep repeating this behavior, always wondering why they feel so miserable and empty. I am not suggesting that one should pretend that everything is all right when it is not; this would serve no purpose but to arouse subconscious rebellion and cause inner turmoil. It is not wise to go through life pretending. Accept that troubles exist and deal with them. You do not have to become negative and depressed because you are concerned with a problem. Look over the situation with a view toward correcting it. If you have done everything you can to rectify a problem, so be it. How can it serve you to descend into a depression because you feel that something is out of your control?

Your disposition is within your control. Your attitude is within your control. The way you think about something is within your control. There are times when it seems impossible to see the sun shining through the fog of our discomfort. Unpleasant thoughts will inevitably arise, but you must not hold on to these thoughts. Let them go. If you hold on to a negative thought, it will create a negative situation. If you touch a hot stove, your reflexes will cause you to pull your hand away before it is severely burned. If you remove your hand quickly enough, it may not get burned at all. Similarly, holding on to a negative thought is dangerous. It is hard work for most of us to integrate positive thinking into our lives, but the result is well worth the effort. Eventually you will not have to work at it because it will become as natural as breathing. If you truly love something or desire to perform a loving action, it will not be a burden to you. The action will be easy. You will want to do whatever is necessary because you will truly understand that each positive, loving action is a step toward your own freedom.

I received a phone call from Lawrence. This was somewhat unusual; normally he would just turn up where I happened to be. He told me he had a free afternoon and would like to come by if it was convenient. I was thrilled. I rushed around getting the apartment in order and made coffee. He arrived at the set time, looking wonderful—Lawrence seldom looked tired, which was remarkable since he was always very busy. He never appeared ruffled or out of sorts, causing everyone he encountered to feel calm in his presence.

He shook my hand, and I offered him a comfortable chair and a cup of coffee. For a while we discussed my life and current work. Lawrence loves to hear about the people I am working with. I told him I was writing about right thinking. "It is amazing to me that people have such trouble seeing that thought is really alive," I observed. "People seem to think that once they have thought something, it just disappears. I want to help them understand that everything in their lives is governed by the way they think. This point is very important, and I don't want my readers to think it's metaphysical mumbo jumbo. Many people deny the existence of anything they don't understand; they fail to realize that just because they have not heard of something does not mean it isn't real and valid. This is such a simple idea. *You are as you think.*

"Isn't it common sense that if you live your life in a shadow of negativity, you will attract negativity? A client of mine was mugged late one afternoon. She called me, quite hysterical. I first checked to see if she was all right physically. She was, thank goodness. She asked me why this had happened. 'There must have been forty people walking down the street, and this mugger singled me out. He was very quiet while he robbed me. He came up behind me and whispered, "Give me your purse and don't make a sound." I didn't know whether he had a weapon and didn't really want to find out. I just handed him my bag and he ran off.'

" 'Do you remember what you were thinking right before this happened?' I asked.

"She sighed and said, 'I'd been having a terrible day. I was feeling angry and resentful about my job, and I had an upset stomach from eating strawberries. I know they don't agree with me, but I ate them anyway because I was angry and didn't care how they made me feel. I was thinking how bad my stomach felt and was angry with myself for eating something I know is bad for my system. I was in a blue funk.'

" 'It seems to me that your negativity attracted this to you,' I said. 'Fortunately you're all right, but don't ignore the valuable lesson in what happened to you. Being wrapped up in your own negative thinking can be dangerous.'

" 'You're right,' she replied. 'I was really off on my own troubled "poor me" trip. I'm lucky that nothing worse happened. I certainly won't walk down the street in such a state again.' "

Lawrence said, "Indeed, it is wise to protect yourself by the quality of your thinking. By doing so you can save yourself a lot of heartbreak."

"Lawrence," I said, "since for many people the selfless point of view—right thinking, that is—doesn't come naturally, it must require self-discipline to make this change in oneself. I've heard you speak of discipline—is that what you mean? I must tell you, I have some trouble with the idea because to me, and maybe a lot of other people, it means having to do something one doesn't want to do."

Lawrence sat back in his chair and smiled. "My child," he said, "you sound so grave!"

I was forced to smile. He was right; I could feel my forehead furrowing into a frown as I spoke. I relaxed and listened.

"Of course discipline is very necessary for one's spiritual development," Lawrence said. "Any major undertaking requires discipline. A great musician or artist lives a life of amazing discipline. It takes many lifetimes to develop a great talent. Discipline is essential in this process, and the true artist accepts this as part of his or her work. True spiritual awakening is perhaps the greatest and most important undertaking of all; it is not surprising that it requires considerable discipline.

"People often rebel against any type of discipline because it reminds them of their childhood, of times when they were forced to do their schoolwork, perhaps, when they would rather have been outside playing with their friends. They feel that it limits their freedom. Simple but true. It is most necessary in the early stages when one is striving to develop new habits. Gradually the new habits are assimilated, and when one experiences the beneficial results, this reinforces one's determination to change. You are free when the wise, selfless action comes naturally, as an expression of your true nature.

"Habits die hard! The old must be replaced with the new. If you remove an old habit without replacing it with a new one, you will feel an emptiness, a hollowness, where the old habit once was. But you can train yourself to replace negativity with thoughts that are positive, productive, and kind. In time this discipline will serve you well, for you will naturally think in a spiritual manner. Look at it this way: If you are used to eating only candy, for a while you have to discipline yourself to eat a balanced diet. In time, as your taste changes and as your body begins to feel better, you will not desire to eat what is not good for you. You will automatically prefer good, healthy food. Discipline, in this case, has served you well and led you to be integrated! This is what you are striving for.

"Discipline should not be equated with perfectionism. There is no perfection on the Earth, and no human being has ever been completely perfect. Merely do the best you can and be satisfied that you are developing at your own rate. We are not competing with anyone else; we can do no better than our own best effort. Do not become depressed and angry with yourself each time you make a mistake. Mistakes are inevitable and are our most valuable learning tool if seen from the proper viewpoint. Accept your mistakes and shortcomings with gratitude for the opportunity to learn from them, and aspire to do better the next time. To agonize over your shortcomings will only cause you to feel that life is hopeless, that you can never do the right thing. This type of thinking will produce negativity and is, in fact, a form of escapism; the idea is, 'If I criticize myself first, no one will be able to criticize me.' Discipline yourself to stop defeating yourself through an overly self-critical attitude. Let go and move forward with your learning.

"If you have a deep-seated psychological problem that hampers your development, you will have to work this out in order to free yourself so that you may progress. You will need help to do this. Do not look upon the need for such help as a sign of weakness. The nature of such problems is that their causes are hidden from our conscious mind and need the insight of a properly trained person with an objective viewpoint to aid us in seeking them out. A good, compassionate therapist can help us immeasurably in this aspect of our spiritual development.

"Often, psychological issues must be worked through in order to lay the foundation for one's new way of thinking. The problem with most therapists is that they deny the existence of anything beyond the physical, and they do not understand the laws of karma and reincarnation. The greatest helper is one who is able to combine psychology and metaphysics. If the two are not working together, the deepest problems often go unsolved. In the future we will see great changes in the treatment of psychological problems. Once the psychological issues have been dealt with, it becomes easier to go forward with new ways of thinking. During therapy you must not allow yourself to become overly self-involved. You mustn't allow your loved one to suffer because you are releasing your complexes. Remain aware of all those around you and how your behavior affects them. Kindness and consideration must not be neglected.

"Another type of problem arises when we can understand something intellectually but our emotions don't react accordingly. This causes internal conflict to which the subconscious mind responds with rage, upsetting the individual's balance. Such emotional understanding cannot be forced. One must slow down a bit to give the emotions time to integrate new information. While you are working out emotional problems, however, try to be especially aware of your attitude toward others. Being uncomfortable as you learn to release these deep feelings does not give you permission to spread discomfort to those around you. This, too, requires discipline.

"All of the problems you encounter are part of the process of spiritual development. There are no shortcuts; you may decide on the pace at which you progress, but you must go through all the steps. This requires discipline. At times it requires *great* discipline. But the end result is your spiritual freedom!"

When Lawrence finished speaking, I remembered what he had told me before about the importance of repetition in learning to practice right thinking. When one is trying to replace a bad habit with a good one, it is necessary to repeat the positive viewpoint constantly until it is firmly planted in one's consciousness. This requires a combination of patience and discipline. I thought about a client of mine who said that she always woke up in a bad mood. She never looked forward to the morning. I asked what her mornings had been like in her home when she was a little girl. She thought about this for a moment, then said, with a trace of surprise in her voice, that it had never occurred to her before but her parents always quarreled in the morning. She then went on to say that in fact there had never been any peace in her home, but the mornings were the worst. I told her that there was no longer any reason for her to awaken in the morning with negative feelings, her childhood was past. I suggested that she tell herself each night before she went to sleep that the morning held great possibilities for good and that she would not allow herself to wake up in a bad mood. It would require some work to train herself to think differently, but it was not impossible. She agreed to try what I suggested.

About a month later she reported that she had gotten over feeling blue in the morning. She had not even realized when the change occurred. "It just sort of snuck up on me," she said. "I don't remember consciously. I did tell myself over and over that the past was the past and that it was no longer necessary for me to hold on to those negative feelings. And then one day I realized that the feelings had been gone for a while and that I'd actually been feeling good every day. What a relief!"

"Where are you?" Lawrence said. I laughed and explained that I had been thinking about all he had been saying and that it reminded me of a client. I told him the story that had just passed through my mind.

"Yes," he replied, "too often we allow ourselves to behave in a certain way through habit. Your client didn't find change very difficult because it is really much easier to be positive than to be negative. Positive thinking makes one feel light and full of goodness. Negative thinking is like being covered with a grimy film. It seeps into one's pores and makes one feel angry and resentful. It is a large part of the reason for illness and feelings of general malaise. Thinking negative thoughts will cause the body to go out of balance. These thoughts will block the flow of energy through the body. One must think properly to remain physically, mentally, and spiritually healthy. Karma, of course, plays a large part in the health of any person, but proper thinking is the most important prescription for good health!"

As Lawrence was leaving he invited me to meet him at Sir William's the following evening. I told him I would be happy to. As usual, he left me feeling a sacred quietness.

A Remarkable Soul Passes Over

My calm was disturbed by the ringing of the telephone. Answering it, I heard the voice of Kathy's sister Teresa. "Mary," she said quietly, "Kathy has passed over." Then she began to cry. We both wept—not for Kathy but for our loss of a dear sister and friend. I felt numb, as one does when hearing the news of a loved one's passing. It doesn't matter that we know in our heart that death is an illusion; we still feel the pain of separation.

I had been with her just the night before, sitting next to her bed, reflecting on all that this dear woman had been through. She had survived cancer for five years, had learned much, and had even been privileged to teach others through her words and her example. Throughout her ordeal she had possessed enormous dignity. No matter how bad things became, she had remained positive and loving. She never became so self-involved that she forgot the feelings of others. Naturally she experienced moments of sadness, but not once in all the years I knew her did she say, "Why me?" Instead she spent her precious time learning about life after death and reincarnation. Until the very end, she remained a source of strength to her family and friends. Her life had not been a long one, measured in years, but it had been a life of quality. It does not matter how much time is granted us but only how we spend that time. That is what is expressed in the Buddhist saying, "A long life is good; a short life is also good."

Kathy was now at peace, I was certain. If anyone had ever

earned the right to peace, it was she. She will be missed by all who came in contact with her. I am grateful beyond words for the jewels of love she has left with me, and she will always remain alive in my thoughts and feelings.

I was again jolted from my thoughts by the ringing of the phone. This time it was Lawrence. He knew. I was not surprised but felt greatly comforted to hear his soothing voice.

"As I left your house I felt that your friend Kathy was passing over from the physical to the spiritual world. I wanted to give you a bit of time alone because I knew you would have to adjust to the news. Please send my heartfelt feelings to her family. They are the ones who will need the comforting; your friend is beyond need. She is surrounded by people she knew in this world who have passed over before her. She was welcomed by her parents, and she felt safe and secure during the transition to the spiritual world. It will take time to adjust to her absence because she was a large part of the lives of many people. You need not speak. I know that words are difficult at this moment. My thoughts and sympathy are with you. Try to rest now. I will see you tomorrow evening."

After saying good-bye to Lawrence, I suddenly felt very tired, as if I couldn't move my limbs or keep my eyes open. I sat back in my chair and dozed off. In a dream I saw Kathy, looking very young and radiant. She told me that all was well and she was happy her ordeal was over. She would miss her husband, family, and friends, but she felt very peaceful knowing that we would all be fine and that she would see us again. She laughed and waved to me, and I awoke. It had been a short dream but extraordinarily bright and vivid. Her hair was luminous and her skin translucent. I awoke feeling peaceful and reassured that indeed all was well with my dear friend. Ah, if all people used the tools to live as she did, we would have a much happier world. Yet the tools are available to every one of us. We are all given the opportunity to deal with difficulties—the key lies in our ability to think properly. Kathy found this freedom, and we were able to learn much by her example.

You can have feelings of sadness or loss, and they do not have to turn into negativity or self-centeredness. One must not confuse sadness with negativity unless the feeling turns into self-pity. I laughed aloud when I thought about my friend and some of the things we had gone through. Kathy had had a great sense of humor and could always find something to joke about, no matter how tragic the situation seemed. I went to bed feeling at peace, knowing that everything was really all right!

The next morning I awoke feeling well rested. I had a busy day ahead of me and was looking forward to the evening at Sir William's. Making some notes as I drank my morning coffee, I reflected on the truth in the idea that life on the Earth plane is really a fantasy. Some people would find this concept difficult to accept, I knew, but it provided food for thought. Thought should be nourishing to the mind and should stimulate one's hunger for knowledge. Many people think unproductively; they are constantly hampered by their inability to free themselves from thoughts of loss and despair. But isn't despair a turning away from the God force that lives within us? This is the higher being, the spiritual being. If we allow ourselves to think of only the physical, the part of us that is finite, then we are running in circles.

Your external life is the direct outcome of your thoughts. Thoughts create living, breathing matter that surrounds the person of the thinker and attracts circumstances to that person. Reality changes with growth and education. Life is eternal; only the physical is temporary. That which is real lasts—the real being, the spiritual man.

The Psychic Sideshow

What good are psychic phenomena unless we use them to free ourselves? Many people get very excited when they see someone supposedly able to bend spoons or walk over hot coals through the use of metaphysical powers, and large amounts of money are being made by people who claim to speak in the voices of beings from ancient times or other planets. What do these things have to do with spiritual development? This reminds me of the story of the student who ran to his master and announced excitedly, "Master, it has taken me forty years, but I have finally learned to walk on water!" The master looked at him and said, "Why did you go to all that trouble? Couldn't you have taken a boat?" What good is spending all one's time trying to learn such things when the time could be used in serving others?

People have misunderstood my gift at times, but this is only to be expected, given the misconceptions and outright fraud frequently perpetrated in the name of metaphysics. As others are born with their own valuable talents for the service of mankind, I was born with a psychic gift. I did not attend groups that teach one how to become psychic, and I do not approve of such groups. To court such abilities is to court disaster if you are not totally motivated to serve. One of my purposes in writing this book has been to attempt to clear up common misunderstandings about psychic powers and the metaphysical world.

If you have a desire to study these topics or to consult a psychic for a reading, consider your motivation. Are you the type of person who runs from reader to reader hoping to hear what you want to hear? A proper professional reading may be of some service to you, but it cannot help you to escape life's trials. In fact, it can become a form of escapism for the person who spends all his time and energy looking for titillation. This type of thrill-seeking often causes nothing but confusion and can be very dangerous to the person's mental stability.

We must learn to make our own decisions. This is difficult, for some, so they try to get someone else to make their decisions. This is not a positive thing to do. Life seems rather dull and monotonous, at times, and metaphysics appears to offer refuge from humdrum daily routines. It is, however, a tool like any other of the tools given us for help and guidance and is not an escape from responsibilities.

Psychism is *not* spirituality. Books and studies of the laws of nature are excellent when they help us to understand and improve our daily lives. Each of us can benefit from good advice, and all of us are free to choose who will advise us. Do not listen to those who tell you they know an easy way to get rid of your past karma. There is no easy way; you must live through it. For every action there is a reaction—this is the law of cause and effect that governs karma. You cannot rid yourself of bad karma, but you can create new good karma. Beware of a reader who asks for large sums of money to release you from some past upset. Such people are charlatans; a true helper would never ask for or accept such a price. I have met quite a few poor, upset souls who gave thousands of dollars to a reader who told them there was a curse on them and the only way to remove it was to pay an astronomical price. This is sheer nonsense. It breaks my heart that people have been taken advantage of in this manner. When someone offers a service, he or she should be paid a fair, agreed-upon fee and no more. Everyone on the Earth plane has to make a living, and this is fine, but you should not be asked for an exorbitant amount of money in order to be helped.

Sometimes you need to see a professional more than once, but that is up to you as the client, and you should never feel pressured to keep going back. This is your free choice.

If you meet a psychic or a reader who is very helpful to you, you may become excited and want to share the experience with everyone you know. This is natural; we all like to share something that we feel has done us good, but many people are not interested in this type of help. This is fine—it isn't for everyone. Try not to pressure people to believe what you believe; it will only cause them to worry and perhaps think you are involving yourself in some type of craziness. Many people do not believe or are not interested in it. In some cases their skepticism derives from misconceptions based on their own or others' negative experiences. In any field there are good and bad workers. How many times have you heard a horror story about an incompetent doctor or a destructive therapist? Just as this doesn't mean all doctors or therapists are bad, so it is true of those working in metaphysics.

There are many people who use their gifts to serve humanity to the best of their abilities, but there are also those who are governed by their own egos and power drives. Choose your counsel wisely.

Do not feel that everyone must accept your belief system, and do not let yourself become so vehement about it that you alienate those around you. Your spiritual development and character have nothing to do with your belief in metaphysics. Many fine people who live fruitful lives never involve themselves in metaphysics. Many people, because of their religious training, feel that anyone who involves himself in the study of reincarnation or life after death is sinning against God. We all have the right to choose our own paths. Mankind has always disagreed on belief systems, and this has led to terrible conflicts throughout history. No single set of beliefs has a monopoly on truth; there are many roads leading to the same destination.

When you are searching for a doctor or even an accountant, you may choose one recommended by a friend or a trusted associate who has used the person's services. This is also not a bad way to choose a spiritual adviser or psychic reader. You might also choose a person because of an article written about his or her work. Do not just pick someone out of the phone book or from a flyer on a bulletin board. Referral and research will help you to find the proper adviser.

Do not follow the advice of someone who tells you to do things in order to get something in return. A wise adviser will give you his or her own insight, but the ultimate decision is yours. You should not feel that you must run to a psychic every time you cannot make a decision on a trivial matter. This is an unhealthy dependence. A good counselor will know that such a dependence is not healthy and will not allow you to become dependent in this manner.

Many excellent books have been published on metaphysical and spiritual subjects, and a good counselor should be able to guide you to them. Many are not easily found, so it would help to be directed to them by someone well read on subjects relating to spiritual development.

Each of us needs guidance, but this does not imply that things can or should be done for us. No one can develop for us. No one is responsible for our decisions. If we do not make wise choices, we sometimes look for a scapegoat: "So-and-so told me to do such-and-such." This is an evasion of personal responsibility for one's life. As children we look for parental guidance until we develop reason because advice is a necessary part of life. But just because someone advises you does not mean that the ultimate decision is not yours alone. Certainly it is wise to listen to advice. It is your decision whether or not to do so. Sometimes the only way to learn is to experience pain, and this is all right if it saves one from future pain.

The Silence

My previous visit had been such an extraordinary experience that I was excited as I prepared for the evening at Sir William's. When I arrived, Sir William greeted me at the door and led me into the study, where he offered me a comfortable chair next to the fireplace. Recorded instrumental music was playing in the background; I did not recognize the piece and asked Sir William about it. He told me it was a piece he had composed in the 1950s. I remembered Lawrence telling me that Sir William was a brilliant musician who had performed all over the world as a young man and had also composed operas. Listening to this music in his home, I was very moved. I had heard nothing quite like it before. Most music has something in common with other music that has gone before it—for example, the principles of Bach have been followed by most classical composers since his time—but this was like something from another sphere. Sir William said, "In the future, mankind will become more aware of the healing force that music possesses. The combination of tones assembled in a certain manner will directly affect the nervous system of the listener and thus aid in balancing the total physical vehicle."

We sat listening for a few minutes longer, and I could feel my whole body relaxing as if I were being given a message. Classical music has always had a very soothing effect on me, but nothing like this.

The piece ended and we sat in comfortable silence for a while. Then Sir William told me that Lawrence would be joining us momentarily but that he had been looking forward to the opportunity of speaking with me alone. He offered me his sympathy on Kathy's passing over and assured me she was doing fine on the other side. "A remarkable soul, your friend," he said. "She served many, and she will be remembered by all as a person of great dignity and courage. Mankind needs heroes and heroines. People like Kathy serve as shining examples to us all."

He then told me that he had heard from Lawrence about the book I was writing and asked me how the work was progressing. I told him I thought it was almost finished and thanked him for the invaluable help he and Lawrence had given me throughout. As he rose to put another log on the fire, he asked, "What exactly is your purpose in writing this book?"

"The central message concerns love and service," I said. "I feel that no happiness, peace, or inner calm is possible for us unless we are living a life of service. It seems to me that we are living in very difficult times and that people have forgotten their true spiritual nature. I've met hundreds, perhaps thousands, of people who all seem to be trying to understand why we are here on this Earth. It's my hope that my book will offer such people a point of view they might find helpful. Also, I'm distressed by the misconceptions people have about metaphysics, and I'd like to dispel some of them by demonstrating how the metaphysical viewpoint can aid us in our search for spiritual freedom."

"Excellent," Sir William said, "and much needed. There is great misunderstanding in the world. You are correct in trying to point out the need for an attitude of service and selflessness. It is all a matter of thought, isn't it? Isn't the outcome of any situation governed by the way we think about it? People have not yet learned how to think properly, and this causes them much heartbreak. There is great nobility in forgetting oneself. Proper thinking is noble thinking. One's thoughts should always be focused on compassion and understanding. One must release self-pity and desire, for these imprison the soul in a cell of selfishness. The higher self that exists within each of us is not controlled by personal desires, which stem from man's lower nature. One need only address the higher self to see how glorious life can be!

"One is not constantly fighting the desire to possess something or someone. One just loves and learns simply to *be*, to do the very best one can each moment and not hold on to negative thoughts. One must open one's eyes for opportunities to serve—they are all around us. All we need is right in front of us. As we grow, our opportunities expand."

The door chimes rang, and Sir William excused himself. After a moment he returned, followed by Lawrence, who smiled and took the chair next to mine. The music had stopped, and the three of us sat together enjoying the silence. It is rare that one can experience such complete comfort in silence when one is with others. The quiet was broken by Sir William's dog who came bounding into the room wagging his tail and dropped a ball at Sir William's feet. Sir William laughed, scratched the dog's head, and said, "We learn much from our little friends who do not speak. These wonderful beings love unconditionally. They serve mankind well by teaching us this fine kind of love."

Tea was served along with sandwiches, fresh fruit, and an assortment of cheeses. Sir William put another recording on the stereo. This piece was light and had an inexplicably humorous tone. We listened as we enjoyed our tea. The dog slept at Sir William's feet, the fire crackled, and the room glowed with warmth and peace. I felt very blessed to sit with these two great souls. What an incomparable opportunity I had been presented to learn and to grow! These men served humanity with every breath they drew.

Already I was thinking: When will I be able to see them again? But then I thought, Just be here now and don't worry about what's next. That will be presented to you when the time is right.

The music changed and Sir William said, "It is the silence between the notes that defines the music. The silence is where the spirit dwells. Listen to the silence and reflect on the sacredness of life."

Sir William reached for my hand, and I reached for Lawrence's. As we sat quietly, connected hand to hand, I could feel their tremendous energy flowing through me. I hoped that in my book I could present adequately the vital importance of service and selflessness, and the freedom that comes from a life lived in gratitude and dedicated to compassion.

I can only do my best.

Index